Capacity Building Series: Volume I

Building Capacity from the Bottom Up

The Key to Sustaining Local Services

*Building Permanent Solutions to
Permanent Problems*

Books in Capacity Building Series

Volume I. *Building Capacity from the Bottom Up:*
The Key to Sustaining Local Services

Volume II. *Decriminalizing Mental Illness: A Practical Model*
for Building Sustainable Crisis Intervention Teams

Volume III. *Accelerating Juvenile Reentry: A Practical Capacity*
Building Model for Sustaining Aftercare

Volume IV. *Accelerating Adult Reentry: A Practical Capacity*
Building Model for Sustaining Post-Release Transitional Services

Capacity Building Series: Volume I

Building Capacity from the Bottom Up

The Key to Sustaining Local Services

James Klopovic
with
Nicole Klopovic

AFFINITAS PUBLISHING

**Capacity Building Series: Volume I. Building Capacity from the Bottom Up:
The Key to Sustaining Local Services
by James Klopovic with Nicole Klopovic**
Copyright © 2024 by James Klopovic

Published in the United States by

AFFINITAS PUBLISHING

Cover and interior design: Nick Zelinger, NZ Graphics
Virtual Assistance: Kelly Johnson, Cornerstone Virtual Assistance, LLC
Editing: Peggy Henrikson, Heart and Soul Editing

Publisher's Cataloging-in-Publication
(Provided by Cassidy Cataloguing Services, Inc.).

Names: Klopovic, James, author. | Klopovic, Nicole, author.
Title: Building capacity from the bottom up : the key to sustaining local services / James Klopovic, with Nicole Klopovic.
Description: 1st edition. | [Morrisville, North Carolina] : Affinitas Publishing, [2024] | Series: Capacity building series ; volume 1 | Includes bibliographical references.
Identifiers: ISBN: 978-0-9982372-3-7 (paperback) | 978-0-9982372-4-4 (hardback) | LCCN: 2024903443
Subjects: LCSH: Human services–Management. | Municipal services–Management. | Community organization. | Organizational effectiveness. | Success in business.
Classification: LCC: HV41 .K56 2024 | DDC: 361.0068–dc23

10 9 8 7 6 5 4 3 2 1

1st Edition

Printed in the United States of America.

To my daughter Nicole Klopovic, who is the reason and inspiration for my legacy Capacity Building Series and my other works. Nicole is cofounder and CEO of The Nicole and James Klopovic Family Charitable Foundation, which lends support to local social programs with funding and knowledge of Capacity Building to encourage:
Permanent Solutions to Permanent Problems.

Difficulty comes from our lack of confidence.
– Seneca

Acknowledgments

This project began with a discussion about how to construct grants that make a difference at the North Carolina Governors Crime Commission in the latter 1990s. Doug Yearwood, my colleague and friend, sparked the conversation and helped me define Capacity Building for the thousands of grants we were involved in for years. Then he encouraged me nearly daily through seven years of research and then writing the Capacity Building Series.

Many, many more people were involved to bring about this book and its three companions. I interviewed dozens of people, and others commented on and critiqued the many new concepts. They were a test of fire for these pages. It would be impossible to name them all, but I still stand on those shoulders!

In addition, I must mention the remarkable publishing crew of Team Affinitas. They take this muddy clay of a writer and carefully mold him into an author. Peggy Henrikson is truly an editor extraordinaire. We've spent untold hours deciding the best way to explain, describe, and promote these ideas. Nick Zelinger is my great graphic designer—tops, really. He takes a plain manuscript and creates something beautiful, a treat to read. And my dear virtual assistant Kelly Johnson is ever helpful with publishing details and internet technology.

Finally, acknowledgements can't be made without mentioning my daughters, Cindy and Nicole, who are in my heart every day, even when we are far apart. Nicole is the co-executer of The Nicole and James Klopovic Family Charitable Foundation, which we formed to support public programs that do good in the world. This Capacity Building Series will be its operating manuals. The Foundation and Nicole are the reasons I write.

*There is no knowable limit to change or growth; and perhaps
there is nothing impossible but thinking makes it so.*
– Will Durant

Thank you all.
James Klopovic

Contents

LIST OF FIGURES AND TABLES xiv

INTRODUCTION TO CAPACITY BUILDING 1

    Why Improve? 3

    Why Go Beyond Community Wellness to Well-Being? 3

    The New Leader 4

    How to Get the Most Out of This Book 4

    Chapter Previews 8

CHAPTER 1: GETTING BEYOND IMPLEMENTATION 9

    Solutions for Implementation That Lead to Permanence 12

    Problems of Process Due to Unpredictability and Chaos 13

    Problems in Stabilizing Local Service Ideas 13

    The Need for a Process That Builds Capacity 15

    An Answer to the Dilemma 16

    The Project Life Cycle Concept 17

        A Paradox 18

        Long-Term Mentality 18

        Planning 19

        Operation 19

        Expansion 20

    The Practicality of Focusing on Local Projects 21

        Productive and Meaningful 22

    Successful Early Intervention 23

        What's Needed 23

        Life Cycle Concept 24

    Determining a Process of Capacity Building 24

    Summary 26

CHAPTER 2: RE-ENVISIONING PUBLIC SERVICES 29

What's Needed and What's Missing 31

Lack of Specific Skills and Measurement of Performance 32

Failure to Gain Funding by Documenting Progress 33

Failure Caused by Misunderstandings and Resistance 34

Other Barriers 34

Need for Matrix, or Network, Solutions in the Public Sector 35

Governance by Matrix 36

Implementation – Impossible or Just a Misunderstanding? 37

The Case for *Why* 40

Cracking the Conundrum of *How* 41

The Concept of the Life Cycle and Capacity Building 42

Enter the Value Broker 44

The Good News 45

Summary 45

CHAPTER 3: DISCOVERING A PROCESS 47

Action Research and Capacity Building 50

An Answer to the Difficulties of Implementation 50

Site Selection 51

Why Local? 51

Other Criteria 52

Iredell County Partnership for Young Children (ICPYC) 53

Pasquotank County – Elizabeth City Drug Task Force 54

Win-Win Resolutions, Inc. 54

Chowan-Perquimans Smart Start Partnership 55

Mediation Center of Eastern Carolina 55

Boys and Girls Club of Henderson County 56

Summary of Sites 56

The Inquiry Process 57

    The Questionnaire 57

Summary 59

CHAPTER 4: CAPACITY BUILDING 61

An Example of Program and Capacity Building 64

    A Change in Focus 65

An Organizational Perspective on Capacity Building 66

    The Physical Site 66

    Capacity Building Capability 66

Practitioners' Insights: Keys to Understanding Project Success 78

Planning and Leadership 81

Capacity Assessment 82

Scope 83

Analysis and Evaluation 84

Developing Reliable Funding 85

Services 86

Staffing 87

    Wholistic Staff Development 88

Overcoming Obstacles 89

Operations 90

Stability and Expansion 90

Initial Impressions of the Intangibles of the Process 93

    A Contrasting Model 94

Regarding the Proposed Steps in the Development Process 95

Essential Questions for a Workable Process 97

Using the Project Life Cycle in Capacity Building 97

Critical Features and Effective Practices 98

PHASE I of the Project Life Cycle: Plan – Design Essential Operations 102

    1.   Nurture and grow key leadership. 102

    2.   Integrate capacity assessment into capacity building. 107

    3.   Determine project scope. 112

    4.   Design the impact analysis and process evaluation. 116

    5.   Nurture relationships for resources development. 123

    6.   Develop performance-oriented services. 126

    7.   Nurture staff by a process of human capacity development. 129

PHASE II of the Project Life Cycle: Operation – Putting the Plan
into Action 133

    8.   Plan operations with the future in mind. 136

    9.   Assess capacity for sustainability. 141

    10. Make scope analysis a continuous part of decision making. 144

    11. Combine process evaluation and impact analysis to optimize
        service delivery. 145

    12. Engage friends in strategic resource development. 147

    13. Nurture performance-oriented service providers. 150

    14. Develop key staff for their human and social capital potential. 153

PHASE III of the Project Life Cycle: Sustainability and Expansion –
Realizing Social Transformation 158

    15. Sustain operations. 160

    16. Plot the long-range strategy and tactics for expansion. 165

Summary 169

CHAPTER 5: THE BUSINESS BENEATH THE BUSINESS 171

Capacity Building for Social Transformation – Unconventional Wisdom 174

    Leadership 175

    Capacity Assessment 176

    Scope 177

    Process Evaluation and Impact Analysis 178

Resources Development 179

Key Staff 180

Services 181

Operation 182

Stabilization and Sustainability 183

Expansion and Transformation 184

Summary 185

CHAPTER 6: LESSONS LEARNED – PRACTITIONER INSIGHTS 187

Summary of Wisdom from Practitioners Getting the Job Done 191

Summary 197

CHAPTER 7: THE CAPACITY BUILDING TOOL 199

Capacity Building from the Bottom Up – A Tool for Local

Public Service Practitioners 201

Summary 206

CHAPTER 8: HOW TO USE THIS CAPACITY BUILDING PROCESS 207

The Model 209

The Process 209

The Project Life Cycle 210

The Capacity Building Checklist 210

The Strength of Community 210

Parting Thoughts: Capacity Building – The Reform Movement 211

GLOSSARY 215

REFERENCES 227

ABOUT THE AUTHOR 247

ENDNOTES 251

LIST OF FIGURES AND TABLES

Figures

Figure 1.1: Study Site Locations, North Carolina 25

Tables

Table 7.1: The Capacity Building Process from the Bottom Up and Back:
PHASES I-III, with Key Action Items and Effective Practices 5

Table 4.1: Site-by-Site Perspective on Critical Elements of the Capacity
Building Process 68

Table 4.2: Practitioner Perspectives on Issues Raised in the Literature 78

Table 4.3: Critical Features and Actions and Their Relevance
to Capacity Building 98

Table 7.1: The Capacity Building Process from the Bottom Up and Back:
PHASES I-III, with Key Action Items and Effective Practices 203

INTRODUCTION TO CAPACITY BUILDING

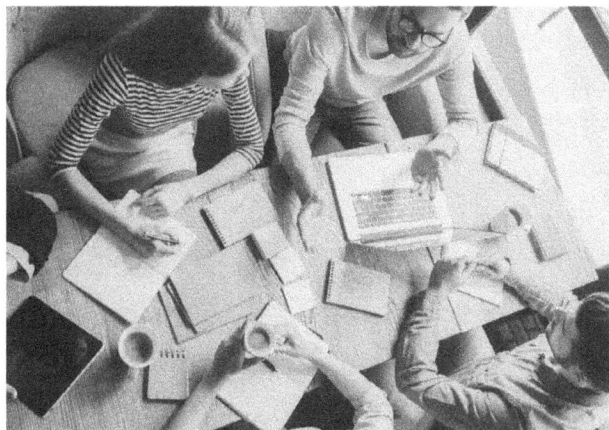

Learn—Think—Do—Then Do It Again

Building Capacity from the Bottom Up builds permanent solutions to permanent problems. Its focus is the community, where problems *and* their resolutions lie. The goal is to move toward community well-being in a practical, methodical, proven way.

The process of building capacity addresses the significant difficulties that local municipalities encounter in bringing productive ideas to fruition and especially sustaining them in solid programs for the good of the community. Capacity refers to all the resources necessary for a successful result, for example: funding, political backing, human resources, technical and marketing support, and professional expertise in the needed areas. This process-oriented method of building capacity targets usually scarce human and material resources for the idea, where they will do the most efficient and effective good.

For example, local leaders realize the importance of preparing children for a good primary school experience and *keeping* them in school until high school graduation. Why is this critical? Staying in school is the best predictor of youth not becoming involved in the criminal justice system. In addition, it's the first step to earning a living wage in a career that will support a family. Local leaders also see the need for aftercare and reentry strategies and a system to prevent incarceration of the mentally ill for misdemeanors.

The Capacity Building Series of books provides blueprints and resources for effectively tackling these thorny issues so communities can thrive. This Volume I is an overview and extensive explanation of the process, and the following three volumes target specific issues.

For a service idea to succeed, it must be seen as a continuous program with the purpose of becoming as permanent as the problem it addresses. The usual approach of viewing a service idea as a terminal project doesn't work long term. Building anything worthwhile takes time and sustained effort. The goal, the vision, is to sustain your idea so it makes measurable improvements. Those results are how you will justify more and permanent funding with commitment. An initial can-do attitude is necessary for sustained effort, which is a function of inspired leadership continuing to magnify enthusiasm for the program.

Answer your most troublesome service concerns.

- *Capacity Building* answers the *how* of community development by attacking and resolving vexing problems involved in providing services.

Follow a sequence of proven, effective practices.

- *Capacity Building* continually asks the correct *how* questions because how leads to action. Only action determines if you are on the right track, but not haphazard action. It needs to be reasonably calculated and executed, with a view to a vision just out of reach. Then reaching it is that much more impactful and rewarding. You move forward, the community progresses.

Target limited resources.

- *Capacity Building* presents a material, significant difference in *how* to lead. It includes stakeholders with key resources and talents germane to the problem. These people possess the means, the way, and the *will* to make a positive difference.

Start small but effectively to sustain your idea.

- *Capacity Building* takes an idea to permanency in the community, where it measurably improves the lot of residents.

Build your idea such that the whole becomes greater than the parts.

- *Capacity Building* is motivational and inspirational. It's not about programming from above through levels of bureaucracy detached from realities on the street. It's about being part of an inspired goal, do I dare say vision, to build productive, proven ideas from the *bottom up* where they will do the most good.

Your first success builds the model and inspiration for continued successes.

Why Improve?

Capacity building as it's practiced now is dissociated from the problem. It has never been meaningfully, systematically studied with the intent of detailing practical, proven lessons and processes, and *documented* with implementation in mind—until now.

Bottom up just *works* better. With this approach, the people of the community define their own problems, gather their own resources, and build their own solutions to solve their own problems. That kind of ownership is inspired, because with the confidence born of a good plan and process, people can find answers to any difficulty. Ask the staff and especially the participants at Triangle Residential Options for Substance Abusers (TROSA) in Durham, North Carolina. It's quite marvelous to witness the impossible being accomplished every day.

Why Go Beyond Community Wellness to Well-Being?

The present goal of local services is often to support the general physical capacities of a public entity. While this is necessary, it's certainly not complete. A township can build a road, fund law enforcement, provide social services, design a park, and build schools. However, what happens when a citizen points out they still have a drug and crime problem, or the schools are undisciplined, or the jail is bulging?

Much more than physical provisions is needed. Well-being means creating conditions where all can live, strive, and thrive with productivity and happiness.

Creating this well-being implies the necessity of a new breed of public servant. These people know they are ultimately responsible for contributing to the strengths of their communities—at the neighborhood, even household, level. It also implies a new way of thinking about community and how to effect good ideas to help solve persistent service problems. The aim of well-being is one reason this series on Capacity Building tackles reentry, a plaguing difficulty for *every* community.

When done right, Capacity Building results in the whole becoming better—much better—than the sum of its parts. It uplifts the whole community.

Lofty talk, this. You must be asking, "What can *I* do about it?!" Well, that's what this book aims to explain in detail.

The New Leader

As this new brand of leader, you are empowered to both serve as a role model and improve the common good. Although this may seem daunting at first, you will find it beyond satisfying, both communally and personally.

Big ideas can come from any inspired brain—and it could be *yours*. It takes willingness and determination to bring that idea to fruition, and you need a proven plan to sustain your idea, which is exactly what this book offers.

As a local leader, you are a keeper of the vision. You continually act ethically and embody character, thus providing inspiration to others. Beyond any attributes of formal education or experience, as a leader of today and especially of tomorrow, you display sincerity, determination, and persistence. You also understand the bottom-up and back-down approach to solving problems, continually improving service and those served. You realize that local problems require local solutions—neighbors coming together. Thus you form and collectively lead local talent and resources with the will to solve *their* problems *their* way. The environment you create is one in which people come to work because they want to be part of something bigger than they are.

The focus *within* leadership needs to be collaboration between all functions necessary to the success of the idea. Why? Public services tend to be insular silos of services that operate to deal with separate problems such as crime and mental illness and juvenile delinquency. How much more efficient and effective they could be if they collaborated. Basically, collaborative effort is how we've survived … and will continue to thrive. This is how the whole becomes greater than the parts—but only when the parts collaborate on the right goal at the right time—a goal just out of reach but vital.

Let's begin with the end. The following checklist of Effective Practices presents a "snapshot" of 21st-century Capacity Building. It provides you with the bricks and mortar to take your idea to permanency. The rest of the book delves into details. It's a good place to start.

HOW TO GET THE MOST OUT OF THIS BOOK

The following checklist is just a few pages by design—simple but not simplistic. It works.

- Review this action-oriented checklist—and think about it.
- Read the book, take notes—and think about it.
- Refer to sections in the book as you develop your program—and act accordingly.

The checklist (repeated on pages 203-205) gives you the sequential process of developing your idea. Correct process is fundamental. It's a proven path to success.

Table 7.1
The Capacity Building Process from the Bottom Up and Back: **PHASES I-III, with Key Action Items and Effective Practices**
PHASE I of the Project Life Cycle: Plan – *Design Essential Operations.*
1. **Key Action Item:** Nurture and grow key leadership.
Effective Practice (EP): Hire the board for individual expertise; nurture them for their primary, long-term capacity building roles of developing relationships and resources.
EP: Make your client base your cheerleaders.
2. Integrate capacity assessment into capacity building.
EP: Use capacity assessment to assist decision making by understanding when and how the community collaboration is working.
3. Determine project scope.
EP: Develop project scope by mapping clientele and community resources.
4. Design the impact analysis and process evaluation.
EP: Combine methods of inquiry to strengthen operations, build capacity, and justify support.
5. Nurture relationships for resources development.
EP: Establish a Commitment Center to gain (financial) commitments from targeted stakeholder groups.
6. Develop performance-oriented services.
EP: Plan for performance-oriented services and providers.
7. Nurture staff by a process of human capacity development.
EP: Draft a comprehensive process of human capacity development based on individualized career development plans.

The Capacity Building Process from the Bottom Up and Back: PHASES I-III, with Key Action Items and Effective Practices
PHASE II of the Project Life Cycle: Operation – *Putting the Plan into Action*
8. Plan operations with the future in mind.
EP: Develop leadership with compassion, empathy, and intelligence.
EP: Refocus the senior staffer from internal operations to external relationship-building and resources development as soon as possible.
EP: Redirect board functions to include operational and oversight duties.
9. Assess capacity for sustainability.
EP: Build capacity assessment into organizational processes.
EP: Develop and implement a sustainability plan based on performance.
10. Make scope analysis a continuous part of decision making.
EP: Develop scope analysis as part of comprehensive, continuous decision making.
11. Combine process evaluation and impact analysis to optimize service delivery.
EP: Set up automation systems to help integrate process monitoring and compliance and performance analysis into daily operations.
12. Engage friends in strategic resource development.
EP: Continue to operate a funding commitment center based on a public engagement strategic plan.
13. Nurture performance-oriented service providers.
EP: Develop career paths for your performance-oriented service partners.
14. Develop key staff for their human and social capital potential.
EP: Nurture staff with a 'hire to retire' process of human capacity development.

The Capacity Building Process from the Bottom Up and Back: PHASES I-III, with Key Action Items and Effective Practices

PHASE III of the Project Life Cycle: *Sustainability and Expansion – Realizing Social Transformation*
15. Sustain operations.
EP: Adjust and sustain operations via a self-accreditation process.
16. Plot the long-range strategy and tactics for expansion.
EP: Form a community transition team to assess current needs and suggest ways to begin closing the service-to-needs gap.

Now you have an overview of how the elements of Capacity Building fit together. The bugs have been worked out. This checklist is your personal consultant at your side. The rest of the book explains each step in detail to answer your questions.

- Herein is *wisdom* attained from experience. Visualize the **Life Cycle** of your idea. This makes your vision real.
- Herein is *logic*. Build your idea with **Critical Actions**—what you need to do when you need to do them. See your project taking shape.
- Herein is *purpose*. **Effective Practices** are just that—effective. You must act, but not haphazardly without a mission.

Process matters. Moving relentlessly, productively, with this proven process is the antidote for confusion and failure. Again, the process is *simple* but not simplistic; it's *suitable* for any good local service idea; and it's *sustainable* as it builds permanency.

One of the best aspects of Capacity Building is that you will mold your program to your local circumstances, politics, and people—and especially to your mix of staff and partners. It will be *yours*.

As you progress, add, edit, and refine your path. That way, you're building your implementation plan of action for your *next* idea—or to help *others* make a permanent difference as well.

The aim is to help create communities where people can live, work, play, be content, and *thrive*.

Capacity Building is 21st-century governance. *Be a leader.*

CHAPTER PREVIEWS

Chapter 1: Getting Beyond Implementation introduces the major task of this work, which is defining and documenting a process for guiding a service idea well beyond the difficulties of implementation to stable fruition.

Chapter 2: Re-envisioning Public Services positions this study within the scholarly work concerning public sector project implementation and policy. Further, it establishes the need for a practitioner-based tool to guide the process of project development from conception to sustained service.

Chapter 3: Discovering a Process explains the case study of successful sites. The study used a questionnaire outlining the life cycle of project development from planning through operation to stability and expansion based on 10 critical features. Questions probed the practical character and nuances of each feature and how they fit into the synergistic whole. Answers became the basis of effective project development.

Chapter 4: Capacity Building presents practical perspectives on the process of capacity building. It comments on the usefulness of the questionnaire and discusses concerns raised by participants. The second half of the chapter details the process.

Chapter 5: Going Bottom Up offers insights about each aspect of capacity building and details each step of the project life cycle. It explains critical features and effective practices and discusses implications for theory, policy and practice, and further research.

Chapter 6: Lessons Learned – Practitioner Insights to Success provides wisdom from "the trenches." It covers aspects of successful capacity building and sustaining a project that derive from the direct experience of project staff.

Chapter 7: The Capacity Building Tool presents an invaluable resource as you work to build, maintain, and sustain your project. This table delineates the entire process of Capacity Building, outlining how a local service idea gets beyond implementation. It includes the major phases in a project's life cycle, the features of each phase, and the effective practices for each feature. Use it as a checklist of actions for success.

Chapter 8: How to Use This Capacity Building Process is an overview, from the Model and Process to the Reform Movement. It wraps it all up in an inspirational package to spur you to action. Now you have a way forward.

Chapter 1

GETTING BEYOND IMPLEMENTATION

Chapter 1

GETTING BEYOND IMPLEMENTATION

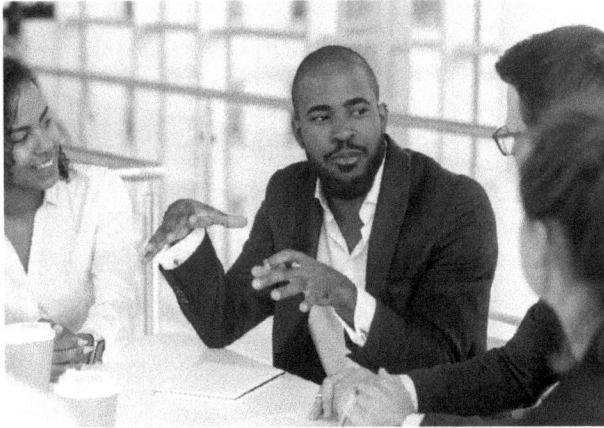

The wicked leader is he who the people despise.
The good leader is he who the people revere.
The great leader is he of whom the people say,
We did it ourselves.
– Lao Tsu, the *Tao Te Ching*

The concept of great leadership presented by Lao Tsu provides the key to some of our most intractable social and governmental ills. Yes, these ills must be addressed one program at a time, which can be glacially slow. But don't get in the way of a mighty glacier! If a community can unite in common purpose, directed by inspired leaders and guided by a targeted local plan, it can solve its biggest social problems.

Where local governments continue to operate within silos of individual services defined by agencies, they achieve only moderate success without meeting escalating needs. Cooperation is not enough. When the serious difficulties of handling mental illness, juvenile delinquency, and adult criminality are tackled by a local *matrix* of specialized services, solutions appear, and these problems diminish. Agencies need to collaborate for the common goal of community well-being—*together* establishing a community where people can live, work, play, and raise their children safely and happily.

> **The efforts of the municipality then evolve from delivering services that support the basics of daily living to developing services that allow people to *thrive*.**

Capacity Building can make the possible real. It guides the determined to dream, create, and build good service programs and sustain them permanently. Work becomes more productive. People can see their idea gathering strength and their efforts reaching goals daily. With program permanency, one problem is answered, allowing others to be addressed. Over time, the community improves, moving toward the ultimate goal of more stable families, neighborhoods, and communities. The efforts of the municipality then evolve from delivering services that support the basics of daily living to developing services that allow people to *thrive*.

Solutions for Implementation That Lead to Permanence

Many promising local service ideas die in the implementation stage before they even get to long-term planning for permanency. Resolving obstacles to implementation presents the biggest challenge facing local public sector practitioners and community advocates. This book proposes solutions for *sustaining* a service with Capacity Building.

How is this accomplished? By organizing the process of program development in a practical, rational way for the long term. Investigation has shown how local communities confront major social problems such as juvenile delinquency, reentry after incarceration, and mental illness. Results offer sound advice on how to develop any good local service idea.

Table 7.1: Capacity Building from the Bottom Up – A Tool for Local Public Service Practitioners on pages 203 to 205 offers the best advice from scores of practitioners running successful services in diverse areas. It covers school readiness, post-release aftercare services beyond reentry for juveniles and adults and keeping those living with mental illness out of the criminal justice system. When cared for properly, these unfortunates in every community become fortunate, productive citizens. These successful programs dramatically demonstrate that building capacity from the bottom up is a proven approach that's widely applicable and easily employed.

The ultimate goal for a service is to make measurable, meaningful improvements in the community. In other words, to be socially transformative. The dynamic of project development is complex.[1] It's complicated by the nature of the public sector,[2] the chaotic nature of taking a service idea to reality,[3] and the unpredictability of all these in combination. The complexity and chaos involved demand an understanding of how to confront and answer these problems. Too many good service ideas are never developed or fail outright because of them. Worse yet, I have observed increased reluctance to even hear of another idea, as a failed idea is rarely forgotten and even becomes nearly legend.

Demands for accountability, funding austerity, and the increasing need for more services require governments to adjust. They need to go from knitting the fabric of services *for* people to teaching people how to knit for *themselves*. Communities could use more collaborative networks of service providers to solve local social problems. Program developers can now use a proven process to answer local service needs while also solving problems of inadequate funding, fractured political will, bureaucracy, and lack of service delivery capacity. Capacity Building fills those needs.

Following is a brief exploration of why project implementation is problematic and the necessity for overcoming persistent obstacles.

Problems of Process Due to Unpredictability and Chaos

What is one of the significant problems stakeholders, decision and policy makers, and especially practitioners have with regard to project development? They have difficulty imagining the sequence of events that result in the prescribed end of community betterment.[4] This struggle is common for those in the public sector and particularly for people involved in community and project development, replicating service ideas, granting, and sub-granting. The need for Capacity Building is remarkable when observed in community after community. The situation shouts for a practical answer.

A successful practitioner once observed it was impossible to document how an idea becomes an established service. She claimed too much was confusing and unpredictable in the long-term process of taking a service idea from concept to successful reality.

Let's look at some of the issues involved.

Problems in Stabilizing Local Service Ideas

Development of local service projects tends to get caught in an endless loop of applying for, spending, and reapplying for money. The source is usually either local tax revenues or yet another terminal source, a soft money grant. This view is short-sighted, for grant money is whimsical, restrictive, and increasingly austere. For that matter, local tax revenues have competing urgent priorities, so a new idea is pushed further down the agenda.

When done correctly, the process of implementing and stabilizing is marked by detailed and lengthy *proper* planning. Many local service projects never develop beyond initial operations before their resources are depleted.

For example, public sector criminal justice service projects at the local level of government have an especially difficult time enduring beyond the startup phase.[5] Too many fail with the boom-and-bust cycle of obtaining funding then finding it inadequate just as the project begins to routinize operations.

Getting beyond the barriers of implementation is vital. Why? Because projects funded from the federal level via grants that pass through state-level organizations represent a remarkably large investment of public resources, especially in terms of time expended.[6] The funds used nationwide over time account for billions of discretionary tax dollars. More disturbing, these federal funds are only *part* of the investment in service project start-ups. State and local governments as well as the private and private nonprofit sectors invest even more. The collective amount wasted is staggering.

An informal, unpublished internal study by the North Carolina Governor's Crime Commission found that only 30 percent of its projects survived even a short time beyond the expiration of initial funding. Plus, many were on their way to dying. When considered nationally, this represents the squandering of billions of dollars each year!

> **Many local service projects never develop beyond initial operations before their resources are depleted.**

Improvement in the implementation and stabilization rates of these local services is especially important because they usually target areas of greatest need and at-risk populations.

Government *does* function and services *are* delivered. But it can and must be better—much better. Failings are often tangled in dynamics such as a lack of qualified staff, inadequate guidance, and lack of project management skills.[7] More specifically, the problems of service project development largely stem from the following common difficulties:[8]

- *Lack of collaboration* – Central offices at the state level are "hands-off" bureaucracies, relinquishing any opportunity to assist the process.

- *Lack of human capital* – Too few appropriately skilled local people were available to take on the duties and responsibilities required by the implementation/stabilization process.

- *Lack of leadership* – Leaders trained and matched to the needs of the evolving project were lacking in every stage of the implementation process.

- *Lack of performance monitoring* – Projects had no meaningful mechanisms to monitor processes (to check efficiency) and assess results (to determine effectiveness).

- *Lack of learning* – Mistakes, or less than productive practices experienced on previous projects, were repeated. No mechanism was available for practitioners to document and archive processes so practitioners could benefit from lessons learned.

- *Lack of research application* – The practical lessons from research weren't applied, or the research didn't communicate findings in a useful manner.

- *Lack of flexibility* – Instructions for implementation tended to be regimented, especially when a government agency was involved, as in the case with grants of federal and state funds. This excluded vital local determination and interpretation of how best to proceed with the project.

These difficulties suggest that any process to build and deliver services needs to address the human dynamics of performance, learning, and flexibility. Beyond merely a list of things to do, a successful plan is supported by a sense of purpose and augmented by a well-considered strategy. Leadership and management need to be inspired, creative, and talented and stakeholders especially patient[9] and determined.

The Need for a Process That Builds Capacity

Formal observations by many scholars over the years since the late 1970s have noted the difficulty of designing and carrying out a public service project.[10, 11, 12, 13, 14] These scholars eloquently described the *what* and perhaps the *why* of the problem of service delivery. However, we've made little progress on *resolving* the problems of implementation to undeniably improve a social condition. We need to understand how to address the problems of project development from idea to permanency so we have solid results to celebrate.

You will see the word *how* frequently. While the who, what, when, and why are good questions for analysis and background, many people tend to get stuck there as it's comfortable to speculate. We must move to the *how,* as only *how* leads to *action,* the only test of whether your idea is working, needs to be adjusted, or should be abandoned. There's no shame in realizing a failure. The pity comes in persisting with the wrong and wasteful endeavor.

Yes, many examples of local service projects have survived and accomplished goals according to their original plans. These include programs for school readiness, case management for at-risk youth, delinquency prevention, and post-release aftercare. Regionally administered and local programs hold great promise.[15] Furthermore, many projects provide examples of success as well as structures to develop new ways of ensuring that service ideas are practical.[16] Then what's the problem? The path to *how* these success stories became socially transformative has never been fully and practically documented.

An Answer to the Dilemma

This book presents a path—a meta-model that borrows from established, productive, and performing service ideas. This path applies to nearly any service idea in most municipalities and, properly followed, may be universally applicable to public services delivery. State and federal policy and decision makers with great concern for delivering services effectively and economically will especially appreciate this approach.

The Capacity Building Model described herein is:

- *Simple* – Because the process of project building is risky and complex, a simple format makes it more useful.

- *Suitable* – It fits any municipality.

- *Sustainable* – Permanence is one of the first things addressed in proper planning.

- *Well defined* – The broad definitions of capacity clarify the process.[17]

- *Efficient* – Service providers must establish efficient operations and reliable operational resources as soon as possible so they can concentrate on the vision, mission, and especially goals of service delivery.

- *Effective* – Measurement is paramount. Capacity Building measures effectiveness so results can be put into cost-effectiveness statements that help budgeteers justify program funding.

- *Socially transformative* – This model explores how to stabilize and position a service project so it becomes socially transformative. It provides various examples that demonstrate the range of Capacity Building's applicability.

The concept of becoming socially transformative is new to developing service projects. Short-term project survival is paramount. Consequently, developers often put little thought and effort into how the idea can support long-term well-being. They may employ a "best practice," whether or not it's suitable. What they need are "effective practices" upon which to construct their models. Most importantly, effective practices make it easier for stakeholders to nurture buy-in. In turn, many times buy-in makes the difference between success and the last gasp of a good idea.

The Project Life Cycle Concept

Conceptualizing the continuum of a useful process is a key to understanding Capacity Building. In this case, the project life cycle is such a key. Everyone understands the concept of a life cycle, and it's easy to teach. So, this guide details the project development life cycle, which has three main phases: *planning, operation, and stability/expansion* for permanency. It's a simple way to communicate the long-term, complex nature of project development while bringing the chaos to heel.

> **First and foremost, the idea must have** *the capacity to make a difference* **in the community.**

The life cycle is found wherever we look, whether we discuss a plant, a person, a piece of machinery, or a service idea. Consider, for example, the process of purchasing and caring for a horse. The purchase is merely the beginning. The long-term plan will span perhaps 25 years of feeding, providing care and veterinary needs, riding, and housing the animal. It must include the associated accouterments for delivering these necessities. Care for the horse will require some sort of barn, water, lighting, and places to store hay and grain as well as a means of waste removal. A potential owner needs to account for all of this and ultimately deal with the horse's last day. That is, if it isn't sold long before then because the life cycle costs have become too prohibitive.

So it is with a project, which we can think of as a living thing. It's born, matures, and hopefully is useful for as long as its service is required. A *program* is required to develop and sustain the *project*.

A Paradox

A major paradox exists in public service project development. Local decision makers and service providers are aware of the essential elements of planning, operating, and expanding an idea; however, they don't work on them in a coherent, organized manner. One project staffer may work on developing the board of directors; another may deal with personnel issues; and yet others may be involved in delivering the service. The board quickly disconnects itself from the rest to work on other "visions." Local leaders agitate for results, and interest is pulled elsewhere. Planning occurs but is usually not part of a sequence of essential activities.

The problem with this paradox is that public professionals are too preoccupied with disconnected busy work to conduct capacity building that will help them get beyond implementation.

Planning must be continuous and for the purpose of establishing the service idea as an interim goal on the way to resolving a problem for as long as that problem exists. First and foremost, the idea must have *the capacity to make a difference* in the community.

A local service idea tends to leap to an unattainable lofty vision without due consideration for how to get there. Those addressing a community need would benefit from *first* having an earnest discussion about the potential survivability of their idea. Many ideas begin as "wonderful visions," but most are impractical. The life cycle then becomes a feasibility study tool. Once feasibility is established, practical planning can begin.

Leaders need to develop a comprehensive plan of critical milestones prior to service delivery. Then that plan must continue to evolve as practitioners learn from and incorporate the experiences of operating it over time in an ever-evolving community.

One of the important aspects of the life cycle concept of project development is to develop a sequence of essential tasks that must guide the project from startup to permanency. The process is then a continuum of repeating tasks rather than a project with a finite ending.

Long-Term Mentality

Speaking and planning in terms of a life cycle instills a long-term mentality into the project. This, in turn, gives necessary pause to every step.

For example, consider leadership that's a continuous presence. These people must evolve as the project ripens from startup to durable entity. The visible charismatic leaders who begin a project will mature with the idea. They will develop different skills and mindsets when they graduate from the foreground of planning to positions somewhat in the background of operations. They'll act as counselors, offering mature advice to an established, functioning entity.

Now let's look at the major phases of the life cycle concept to sustain the idea: Planning, Operation, and Expansion.

Planning

Planning is the first phase of the project development process. This stage encompasses conceptualizing the idea for service. It then establishes a progression of critical milestones or features and activities necessary to guide the idea to an efficient and effective operation. Some of the best plans begin with the vision for what the idea can accomplish then reverse engineer how to get there. Planners reverse gears through what must be done to get to the vision right down to what must be done in the present day and even the immediate moment. This connects the vision with precise actions to get there. Consider it *the business plan.*

Operation

While planning is marked by work and activity, operation transforms the plan into daily tasks that accomplish measurable goals. Operation is where the realities and practical necessities of the work of problem solving modify the intentions and speculations of the planning phase. Leadership now changes from the speculative nature of planning to the work of turning resources into community betterment and well-being. Operation brings:

- *Capacity assessment* – Leaders identify what can and especially what cannot be done according to the community's ability to deliver the stated service.

- *Determination of project scope* – Leaders assess and determine the scope of what the project should and can do.

- *Measurement of goal achievement* – Team members make processes efficient and goal oriented and begin measuring impact and effectiveness.

- *Development of resources* – Participants gain and maintain collaborative partnerships to continually replenish support and resource streams.

- *Establishment of performance* – Service providers become performance oriented and work with the initial project team.

- *Formation of teamwork* – Staff members work together as a team for mutual benefit.

For the service idea to bear fruit requires daily work, continuous, measurable performance, and an actual narrowing of the gap between services and service needs. Through operation of the plan of action, the plan is adjusted to meet the real and fluid demands of people, places, and circumstances.

Expansion

Successful project expansion is possible only when a project is self-sustaining. This occurs when the project is generating, or has access to, all resources necessary for continuous operation. These include, but are not limited to, reasonably stable sources of funding. Money is only one of several categories of resources that must be available. Some of the best, most stable programs work on attracting then grooming staff. They have creative ways of getting what they need, such as donated food for their cafeteria, and make a herculean effort to acquire donated items such as furniture, supplies, and materials.

The stabilization necessary for expansion requires a state of project maturity. In this state, project principals can assess service needs and begin to narrow the gap between the services offered and those that are needed, as political will, personal energies, and resources allow.[18] This implies the impulse to expand too far, too wide, too soon. Expansion is incremental as will and resources allow, even if it means serving only one or two more souls. Few service ideas achieve this desired stage of development. Let me mention TROSA again. Kevin McDonald, the founder, proved his idea for nearly 30 years before he opened a satellite facility. And, yes, it is a success.

Moving from maturity to project expansion should be the intermediate goal of all public service projects. The long-term goal is to successfully address the service requirements of the target population in a defined area, which in turn leads to a more wholesome community. Stabilization should be just another milestone on the trajectory of realizing the capacity to transform a problematic social condition. The well-conceived plan anticipates from the outset the critical activities that progress through operations and stability to transformative capacity.

Luckily, successful community projects exist that exemplify lessons learned and define a practical practitioner-oriented implementation process. However, the public process of instituting new ideas is imperfect and success rates demand improvement. By addressing such imperfections, improvement in project implementation can evolve. Even minor improvements in stabilization rates of these projects can have significant effects in the better use and proper allocation of exceedingly limited means, including money and resources, human capital, and time.

The Practicality of Focusing on Local Projects

Many local service projects address the needs of children and young adults because addressing the "tangled roots"[19] of dysfunction reduces demand on institutions. Those most affected are usually human and social services, courts, corrections, and law enforcement, which deal with juvenile delinquency, criminality, and victimization. Currently, public officials and program leaders focus on attacking social dysfunction head on. It's dramatic to be "tough on crime." That approach works largely when something goes wrong. For example, a child is arrested for delinquency or a minor crime and put into detention. The question to ask is, what brought this youngster to criminality in the first place? Capacity Building answers this concern.

Successful project expansion is possible only when a project is self-sustaining.

The matter of creating a positive difference in the community normally does not call into question *what* to do to serve targeted populations; there are many great ideas that go wanting. The question is how to establish the service idea *early* in the chain of outcomes to help the individual to independence.

Project staff need assistance with the behavioral, political, bureaucratic, organizational, and administrative tasks of building the necessary support systems for their service. The urgency of the moment, and particularly the concern for funding, distracts from the tasks of properly implementing the idea with sustainability in mind.

Stakeholders tend to react to a criminological problem, for example, by saying, "Sure, I can [attack our gang problem, fight juvenile delinquency, reduce prison and jail populations]; just give me the money." Often, only token requests for funding support are made for project implementation, and *no* requests anticipate what needs to happen long term. When funding does materialize, it's applied with rigor and purpose to support the targeted services; *but* those in charge do *no* capacity building, thus dooming their

> Our major public institutions need to partner with local decision makers and service providers to a much greater degree. Together, they can best define a problem to mutually solve and determine resources to share.

project to failure. Many, sadly, seem surprised when the wished for, hoped for, planned for continuation of funding, as announced when the project began, *stops*.

Further, decisions in the public sector are not the case of a simple choice between this program and that program, which may be undertaken later. In a world of limited resources, it's a case of what can be done *at the expense of, not in addition to,* another program. Therefore, it's critical that the chosen idea be feasible and have potential for significant impact on the community. Indeed, only the best, preferably research-based, cost-effective ideas must be considered.

The key is to thoroughly plan *then* provide the service, in that order. Once an idea is implemented, a cooperative, concerted effort is necessary to stabilize the idea. In reality, this order is often reversed, with planning done as an afterthought. The focus seems to be getting the service numbers up, which usually has little to do with any measurable, positive effect on the problem at hand or the community.

Bottom-up, self-sufficient local project development is more practical than a top-down (federal) approach. Local bureaucracy with local determination is more manageable than the complex approach of working through state and federal agencies. Any sweeping proposal, such as those pronounced from federal or state governments, is often too difficult to implement at the local level.[20]

Besides being simpler to manage, ideas generated locally are usually more realistic and vested with the power of individual commitment. When focused, such commitment can overcome "impossible" odds.

Productive and Meaningful

To gain traction, the development idea needs to be as productive and meaningful as possible to stakeholders. This is crucial considering the large investment of limited time, overburdened human capital, and scarce resources, especially money, required.

If collaboration is involved with public agencies and systems such as our health services and the criminal justice system, the most effective collaboration is bottom up. Our major public institutions need to partner with local decision makers and service providers to a much greater degree. Together, they can best define a problem to mutually solve and determine resources to share. With inspired, proven leadership, this is how matrix solutions evolve to resolve a locally defined problem.

Successful Early Intervention

Local government early intervention programs that keep children in school are good policy because they also keep children out of trouble.[21] Take school readiness for instance. A significant number of children are not mentally or physically ready, nor are they skilled enough, to start kindergarten.[22] Many at-risk children could be ready to learn in kindergarten given the services offered via local school readiness programs. These include targeted prenatal care, immunizations, well-baby classes, nutrition programs, and preschool. These particular basic, nearly intuitive service programs are relevant to the issue of capacity building because they have extreme difficulties starting up and remaining viable. This is true even though they're historically a productive use of resources. An associated problem is that public decision makers tend to optimistically think big but plan small. Success is enhanced by thinking small and planning big.

It makes sense to initiate these local programs because they're feasible and cost-effective according to a number of studies.[23] They increase learning skill, social and scholastic development, IQ, vocabulary, and total workforce capability.[24] The cumulative effect of simply establishing more of these proven preventive programs that focus on young children and their parents would be demonstrable. Likewise, efforts to reduce prison populations are cost effective and easily replicable with a model for their implementation.

What's Needed

It's not that decision makers and practitioners in the public sector don't know what works. Rather: *"… it is that what works requires organizational assessment and change, systemic commitment and continuous monitoring and evaluation."*[25]

In other words, service providers need the *how*—the process and the plan—for getting their ideas into the community for the long term. If the *how* of programming isn't emphasized, the risks are fragmented, ineffectual services[26] or project failure even after extraordinary effort. Proper planning minimizes this reality.

Numerous exemplary service programs or projects have made dramatic improvements in performance by making and understanding a commitment to programming excellence.[27] Yet, performance-based programming remains elusive. Bureaucracy hinders the kind of performance and accountability required by the public. Improved programming processes can ensure that projects perform more successfully. How? A major portion of a good implementation process is assessment. The process assesses how well a project is realizing stated goals and contributing to community wellness (improving social dysfunction) and well-being (maintaining services that enhance quality of life).

Life Cycle Concept

The discussion thus far suggests that a successful project startup needs the following three fundamental elements:

- *A tool to guide the process* – The sequence of essential actions matters.

- *Much improved practical understanding* – An action must be practical to be implemented.

- *Meaningful measurement of performance* – Everyone even remotely concerned with a program, must know how and how well it is working.

Other preconditions for success are also required, such as having enough political will and resources to see the project through. However, these three primary elements are the heart of project development based on capacity building. The underpinning of these three elements is the concept of the project's life cycle, or phases progressing from concept to transformative capacity. It's helpful for local stakeholders and decision makers to understand the activities in the practitioner-preferred sequence necessary to accomplish each major milestone. The progression is logical, thus understandable and very doable. Let's see what it involves.

Determining a Process of Capacity Building

To establish a firm idea of what works, we drew on real-world experience with projects that succeeded, struggled, or failed outright. We also culled the opinions of experts and practitioners at certain study sites. Because of the complexities of project development, the focus of this work is on *a* process, not *the* process of capacity building for a socially transformative program. It matters that this take on Capacity Building isn't theory. It's based on what works in a *particular community* and how to implement the sequence of *essential actions* to build permanency in that community.

Certain relevant criteria were used in selecting study sites. The criteria required a local service project that was either successful or unsuccessful as determined by independence from startup funding. The study was conducted at six North Carolina sites that existed at the time of this study. Of course, site personnel had to be willing to participate. When the study sites were pin-mapped, they painted a representative and diverse sample of startup projects that spanned the considerable length, breadth, and characteristics of North Carolina. (See Figure 1.1.)

**Figure 1.1: Study Site Locations,
North Carolina**

These sites consisted of the following local programs:

1. *The Iredell County Partnership for Young Children* – Providing school readiness services for at-risk families

2. *The Pasquotank County - Elizabeth City Drug Task Force* – Providing investigations into illegal drug distribution to prevent juvenile drug use and trafficking

3. *Win-Win Resolutions, Inc.* – Teaching peer mediation and conflict resolution to high needs primary and secondary school students

4. *Chowan Perquimans Smart Start Partnership* – Providing school readiness services for at-risk children from high needs families

5. *Mediation Center of Eastern Carolina* – Providing mediation and Teen Court services

6. *Boys and Girls Club of Henderson County* – Providing out-of-school services for high needs middle and high school students

The more than two dozen respondents at these sites are the main source of perspective, insight, and practical wisdom reflected in these pages. Every respondent was candid and even eager to share what and how they were providing services.

The course of project development has been aptly described as a journey with all the implications, activities, and work of taking a lengthy trip. But a trip ends. The journey of project development continuously transforms itself. It involves cycles of action and reflection. Practitioners must constantly seek to understand and influence the evolving circumstances of social problem-solving in the dynamic of their community.

> **Sustainability is dynamic in that it evolves as its context evolves with changes in personnel, regulations, duties, responsibilities, and politics.**

In reviewing their experiences via the life-cycle process, practitioners came to new understandings of what they did and what they might need to do to improve present or future operations.

Sustainability for any service project requires the project to generate its own operational means for continuance. It needs to produce adequate ecological,[28] operational, material, financial, and human resources to keep functioning. A sustained service project has long-term viability by continuing to provide beneficial service after major financial, managerial, and technical support from external donors terminates.[29] Ideally, a service project should generate its own income streams, is considered a standard part of local services, and does measurable, meaningful good.

Sustainability is dynamic in that it evolves as its context evolves with changes in personnel, regulations, duties, responsibilities, and politics. That said, if it ceases to make improvements in the target population and contribute to the community at large, it should cease operations.

Note also that the stage at which a project becomes self-sustaining directly precedes the stage at which it becomes fully transformational. Sustainability then, is the capacity of a service project to endure beyond implementation to continuously improve the community.

Summary

Chapter 1 introduced the major task of this work, which is defining and documenting a process for guiding a service idea well beyond the difficulties of implementation to stable fruition. Municipal professionals need to know there's a way to take a good service idea from conception to sustainable permanence. They can learn how to stop the cycle of enthusiastic implementation followed by defeating exasperation, resignation, and failure—which is repeated with the next "best" idea.

The discussion now moves to what is gleaned from the literature concerning public policy and the process of capacity building for social transformation. Chapter 2 focuses on the specific problem faced by government, especially local, of *how* to successfully complete the life cycle of service projects and make them permanent.

Chapter 2

RE-ENVISIONING PUBLIC SERVICES

Chapter 2

RE-ENVISIONING PUBLIC SERVICES

"The remarkable thing is that new programs work at all."
– Jeffrey L. Pressman and Aaron Wildavsky

Governments, especially local municipalities, need guidance to help local service ideas evolve from their initial goals toward sustainable services.[30] Such evolution presents significant opportunities to impact the well-being of communities. Creating a place where people can thrive and be happy is—or should be—the ultimate purpose of governance, especially of local municipalities.

To best accomplish this task of nurturing well-being, we need to transition from top-down, centrally controlled government operations to a combination of agency and networked, diffuse solutions.[31] Government must function more collaboratively to adequately deliver goods and services. Public administration needs to move away from hierarchical control to encouraging wider participation and capacity building.[32]

What's Needed and What's Missing

The United Nations Development Programme[33] states that the modern democratic (local) public agency should be participatory, transparent, accountable, effective, and equitable. In other words, public agencies should provide value according to the needs of the community—the end point of public policy and services. Even though local governments are ahead of federal and state agencies in developing stable services,[34] local municipalities have little capacity for delivering performance-driven operations.[35]

There's limited time at the local level for new projects and less time to monitor top-down specified performance measures. The public service culture of policy compliance and risk aversion is not an environment for innovation. It's been noted that the Australian response to new public management by collaborative networks (matrix solutions) has been hampered by halting attempts at marketing, incompatible corporate management techniques, restrictive performance regulation, and a rush to privatization and decentralization. The predictable result is fragmented services, loss of policy control, ambiguous accountability, more politicization, and more complicated management.[36] Consequently, little is learned about moving beyond the provision of basic local services to social problem solving.[37] The lion's share of resources, people, and political will go to business as usual. We leave needs unsatisfied and never even see opportunities. We don't realize what we're losing.

Evaluating best practices, promising practices, or best-value programs actually diverts resources from basic required service activities that no one evaluates.[38] Even if evaluation is done, it doesn't usually relate reliable, valid information on the impact and efficiency of processes; thus, results are subject to much debate, leading to more doubt about the pathways to reform. New managerial policies by networked solutions at the local level and process-based programming promise a way out of the stagnation.[39]

> **The public service culture of policy compliance and risk aversion is not an environment for innovation.**

Lack of Specific Skills and Measurement of Performance

Unfortunately, however, the work of developing transformative service projects is technically based and not easily accomplished. Besides general proficiency with automation, staff involved in service idea development need to have further skills. They need to be proficient in job-relevant data collection, certain kinds of analysis, and certainly in implementing data-based action. In fact, researchers have described the prospect of moving toward more efficient and effective public processes as "bleak," mainly because stakeholders lack appropriate skills.[40]

It takes social science plus practical expertise to implement research-based best-*value* ideas, understand and keep processes moving toward goal accomplishment, and determine performance and results.

The less-than-productive debate about *what* needs to be done continues, whereas the *how* seems to be lacking. Service practitioners have no way of knowing whether they're taking the right path for service delivery and if they're making progress in shaping community well-being. Measuring actions meant to improve the citizenry is quite elusive due to difficulties in defining units of meaningful measurement and scarce and tough-to-gather data.[41] Thus, public performance measurement is distorted or simply incomplete and inadequate.[42]

Failure to Gain Funding by Documenting Progress

Let me stress the wisdom of documenting performance. Demonstrating progress with analysis and irrefutable numbers is the crucial element in winning continued funding or any funding at all. Present the cost-*effectiveness* argument tailored to the concerns and needs of your budgeteers. Present the tradeoffs of not developing your idea. Anticipate questions with rehearsed answers. Show respect and you will earn respect. Nothing is guaranteed, but a solid dollar-and-cents position will stand even against other "discretionary" requests. You may even attract an exemplary beneficiary. Persistence pays; you may come up short, but you've made and strengthened the next presentation. You must survive at budget time or your project will fail. Now let's continue the discussion on present performance measurement.

For example, most measures involve the numbers of people attending a program, not whether they've improved by experiencing a given service. It's difficult and expensive to conduct long-term studies on how a program is affecting behavior; therefore few are done—and those are subject to valid criticism. This lack of performance data and subsequent suggestions for how to develop a service idea cause misleading strategic and managerial decisions with negative long-term results.[43]

Many times, public agencies are even worse off for having attempted to assess performance. In fact, researchers discovered that the cost of serving a client *increased* as the concern for efficiency and effectiveness went up. This concern drove agencies from one impractical "best practice" to another without first stabilizing their service processes.[44] (Let me add that there's no such thing as a "best practice" for services. What is good at one locale has little to do with the dynamics of another. More about this further on.)

However, the computation of impact is usually done out of sequence, if it is done at all. Such measures are important only *after* a systemic, preventive, and trans-

> **A premature focus on results distracts resources from systemic transformation and positive change in the community.**

formative answer to the problem is put into place. A premature focus on results distracts resources from systemic transformation and positive change in the community.

Failure Caused by Misunderstandings and Resistance

Local service projects fail for many reasons. Most of them relate to practitioners' lack of understanding of *how* to make their ideas work.[45] Essentially, they fail to design their transformative capacity adequately and make daily operations efficient and effective. Most of all, they fail to carry out the detailed long-term planning that leads to self-renewing services.

In addition, practitioners always face the obstacle of the human dynamic. It's quite tricky to change the pattern of work habits in the public sector. Many factors undermine the prospect of promising change that translates into improvements in community well-being. These include:[46]

- *Negative attitudes* – People often resist and aren't open to change.

- *Complex dynamics* – Having to work in a network can introduce more complicated interactions.

- *Lack of receptivity to newness* – People resist new modes of service delivery.

- *Lack of clarity* – People can be confused about the service idea itself.

Being in a top-down organization and in control can be more comfortable than working in a network of providers. However, it hamstrings the necessary connection and collaboration with the community needed to solve local-level problems. The human barrier to change is considered cultural.[47] Thus public sector change is slow and agonizing even with the advantage of inspirational leadership and a vehicle for understanding and accomplishing productive reform.

Other Barriers

Yet, increasing numbers of exemplary local ideas are making a *systemic,* positive, measurable difference in their communities. Consider: North Carolina Smart Start (active in 50 states), Boys and Girls Clubs (active in 50 states), the Triangle Residential Option for Substance Abusers (active and expanding in North Carolina), the Missouri Model for intensive aftercare (still active), and Crisis Intervention Teams (a national model). Even successful programs are not without their difficulties, however, mainly in building project operational capacity. The significant barriers to overcome include:[48]

- *People* – lack of qualified people to engineer positive change
- *Resources* – lack of funding
- *Culture* – a risk-averse public culture, politics, and inertia

These happen to be the very same difficulties pointed out decades ago![49] The implication is that practitioners are caught in a loop of continuously rediscovering the practicalities of project development and making the same mistakes over and over. Misunderstanding implementation is the hamster wheel of current public services delivery.

Having no practical theory of capacity-oriented project development from which to learn, practitioners make little progress beyond implementation compared to what they could be accomplishing.

Need for Matrix, or Network, Solutions in the Public Sector

For our purposes here, a matrix solution is an assembly of select talent and resources necessary to deliver a service that answers a locally defined service problem or need. As logical as this approach is, it barely exists. When it does, solutions tend to be cobbled together in a haphazard way. The program is implemented until "success" is declared; then the effort either limps along or fades away.

However, a trend is gaining steam to manage public programs using networks of services. It's motivated by the realization that government *cannot* adequately address social needs nor resolve social problems with isolated agency services. Teamwork is required—no, mandatory.

With local services combining in networks to resolve an issue comes a new strategy.[50] Networking in the public sector handles accountability and performance by mustering the power of self-directed, problem-solving groups of stakeholders When properly founded on building resource capacity, matrices complement and complete agency services. We're seeing this amped-up effectiveness in school readiness and post-release, or aftercare, programming. Top-down agency control is giving way to expanded and improved services through the cooperation of service networks.

Governance by Matrix

Governance simply describes how an organization controls its functions.[51] Governance by matrix solutions means doing public business by negotiating mutual decisions and accommodating rather than controlling stakeholders. In other words, managers enable the self-governing capacities of stakeholders[52] involved in a certain problem, service, or purpose. It's a matter of coordinating resources such as money, technology, and people for public benefit,[53] resulting in productive collaboration instead of merely casual cooperation.

Networking, or building matrices, is a critical factor in governance going forward—from the bottom up and back down again, while learning progresses with each cycle. Those lessons are put to targeted purpose. Hence the idea progresses to stability then to permanency. Public services become more accessible to citizens by being more responsive *and* accountable and by being efficient, effective, and equitable.[54]

Traditional agency organization and control have their place. However, the evolving government manager needs to recognize when to exercise authority and when to facilitate a networked, communal solution to a service demand or problem. The culture of control needs to change to one marked by mutual trust, communication, coordinated processes, and shared information.[55] It's a situational melding of control and coordination with the aim of collaboration.[56] This new governance process may be coordinated by a third-party facilitator or facilitators,[57] who ideally are inspired and inspiring leaders who develop themselves and are comfortable in this new role.

National and state officials struggle just to define this new governance by markets, technology, and networks,[58] so it's no wonder local officials and practitioners find it difficult to implement this novel results-oriented paradigm. A marked characteristic of the collaborative way of conducting public business is that limited resources, especially the human kind, must be leveraged[59] so the whole becomes greater than the sum of the parts. But leverage needs structure. This new paradigm[60] requires a conceptual reference and a sequence of procedures that facilitate the discovery of problem *solutions*. It needs a proven, easy-to-implement-and-sustain capacity building process.

This process also needs to increase participation and the capabilities of stakeholder groups. In turn, this implies that staff at

> **The culture of control needs to change to one marked by mutual trust, communication, coordinated processes, and shared information.[55]**

service-oriented public agencies need to be involved with building capacity. A main focus of the Capacity Building process as it's described here is developing the funding streams necessary to resolve problems.

Implementation – Impossible or Just a Misunderstanding?

How is implementation even possible? A review of difficulties that arise[61] provides insight into how to design a *workable* process of implementation.

- *External factors* – Project stakeholders usually can't control political or physical factors. These alone can stop a project in its formative tracks. For example, federal administration has been known to summarily cancel or reduce major funding that supports criminal justice and delinquency prevention startup projects.[62] Local projects that depend on funding suddenly and unexpectedly shut down. The stigma is worse than not starting at all as it is labeled or thought of as a "failure."

  This problem of uncontrollable and unknown factors points to gaps in policy and strategic thinking.[63] Policy makers, for example, may suggest a program then demand hasty thus unrealistic proof of results from investments of public resources. Proof then is short term, of little relevance, and can be manufactured. The fallacy of hasty results is that tactic, however, may not be measurable for years, even decades. A case in point is school readiness programming. Many unanticipated issues can arise in those years.

- *Logistics* – Accessing resources when and where they're needed and in the necessary quantities is also a critical constraint. Furthermore, what if those resources are highly skilled, motivated, reliable, yet human, complicated, and fallible staffers?

  Further, logistics compound program startup problems: For instance, adding a multilayered, bureaucratic supply chain that's geographically remote complicates issues.

- *Misunderstanding of cause and effect* – These two aspects are readily misinterpreted. Stakeholders often aren't clear about the problems they're answering and the goals they must therefore accomplish. Chosen policy and subsequent action may be impractical. Governmental top-down directives are fundamentally flawed by being disconnected from the intended recipients. Therefore, the directives misinterpret a service and how it will perform when delivered.[64]

Finally, the recipient further misinterprets the instruction. In addition, top-down directives from the federal level, through the state to the local municipality, are increasingly muddled at each level, thus progressively difficult to implement. This is a waste of resources, as it's the local level of government that determines what and how directives are digested and implemented … if at all.

Multiply this lack of communication or misconstrued intention by the many levels of people involved in project development, and a small world of whirling chaos may well ensue.[65]

- *Disconnected goals* – Goal setting at the top is disconnected from implementation. It rarely works as intended. Plus, bottom-up and negotiated leadership as often practiced are likewise flawed.[66] An attempt to understand the how (cause) of achieving self-sufficiency (effect) needs to be a mutual effort between the organizational hierarchy and project stakeholders.[67] This understanding must be practical and contextual.

- *Misunderstanding of cause and effect relationship* – This is different from misunderstanding the basic problem that the service seeks to resolve. Rather, it's a lack of appreciation for the compounding effect of multiple stakeholders. Every decision-making stakeholder added to the chain of cause and effect presents another chance for misinterpretation, delay, or outright obstruction.[68] Some people object to or muddy plans simply because they can. This effect is cumulative and geometric and increases the chance of failure. Project development becomes a critique of personalities rather than a productive improvement of the process. The lesson for project developers? Carefully consider the incremental cost and benefit of every entity or person added to the hierarchy or stakeholder group involved in the project.

- *Lack of a method for consensus* – Purposes of the project must be understood and agreed upon. Many times, arriving at consensus is all but impossible because project staff usually lack a method for considering the views of multiple, need-to-know stakeholders.

- *Lack of an understandable order of tasks* – Putting a directive into effect doesn't consider the practical order of tasks in terms that stakeholders can put to work. Most directives for program implementation discuss the process in a fragmented manner if at *all.* That is, project development is considered topically, one involved entity at a time, with little consideration of the necessary connectedness of one function to the next (e.g., staffing, capacity assessment, and resources development).[69] To be effective, critical functions need to be interconnected, even feed off one another, to strengthen the whole. The order of goal-oriented planning, operation, and expansion is at the heart of these pages, which aim to resolve this issue.

- *Lack of communication and coordination* – The kind of true collaboration needed in the public sector and expected from project implementers simply doesn't happen.[70] Any bureaucracy is compartmentalized. Enclaves of people have their own views of their world, especially concerning policy/project directives and how to interpret them. Or they don't interpret them at all.[71] Consider that many projects are conducted with the direct involvement of all three levels of government. Add to this mix the private sector *and* the nonprofit sector, all with multiple agencies and organizations represented directly or tacitly.

- *Unobtainable ideal compliance* – Contemplation of the public sector agency mindset reveals an unfortunate tendency. Staff are often not only reluctant to comply with difficult programming directives but often meet them with skepticism—or outright obstructionism.[72] In the end, it is local people who decide *what* is implemented and *how* well a top-down idea works, sometimes if at all.

What is needed for resolution of these difficulties? Inspired leadership and a clear process of program development produces a continuous cycle of community betterment and well-being.

The Case for *Why*

Despite the difficulties in implementation, local service programs that are feasible have proven to be well worth the effort and resources invested. Many involve assisting children and young adults or seek to help adults avoid dependency on public services and becoming involved in the criminal justice system. All are expensive and have

> **Inspired leadership and a clear process of program development produces a continuous cycle of community betterment and well-being.**

limited public funding and, especially, human capital. It's common sense and good policy to address the needs of children and youth to keep them in school and on a path to productive citizenship. Likewise, it's sensible to keep a former inmate from returning to criminal activity or steer a mental health consumer away from court action and or the criminal justice system to appropriate community-based services. For success to those ends, such programs need to have a better survival rate.[73]

Local governmental early intervention programs are not only good policy,[74] but research shows them to also be cost-effective.[75] For example, the programs directed to children can increase learning skills, social and scholastic development, IQ, vocabulary, and total workforce capability.[76] Very important are the consequences of improved self-esteem. When considering programs that focus on youth, opportunities for broader application are numerous, especially because *any* youngster can make bad decisions and run afoul of the law. The cumulative effect of more of these programs would be socially transformative.[77]

Likewise, when a program diverts someone with mental health issues from jail to appropriate therapy, not only does the person receive the right kind of help, but the allocation of scarce resources is more accurate and frugal. The best part of diverting someone from court involvement is that services are available at a fraction of the cost of public agency involvement. And a diversion of a mental health consumer can be as simple as empowering a police officer to take a disturbed person home to family.

The prudence of focusing resources on youth is compelling considering the persuasive case that *all* children are at-risk.[78] Children from upper socioeconomic backgrounds have disposable income that can drive experimentation with risky behaviors. At the very least, any young demographic will have a significant number who will drink alcohol, experiment with sex, smoke or chew, take illegal substances, and drink and drive. These problems are intergenerational, persist, and demand solutions, especially at the community level—and programs *do* exist that demonstrate how to make a difference.[79]

At the time of this writing, the return on investment to society from local intervention projects is dramatic, fiscally as well as socially.

> **Local youth-based service programming can help reduce the multiple burdens of overextended social services.**

For every dollar spent, preschool programming, for example, returned $7.14 to society in increased economic well-being and tax revenues.[80] These financial returns consider such societal benefits as earned careers, reduced spending on remedial education, and reduced criminal justice involvement and crime. Many of these indicators also apply to former inmates who learn a skill that results in a career-oriented job, thus earning them a place back in society. The community reaped returns of $6.11 per dollar for extended intervention programs and $1.66 per dollar invested for school-age intervention programs.[81] Experience demonstrates that monetary returns to public coffers increase over time. The earlier in the lives of youth these preventive programs are introduced, the more dramatic the societal return.

Local youth-based service programming can help reduce the multiple burdens of overextended social services. For example, historically large prison populations that continue to grow could be reduced. Research repeatedly demonstrates that programs that keep young people in school effectively keep them out of a jail cell.[82] Unfortunately, experience relates that these successful projects are a scant few of all the good ideas that otherwise fail or never begin.[83]

Cracking the Conundrum of *How*

An analysis of the governance of crime reduction programs in Australia and the United Kingdom discovered that implementation should essentially consider people, process, and performance.[84] The tenets of new public management suggest processes should be flexible and cost conscious. They need to value people (staff, consumers, and stakeholders), honor technical competence, foster hands-on management, and be performance/results oriented.[85]

A process of capacity building should provide the infrastructure of positive change and would better serve as a matrix—a networked learning organization, motivated by the logistics of action.[86] However, analysts and social scientists stopped short of discussing *how* to develop these skills and *how* to put them to work on something proven, productive, and promising.

Other researchers[87] have suggested that (project) capacity ought to be considered ecologically, that is economically, politically, and situationally. Economics must be a consideration mainly because if resources aren't dependable and the idea isn't self-sustaining, the project dies. Politically, the project requires a nucleus of people with the long-term will to tackle a problem and see project building through to self-sustaining existence and transformational results. Proper project development is vitally important as every locale presents an entirely different set of circumstances that define how the project should be built to survive.

These observations only raise more questions about capacity building. *How* do practitioners build economic, political, and situational capacity? Does the literature take us any closer to cracking the implementation conundrum observed decades ago?[88]

The Department of Health and Human Services is just one source that profiles examples of projects that are doing well.[89] These profiles focus on the service at hand and only hint at what constitutes success. For example, a study of the Child Care Partnership Project, a public/private partnership for child care, counsels practitioners to establish goals, measure progress, include stakeholders, market their successes, and establish governance. Again, these same observations were made years ago![90] Field experience reveals that practitioners are aware of these themes of project success and failure. Yet they, too, falter on answering what to do next when an idea demonstrates a glimmer of promise.

Coming to the rescue when used wisely is the methodology of Capacity Building, which incorporates the concept of a project's life cycle.

The Concept of the Life Cycle and Capacity Building

A point of departure is needed describing how public services will be delivered within the new realities of increased civic demands and decreased public capacity to deliver.[91] That point of departure for the public sector is the concept of the life cycle, used in nearly every discipline from engineering to psychiatry. It provides a way to organize the chaos and complexity of project building that's relatively easy to grasp. Via the life cycle of project development, stakeholders can more readily see their organizations and service ideas develop methodically. They can watch the vision take shape and are vitalized by the energy of emerging, incremental successes.

The closest application of a life cycle to that of developing a service project is in (corporate) organizational development.[92] Organizational theory recognizes that the organization develops along a life cycle that's comprised of critical factors.[93] These factors move predictably through stages, but in different ways, depending on the organization[94] and require different skills at each stage.[95] However, the stages aren't well defined,[96] especially in terms of building capacity, or the functional and business support to deliver a service.

The literature does suggest some of the characteristics of what a model of capacity building should embody. Researchers have observed that a programmatic idea must include the operational systems, support structures, and project-appropriate operational processes that will sustain that idea in the community.[97] However, they stop short of the next steps.

Let's explore what the literature suggests local service capacity building should be.[98] Successful policing projects for example, and the literature for improving the effectiveness of program delivery suggest the following requirements:

> **Proper project development is vitally important as every locale presents an entirely different set of circumstances that define how the project should be built to survive.**

- *Support* – Support needs to be adequate, flexible, and guided by an established process. Means must lead demand.

- *Organizational control* – Control can be central, but over-control by hierarchy must be moderated via a learning, collaborative partnership; top down, bottom up, and back again, improving with each iteration.

- *Research and evaluation* – Services need to have a research basis and an evaluation component that consider process improvement and meaningful goal accomplishment.

- *Data management* – Knowledge and information must be managed. In particular, there needs to be a way to capture, archive, and especially disseminate practices that prove to be productive.

- *Funding* – While operational resources are much more than funding, funding needs to be developed from multiple sources, with each linked to programming productivity and outcome.

These general characteristics describe a program that develops service delivery capacity with the intention of becoming permanent and having a marked positive effect on the community. It also highlights enlightened leaders who listen to and learn from staff. That said, the public sector must reform from the bottom up to be able to deliver services as efficiently and effectively as possible—and, unfortunately, inertia prevails.

Theories abound, but little is said from the practitioner's much more realistic ground view. One theory that moves closer to the kind of advice needed suggests keeping in mind the Five E's of performance-based public management:[99]

- *Economy* – Treat resources, especially human resources, as limited and very dear.

- *Efficiency* – Do the work at hand correctly.

- *Effectiveness* – Do the correct work, preferably based on performance data.

- *Experimentation* – Be flexible when conducting any plan, adapting it to situational realities.

- *Eclecticism* – Be inclusive, based on the ability to contribute to the purpose at hand.

According to this theorist, eclecticism, which includes learning from what is done and acting on it locally, is the greatest determinant of project success.[100] Again, this recognizes the vital nature of doing things locally, from the bottom up. Bottom up is where the problems and answers lie. More importantly, it's where the human factor is most capable. It's about people solving the problems they want to solve their way.

Although these are valid points, they don't describe *how* to put these ideas and observations into practical work. The answers to effective service project capacity building are as elusive as they are necessary to discover. The job of discovering how to build an idea falls to the public professional, the practitioner in our towns and cities.

Enter the Value Broker

Government leaders seem to be realizing that collaboration with local municipalities requires public agency careerists as value brokers—a new paradigm. The transformational public careerist is one who understands organizations, culture, and especially the processes with which they must operate. He or she is one who sees the future and can communicate the inspiring vision as well as motivate staff to take the sequenced actions to achieve it.[101]

When it comes down to successfully meeting the demands of delivering public sector services, success is largely dependent on people who can do the following:

- Think strategically
- Get results through people
- Cultivate relationships
- Lead by example
- Communicate effectively[102]

In other words, the public leader of today should develop and be equipped with transformational skills[103] and the means or tools with which to put them to work.[104] Local

> **Government leaders seem to be realizing that collaboration with local municipalities requires public agency careerists as value brokers—a new paradigm.**

service project development demands the skills of the enlightened public professional as value broker. Like other theories, however, this one stops short of suggesting a practical way to apply transformational skills—especially those of value broker.

As observed in years of field experience, the dramatic fact is that nearly everyone has it in themselves to be this value broker. Thus anyone might simply say, "Yes we can"—then *do* it.

The Good News

Public professionals are searching for a way to put together long-lasting projects marked by planning that includes markets, community input, technology, problem-solving relationships, and growth.[105]

The good news is many public service projects *do* work. Projects *do* achieve goals. They *do* become self-sustaining and permanent in the community. Some *do* provide examples that prove appropriate behavior can be molded. Some *do* develop in a cooperative and collaborative (yet "messy") way.[106] So we *do have* examples for how a process can and perhaps should be shaped. Plus, the literature suggests that long-range capacity building *can* be described.[107]

Stay tuned for just such a description.

Summary

Building Capacity from the Bottom Up focuses on service project development at the local level because many municipal service ideas focus on prevention and intervention, which are each a sensible and cost-effective use of resources. Prevention and intervention are examples of the *Why* of service programs.

This chapter explored the difficulties municipalities face in developing these programs and factors to consider and incorporate for success. It also introduced the re-envisioning of public service programming as the product of networking among community service practitioners. The result is a matrix of service providers who plan and work in cooperation to fulfill a community's needs.

The next chapter elaborates on the *How*. It explores a practical process of implementing a local service idea with permanency and socially transformative capacity in mind.

Chapter 3

DISCOVERING A PROCESS

Chapter 3

DISCOVERING A PROCESS

When you are asked if you can do a job, tell 'em, "Certainly I can!"
Then get busy and find out how to do it.
– Theodore Roosevelt

This chapter describes how the process of local services capacity building was researched, discovered, and developed. Its purpose is to strengthen the validity and wide applicability of capacity building to local municipalities. It introduces the investigatory methods used to detail this type of capacity building, taking a service idea from conception to self-renewal and permanency.

Ultimately just about any idea in the public arena could be developed to transform social conditions. Defining a novel way to develop local service ideas to a state of generating continuous operating resources, or self-renewal, is only a beginning. Once it's documented, the process will continue to evolve every time it's applied. Many workable ideas for services become obvious once practitioners learn the skills of capacity building. The key to success is application. The Capacity Building model needs repeated testing in the field with actual social problem-solving ideas. The best way to learn about the process and how to apply what you discover is via action research.

Action Research and Capacity Building

Action research is a *systematic* inquiry[108] that's *data-driven*[109] *within a fluid social context.*[110] Its product is *learning,*[111] and its outcome is *dynamic change.*[112] It fits the study and description of a novel capacity building process for local service ideas mainly because it's *flexible.* Flexibility is required to investigate the fluid organizational, social, and behavioral dynamics of local project development.

Action research involves continuous refinement that's essential to capturing the emergent nature of taking a service idea from conception to productive permanency. Service projects and action research and are mutually inclusive as each aims for social transformation.[113] The action research paradigm seeks to coalesce networks of community advocates for problem-solving. This will lead to self-renewing local service ideas when using the process defined within these pages.

An Answer to the Difficulties of Implementation

Analysis of how multiple, diverse sites functioned and interviews over four years produced a process that answers the difficulties of implementation with the view of sustaining a local service idea.

> The key to success is application. The Capacity Building model needs repeated testing in the field with actual social problem-solving ideas.

These results can be applied to various service ideas such as school readiness, aftercare for adults and adolescents, and decriminalizing mental illness. The diversity of these programs demonstrates the wide application Capacity Building has in the public sector.

The following sections provide a brief overview of the action research steps of planning, acting, observing, and documenting, with the all-important continuous reflection.

Practitioners tested the life cycle process and proved it practical, efficient, and effective and, most important, replicable. Interviewees discussed which suggestions reflected the most useful practices to accomplish a certain feature and offered revealing insights into the intangibles of capacity building. We then refined these experiences to practical, useful lessons learned that could be generalized. We continually adjusted emergent themes relative to building a universally applicable model for local services capacity building.[114]

Action inquiry provided the model for reflection, investigatory discipline, and the real possibility of social change when practitioners applied the practical *process* of capacity building. Capacity Building for local services delivery proved to be a viable tool and part of how municipal governance can be improved, if only by effecting a much better allocation of scarce public resources. The process will guide practitioners in making a significant difference in well-being with and in their communities. *Ideas can become reality.*

Site Selection

Investigation sites represent a reasonable range of local service projects in a variety of municipalities in a representative state, North Carolina. Because considerable effort and time would be invested in each site visit, the winnowing process was meticulous. At the time, 445 grants were actively under management, representing different locales and a wide range of service ideas. Therefore, winnowing had to result in the few sites that would be productive to visit. (See Figure 1-1: Study Site Locations, North Carolina, on page 25.)

Why Local?

The research team confined the inquiry to local government service projects for various reasons. First, the local government level is where service project capacity building can provide the practical model for eventual and much wider dissemination and application. Many projects at the state and institutional levels are complicated by being buried in large bureaucracies. They're a small part of a much larger whole and lack the compact nature and unity of a local project. Other projects have little or no appropriate process component, and may focus, for example, on a one-time procurement. Most important, the local level is where social problems *and* their solutions are rooted.

In addition, we selected local government entities because they're closer to the difficulties of social dysfunctions that drain the community, public services, and in this case, the criminal justice system. Local projects are preventive in nature and have the potential of meaningful return on the investment of money, resources, and especially time. Furthermore, the local level tends to allocate scarce resources more efficiently than state or federal programs that are dissociated philosophically, physically, and bureaucratically from the point of impact of invested resources. For example, local alternatives such as after-school programs are highly productive compared to the cost of an institutional, criminal justice system response to (juvenile) mischief, delinquency, and crime.

It's important to learn from these local preventive programs because they tend to resolve social problems ahead of involvement in or dependency on expensive state

> Capacity Building for local services delivery proved to be a viable tool and part of how municipal governance can be improved, if only by effecting a much better allocation of scarce public resources.

and federal public resources. Studying service at the local level means processes and answers to questions will be in context and in terms familiar to the stakeholders who employ the process.

Other Criteria

Operational stability *after* initial project funding expired is the first major goal of project development, so this was reflected in the selection process. Alternative sources of funding indicate project maturity. Without this simple funds-based definition of success, selection of study sites would have been much more complicated. This criterion was useful when sifting through hundreds of possible service projects, many of which ended or changed focus when the grant expired.

Careful consideration was given to whether struggling projects should be added to the list of study sites to add perspective to the study. It was ultimately acknowledged that *all* projects struggle; it's the nature of the business and doesn't imply failure. We could harvest a wealth of pertinent information from sites without being judgmental. Therefore, the criterion of struggling would not be significantly helpful to the analyses.

Eighty-eight projects were originally proposed by senior state-level community planners. Service had to be the major function. Many study sites proposed by the senior planners were dismissed because they failed to meet the above criteria. We screened 24 by telephone with a screening questionnaire to settle on the six study sites.

As part of the site screening process, we ensured as much as possible that the site qualified for our study purposes, respondents were comfortable participating in an inquiry, and they had time for interviews. The sites were where the practitioners and stakeholders worked, where documents resided, where process occurred, and where the vital context would be evident.

When project winnowing began, we considered the original problem that the potential study site sought to resolve. The identified problem is a basic indicator of what the project is about and what kind of solution stakeholders might seek to develop. We sought projects that worked with large local issues. For example, lack of school readiness, reentry, adult/juvenile aftercare, decriminalizing mental illness, or illicit drug trafficking was preferable to a site seeking to improve the operational efficiency of a local government agency. We discussed the service with practitioners to get an impression of its relevance for sharing lessons learned with other jurisdictions.

Replicability of a service was critical because transporting or scaling a proven idea is wickedly difficult. No municipality is the same as another, if only for the fact that different people are involved. In terms of community development, the service idea had to have potential for development in other municipalities.

We looked for projects with organizational and administrative functions separate from a municipal agency. This independence indicated their size, complexity, sophistication, and longevity would likely have a meaningful effect in the community. A substantial annual budget that supported a few full-time employees also implied size and complexity.

Iredell County Partnership for Young Children (ICPYC)

The North Carolina Smart Start program at the time of this inquiry had partnerships at the county level that focused services on school readiness. These partnerships, exemplified by the Iredell Partnership, use a model that forms collaborations between interest groups. The groups deliver school readiness services to preschool-age children and their parents and educate the public on the needs of young children, especially those at risk.[115]

Iredell's services are in four main areas:

- *Partnership child care* – offering referrals, parent education, training, consultation, and public awareness

- *Early learning resources* – providing stakeholders, mainly teachers and parents, with teaching tools, supplies, research, and the paraphernalia of school readiness

- *Health* – offering childhood screening for general health, vision, dental, and nutritional screening and needs

- *Family support* – Enabling parents to be teachers of their children

The selected programs exemplify matrix solutions, a hallmark of 21st-century governance, which focuses ad hoc groups of stakeholders specifically chosen to solve local service needs. With this approach, we could observe the coalescing of those involved into a collaborative whole where the whole is greater than the sum. In other words, staff were more than mission oriented; they were vision driven. This aspect was important to the researchers, as this intangible is a significant aspect of permanent success.

Pasquotank County - Elizabeth City Drug Task Force

The Pasquotank County Sheriff's Office in Elizabeth City, North Carolina, is the site of a long-standing drug task force.

It has been operating since the mid-1990s and was originally started by state and federal funds. The task force includes two sheriff's deputies. Its primary function is investigations of illegal narcotics, with the goal of stopping juvenile drug abuse and trafficking of illegal substances. The team is supported by the sheriff, who sees that the county commissioners include funds for the unit in his annual budget. Some of their measures of success include the number of weapons and drugs seized and the reduction of drive-by shootings. Staff are committed to the project, a well-developed operation that includes partnership arrangements, analysis and training functions, and written operational procedures. This client-oriented local project serves the citizens of Pasquotank County. (Note: At the time of this publication, it appears the ECDTF no longer functions as it did when the investigation was completed. This top-down idea, largely funded with grants, appears to have ended. It exemplifies the risk of not planning for permanency with local resources.)

Win-Win Resolutions, Inc.

Win-Win Resolutions seeks to guide primary and secondary students in developing social skills. Win-Win began in 2000 and is supported by a combination of revenue streams from local and grant sources. Services are concentrated on anger management and conflict resolution via a therapeutic drama model. It serves children, young adults, parents, and teachers in the Guilford County area. While the program is designed for all students, it targets schools with the greatest number of at-risk students.

Significantly, Win-Win is headquartered in downtown Greensboro, North Carolina, the site of one of this nation's most significant civil rights events, the Woolworth sit-in. The whites-only lunch counter, where, in the 1960s, four youthful

African Americans sat in protest, is now an icon in our National American History Museum in Washington, D.C. Win-Win still struggles with some of the same issues that were the focus of the protests immortalized by an act of civil disobedience at a lunch counter.

Chowan-Perquimans Smart Start Partnership

The Chowan-Perquimans Smart Start Partnership provides kindergarten readiness services and counseling in rural coastal counties of eastern North Carolina. Staff offer programs such as parenting classes and support for childcare facilities and services, child care health/safety/wellness training, and literacy outreach. They determine effectiveness by measuring the number of targeted children who are ready for kindergarten each year. Staff also obtain feedback from teachers on how class management has improved, as well as feedback from parents who report better parenting skills.

The program was considered relatively successful while operating on startup grants. Operationally, it was found to be a comparatively sophisticated project as it's part of the overarching state-supported Smart Start school readiness policy.

Mediation Center of Eastern Carolina

The Mediation Center of Eastern Carolina (MCEC) is an umbrella agency that supports an array of local services at several sites. The Mediation Center is a nonprofit organization focused on two main services: teaching conflict resolution/mediation skills and Teen Court.

Teen Court is a model of a successful local service idea as it's a community-based alternative to juvenile court for first-time minor misdemeanor offenders ages 10 to

> The selected programs exemplify matrix solutions, a hallmark of 21st-century governance, which focuses ad hoc groups of stakeholders specifically chosen to solve local service needs.

17. It can be set up in almost any community and easily saves costs by avoiding formal court proceedings. Offenders who successfully complete Teen Court at the MCEC avoid juvenile court and the stigma of a criminal record.

Sanctions such as Teen Court jury service, anger management, and bullying prevention are decided by a court of peers under the supervision of a judge and court officials. Overall, the Mediation Center seeks to develop community capacity to address problems of juvenile delinquency and the friction of cultural differences.

The main service, Teen Court, presents interesting investigation opportunities. Many Teen Courts operate throughout the state as a widely distributed microcosm of all the processes that occur in local service project development.

Measurements of success include the reduction of recidivism rates, the completion rates for sanctions adjudicated, and pre- and post-test attitudinal measures.

Boys and Girls Club of Henderson County

This youth program in Hendersonville, North Carolina, targets minority youth who mostly live in single-parent households and qualify for the free lunch program via their schools. Its aim is to keep these youngsters in school by offering a range of social skills training, mentoring, and academic tutoring.

At the time of this study, the program had an annual budget of $780,000, which largely supported a staff of six full- and part-time administrative personnel and service providers. It's incorporated as an independent 501(c)(3) nonprofit entity[116] and creatively funded from several sources of grant and local monies.

Measures of success focus on the reduction of target population contacts with law enforcement, fights that disturb the peace, detentions, and increased academic performance. It advances the Boys and Girls Club model that's been evolving for more than a century by having its roots in post-Civil War care of orphaned boys. Its sophistication leads the community to consider this project an example of how a service should be delivered.

> **Teen Court is a model of a successful local service idea as it's a community-based alternative to juvenile court for first-time minor misdemeanor offenders ages 10 to 17.**

Summary of Sites

When the selected sites were highlighted on a road map of North Carolina, they painted a representative and diverse sample of sponsored start-up projects. (See Figure 1.1: Study Site Locations, North Carolina, page 25.) Demographically, they encompassed rural, urban, and metropolitan locations that spanned the considerable length of North Carolina from the western mountains, through the Central Piedmont, to the eastern coast.

They're located in and are supported by their municipalities. Organizationally, they range from an independent nonprofit, the Boys and Girls Club of Henderson, to part of a long-established, overarching organization, exemplified by the Iredell County Partnership for Children.

These projects are mature in that they have progressed through the three phases of development—planning, operation, and stability—sought in this study. Collectively, they provided a wealth of data that tested the life cycle process and brought to life the suggested features of the Capacity Building concept.

The Inquiry Process

This study involved the following four stages:

1. Develop an interview questionnaire.
2. Conduct the site visits.
3. Analyze results.
4. Report results.

First, we'll consider the questionnaire. Note that there's usually a distinction between a questionnaire and an interview, but those terms are used interchangeably herein, depending on the context.

The Questionnaire

The initial task was to simplify and refine an unpiloted interview instrument (questionnaire). The instrument was then used in the field. Multiple respondents reflected on the instrument's suitability for investigating the dimensions and dynamics of capacity building. The goal was to establish a theory of capacity building and determine a narrative for the process from the various community experiments under study. Equally important was to discover some of the behavioral, physical, and operational aspects of the life cycle. These intangibles are critical to a project's success in reaching operational stability and longevity.

The questionnaire was based on the essential features of service idea development. Questions probed the practical character and nuances of each feature and how it fit into the synergistic whole. Following is a list of the key features according to stakeholders. The features and how they fit into the phases of the project life style will be described in detail in *Chapter 4: Capacity Building*.

- *Needs assessment* – Gathering data, defining the problem, assessing resources, target populations, and target areas

- *Project scope* – Determining vision, mission, goals, challenges, leadership involvement, alternative solutions, and focus of resources

- *Project impact analysis and process evaluation* – Determining measures of success, measuring results/effectiveness, monitoring process, targeting resources, determining goal orientation by staff, and justifying resources

- *Resources* – Developing resources, developing funding streams, planning and managing finances, developing support, planning marketing, and determining conflicts of interest

- *Services* – Targeting services, determining services accessibility, developing goal-oriented service providers and other qualities and qualifications of service providers, evaluating service performance and goal orientation

- *Key staff* – Developing a cohesive team, determining job titles and descriptions and the desired qualities and qualifications of key staff

- *Administrative structure and operation* – Determining administrative structure and means of staff development, securing facilities and resources, keeping records and maintaining data, setting up communication and automation, determining staff duties and responsibilities, defining/limiting the project scope, solving operational problems, and determining management style

- *Service-to-needs gap* – Assessing the gap between existing and needed services, focusing on target population and areas, identifying shortfalls in service needs and available resources to fill them

- *Long-range community development statement, strategy, and tactics for expansion* – Relating vision, mission, and goals to essential resources for expansion, essential staffing, essential partners, timelines, expansion readiness, and obstacles to expansion

The questionnaire was designed to prompt as much necessary discussion, introspection, and explanation as possible. At the same time, it kept the interviews focused on understanding nuances of relevant knowledge and capacity building. Therefore, answers to the questionnaire became the blueprint for the resultant process.

More specifically, we used the instrument to interview 22 respondents. These included seven senior staff (usually the executive directors), six division directors, seven staff members, and two board members. Informally, we engaged eight other stakeholders, including clients, students, parents, and community members in conversations about their experiences with their respective projects. Interviewing this many respondents with a large instrument allowed probing deeply and comprehensively into how they conducted or experienced their projects.

Summary

This chapter detailed the means used to understand the process of capacity building. The case study is the most suitable method to understand the behavioral environment of a practitioner-based process that guides a local service idea from conception to permanency in the local community. The study used a questionnaire (or interview instrument) outlining the life cycle of project development from planning through operation to stability and expansion based on critical features. Those features then became the bases for Effective Practices, or actions necessary to sustain an idea for local services. This laid the groundwork for analysis, whereby we could tell the story of project stabilization and building the capacity to transform, which follow in the next chapter.

Chapter 4

CAPACITY BUILDING

Chapter 4

CAPACITY BUILDING

*" . . . consistency of mind, persistency of purpose
and the grand simplicity of decision . . ."*
– Winston Churchill

This chapter considers how the process of capacity building evolved via the perspectives of practitioners at each site, how the questionnaire was used, and subsequent issues raised by respondents. As expected, the respondents provided insightful and, at times, profound observations and practical interpretations of complex issues.

Investigators were fortunate that practitioners were willing to share how their work is accomplished and how they became agents of transformation in their communities. *They know their knitting.* In fact, they pave the way for evolving leadership that's more effective in modern governance. That is, they contribute to individual, agency, and community well-being—usually via matrix solutions to resolve social difficulties.

The knitting analogy provides a way to view project development. Knitting is basically a repetitive but skilled task of turning yarn into clothing. Insight comes over time and only by concentrating on the basics. Variations of basic stitches and techniques produce beautiful and useful articles. However, if any of the basic techniques are ignored, the whole project can unravel. The

> **The philosophy is to always do only what can be reasonably accomplished well and with lasting, positive results.**

same is true of capacity building, a major theme in the study of local service programs. In capacity building, several elements are "knit" together into "whole cloth." Each strand is important. Each continuously gathers strength from the others as project capacity evolves, perspectives on the social environment expand, and social capital increases.

As with knitting, if you wish to build a public program, you need to begin with the desired results in mind so you can decide what's needed to achieve the vision. You might want to select one of your most difficult problems in one of your most difficult areas with one of your most difficult-to-serve populations. Why? Because arguments against the intervention can be countered with, "If it works there, it will work anywhere." (A good example is the Boys and Girls Club of Henderson County.)[117] Your program can then serve as an example for other agencies and champions, who can learn from what you established over years of trial and error. Local innovators can perhaps begin with easier projects in better areas with more amenable populations to fill the services-to-needs gap in their community. The philosophy is to always do only what can be reasonably accomplished well and with lasting, positive results. Plan for permanency. Bite off a little less than you can chew so you may confront any problem and learn: Less, much less, is much more.

An Example of Program and Capacity Building

In the early 1990s, the State of North Carolina focused on solving the problem of school violence. We began research[118] by determining the most efficient and effective intervention to help maintain order in primary and secondary schools to enhance the educational environment. This work initiated thinking around the process of capacity building in the public sector.

We learned from a community with a high school where teachers *actually locked themselves in their classrooms* to keep intruders from disrupting classes. The community's dynamic chief of police saw the need and potential for resolving the safety issues of a struggling public school. Despite his stringent budget, he was willing to commit manpower, time, and resources to resolving the problem. The chief became the project's essential champion—one of several champions resulting from his example. In turn, the site became one of those that exemplifies the statement, "If it works here, it will work anywhere."

A Change in Focus

The intervention in this case was the School Resource Officer (SRO) program. The initial reaction of the community to putting an armed officer in a "gun-free" environment was swift and obstinate. We heard over and over from parents, "You are *not* going to put a gun totin' officer in *my* school." A student addressed that issue emphatically: "If you think the officer's gun is the only one at school, ya gotta be kidding."

The program eventually changed its focus from controlling and enforcing behavior to a model of prevention and participation. Instead of determining the effects of putting a sworn officer in uniform with a gun in schools, initiators looked at how an officer could become part of the school administration, staff, and the student body. This change began the work of answering the more valuable question of *how* rather than what or why. The question here was: *How* can an officer be placed in a school to reduce or eliminate school disruption by promoting a safe and secure learning environment?

Answering the rather academic questions of what or why *distracts* from the essential question of *how* to deliver an effective service. In other words, we looked at building capacity for the idea, not to simply justify a decision to put a sworn officer in the classroom. For instance, while the officer could arrest a student, it was more important that the officer teach and model responsible behavior. The badge and uniform needed to represent a peaceful authority, not more of the "cuff 'em and stuff 'em" view of policing, which is far from the "protect and serve" overwhelming motivation.

A volunteer sworn officer was handpicked by the police chief to help determine how best to train and redefine the roles of the school resource officers. He especially worked on possibilities for cooperation and collaboration between the schools and the officers. A sworn officer has authority and jurisdiction that begins where that of the schools end, and the goal was a good marriage of duties and responsibilities. The results far exceeded expectations.

When this experiment began in the mid 1990s, North Carolina already had about 250 SROs statewide. After introducing the new model, the job evolved to take on a proactive perspective. The officers began integrating into the fabric of the school to become advocate role models rather than control-oriented disciplinarians. This approach recognizes the potential and strengths of youth instead of regarding a wayward youngster as a problem to punish. By February 2019, North Carolina had over 1,200 SROs and some of the safest schools in the nation according to the state's Division of Juvenile Justice and Delinquency Prevention.[119] The SRO program scaled up to meet the need by becoming a permanent, stable part of local services. Capacity building is rooted in successful projects such as the SRO program.

An Organizational Perspective on Capacity Building

A comparison of the study sites offers insight into the lessons gleaned that formed the composite process of Capacity Building. While all sites are enjoying longevity, Iredell Smart Start and the Boys and Girls Club, for example, enjoy a level of maturity that allowed them to begin to expand services and measurably improve community well-being. Staff and stakeholders provided vital insights and effective practices relative to the elusive expansion phase.

The Physical Site

The physical aspects of the service site are important, as place has nearly as much influence as process in the success of a service idea. Four walls can reflect inspired leadership, meaningful hard work, efficiency, effectiveness, equity, and positive change in lives. This is true of the Henderson Boys and Girls Club, where we noted the walls were festooned with the artifacts of success and promise. Place can be symbolic, as with Win-Win Resolutions. As previously mentioned, it's based just around the corner from the location of the historic Woolworth's lunch counter civil rights sit-in. Who can refute what such a location says about Win-Win's mission to reduce violence and prejudice in schools and communities?

Capacity Building offers a stark comparison and testament for bottom-up collaborative networked governance versus top-down government.

Capacity Building Capability

The sites offered contrast and depth with their various degrees of maturity and their understanding of what it takes to endure:

- The Iredell Partnership and the Boys and Girls Club were extremely strong and supported each other well.

- The Win-Win and Mediation Center of Eastern Carolina (MCEC) sites were still building or rebuilding capacity.

- The Pasquotank Drug Task Force and Chowan Smart Start provided contrast to capacity building because they continued largely by complying with federal, state, and local policy and directives.

    The Pasquotank County–Elizabeth City Drug Task Force became a study in the importance of securing self-renewing resources with planning and early in implementation. Long after the site visits were complete and writing began, a large part of its funding, which came from federal grants, or soft funding, did not renew. Consequently, the Task Force was reduced to two investigators as the county could not assume the funding shortfall and eventually ceased to exist in that form. By comparison, other study sites with multiple sources of funding are still functioning and accomplishing original goals, even in extremely austere times and conditions. This demonstrates the difficulty of depending on soft funding.

Capacity Building offers a stark comparison and testament for bottom-up collaborative networked govern*ance* versus top-down govern*ment*. A comparative analysis offers additional insights.

On the following page, Table 4.1 compares the maturity and thoroughness of capacity building between sites. It represents the range of project actualization, from compliance to directives, as with Pasquotank and Chowan, to the degree of acceptance into the community as institutions of leadership and change, as with Iredell and the Boys and Girls Club. The visual comparison is stark.

When we completed the site visits, we talked with senior community development specialists and analysts to determine how the sites compared in each of eight key elements of capacity building. A "Y," signifying yes, means the site displayed mature capacity building for the feature in question. Discussion of the various interpretations of each feature follows the table.

Table 4.1: Site-by-Site Perspective on Critical Elements of the Capacity Building Process

Elements of Capacity Building	Sites					
	ICPYC	Pasquotank	Win-Win	Chowan SS	MCEC	B&GC
Performance	Y					Y
Staff	Y				Y	Y
Leadership	Y				Y	Y
Organization	Y		Y		Y	Y
Community	Y				Y	Y
Resources	Y		Y			Y
Process	Y		Y		Y	Y
Services	Y		Y	Y		Y

Iredell County Partnership for Young Children

At the time of this writing, the ICPYC is one of 80 partnerships under the state-sponsored Smart Start school readiness program supported and guided by the General Assembly via the North Carolina Partnership for Children (NCPC). The state recognizes and supports the need to see "That every child in North Carolina arrives at school healthy and ready to succeed."[120]

Everything about Iredell speaks of a well-run initiative. It exemplifies the ways in which local public services can stabilize and expand to begin to close the service/needs gap, in this case, for school readiness.

The Partnership prepares at-risk children for school by involving them and their families with health services, childcare, and parenting classes. In many ways, the ICPYC is the ideal local public service provider, in that it:

- Has the umbrella support of the state general assembly and the office of the governor.

- Enjoys county political support and growing recognition by target populations.

- Offers a range of networked services targeted at the overall mission of school readiness for children ages zero to five.

- Exhibits good business sense with an effectively functioning business infrastructure, such as departments for administration, fiscal management, and human resources.

- Has local determination, collaboration, and support.

Site leaders were considering expanding into other at-risk neighborhoods. This was seen as a speculative move as resources must precede the expansion; availability was not guaranteed. Scaling up or replicating represents a significant conundrum for successful projects, and their struggle with this is a laboratory for local expansion efforts. It exemplifies the bottom-up, strengths-based philosophy of resolving a problem and focus toward the target population of at-risk youth and families. Iredell is an excellent model of how to transition an idea from conception to fruition.

> The Iredell site exemplifies how to synergize federal, state, and especially local resources toward a specific, locally defined problem—in this case, school readiness.

The Partnership lives its vision:

All children in Iredell County will have strong, stable, and capable families who are knowledgeable about parenting and child development, and who effectively fulfill their roles as the primary providers, nurturers and teachers helping their children reach their full potential.

And its mission:

To build a comprehensive network of services to meet the needs of families with children from zero to five years to ensure that all children are healthy and ready to succeed in school and in life.

Iredell represents a good idea—school readiness—that has reached the state of transformational capability. More Iredell County children than ever start school ready to learn. It makes a difference in the community *from the perspective of the service consumer.* This Partnership and the Boys and Girls Club understand and demonstrate how to build capacity that results in meaningful social transformation.

> **If the idea is sound and key staff are inspired, success is assured.**

That said, Iredell's struggle has been substantial. The program developers faced the usual threats to establishing their idea: (political) opposition, lack of acceptance in the community, and insufficient funds for needed services. The Boys and Girls Club also faced such hurdles—but that model has been working out the kinks of their business for over 150 years! The ICPYC and the Boys and Girls Club exemplify the long-term view of vision and mission and the constant shaping of processes to realize their potential. The staff at Iredell, for example, have stabilized operations and are expanding their services. Each successful service proved persistence matters. If the idea is sound and key staff are inspired, success is assured.

Iredell is a superior experiment in the most significant aspects of local community development. We found that with Iredell, we could easily:

- Study and implement the life cycle of project development.
- Test the trustworthiness of the critical features.
- Better understand the nature and achievement of capacity.
- Discover in depth the unknowns beyond the barriers of implementation.

The fact that staff were working on closing the gap between existing and needed services added insight to the largest unknown of local service project developments: how to make a transformative difference in the community.

As an expression of social capital in action, Iredell incorporates the following:

- *New governance* – The project exemplifies matrix solutions and value-brokering.

- *Adaptation* – It adapts its evolving theory to problem resolution.

- *Accommodation* – It accommodates conventional top-down administration, the practical execution of policy, and the productive use of politics.

- *Bottom-up approach* – All the while, it delivers a community service from the bottom up.

The Iredell project represents the full flowering of the capacity building process that emerges from practical investigation and reflection.

The Pasquotank County – Elizabeth City Drug Task Force

Pasquotank County illegal drug interdiction is the responsibility of the sheriff's office. The task force had been operating for about 10 years at the time of the field work

> **Pasquotank represented the effect of policy and the need for compliance. These priorities overshadowed the need to continuously improve, which is integral to the capacity building process.**

for this study. The team of two investigators targeted mid-level traffickers of illegal substances. The team was quite proficient and effective in pursuing and investigating traffickers, so cases led to convictions by the federal prosecutor.

At first impression of the study site, the Task Force garage appeared to have been abandoned, which was by intention except for the new cruisers parked in front. The building had not been maintained properly for years. The yard was overgrown with grass and weeds and studded with abandoned, confiscated, and parked vehicles. Little order was evident. The realization then dawned that the old, two-bay maintenance shed had been kept in service because it was a "perfect" cover for narcotics investigation.

Pasquotank remained a function of two quite capable investigators and the sheriff. Thus, we found little to study regarding each of the features of capacity building. The scope of the Task Force was the predetermined drug investigations. These were carried out by only the two investigators. The project didn't have to assess community need relative to the resources to address it.

The detectives in the Task Force were the main site respondents, and their major contributions were directed to the understanding of Phase II of the life cycle— Operations.

Pasquotank represented the effect of policy and the need for compliance. These priorities overshadowed the need to continuously improve, which is integral to the capacity building process. A major concern, however, was the project's dependency on federal funding, which had to be renewed regularly and was subject to cancellation.

Why did we include Pasquotank in the study? It made for a good comparison. It was a successful compliance-oriented project as opposed to successful projects built on the capacity building model. In comparison to the other sites, Pasquotank was a product of top-down federal policy, technical assistance, and funding for a narrowly defined purpose—to interdict drug trafficking. The project did not consider the roots of the drug problem or if anything could be done to stop the problem from manifesting in the community. It only answered the mandate to build a case for incarcerating drug offenders, successfully making arrests that resulted in incarceration. No figures were available as to the effect on or mitigation of the local drug problem. However, it was a good example of a process driven by compliance.

Win-Win Resolutions, Inc.

The founding executive director of Win-Win wanted her idea used as a national model. Therefore, the service was built with replication in mind.

The vision of the project remains:

To create a world where people live, learn and work in inclusive, harmonious communities.

Which translates to its mission:

To reduce violence and prejudice in schools and communities by teaching conflict resolution and positive social skills through interactive drama.

Win-Win is a tenant in a multistory former bank building, which is well maintained and now serves an array of nonprofit businesses. The office is a small suite consisting of a reception area, three offices, and a copy/storage room barely large enough for the copier, some boxes, and a wall hanging.

Win-Win is a true local idea from and of the community, held together by the original champion of the idea. It's a study in evolving process, alternating between daily operations and expansion.

The project provided perspective on the dynamics of a good idea and its staff, who continue to grapple with the issues of capacity building. Developers were initially concerned with the basics of establishing the idea. For example, they devoted much of their time to stabilizing funding streams, developing the board, establishing human capital, building the organization, and developing their relationship with the various stakeholders. Staff endeavored to find a permanent place in the community by working with support agencies such as the local school board and municipal government.

Staff, most notably the executive director and senior Win-Win staff, contributed the most to understanding operations, especially resources development.

At the time of the study, Win-Win was a laboratory of developing processes aimed at what lies beyond implementation alone. It was exploring basic questions of how to shape leadership, how to develop funding streams, and what its relationship was with the community. It was a model of a service idea that was young in its life cycle, attempting to assess how to operate and develop capacity.

At present, the Win-Win idea of teaching social competencies in at-risk schools has survived well and the program is going strong, a testament to the commitment of its leadership, staff, and an idea built on sustaining capacity.

Chowan Perquimans Smart Start Partnership

The Chowan Perquimans Smart Start Partnership for Children is part of the same network of school readiness programs as Iredell's.

Chowan Perquimans stakeholders see their vision as:

Bringing people and organizations together to work with and for parents and children in order to maximize school preparedness and ultimately develop future productive citizens.

Programs and services are guided by their mission to:

Facilitate collaboration and coordination of comprehensive family support services for all children to maximize school preparedness and to ultimately develop future productive children.[121]

Beside school readiness, this program seeks to ensure that its two county childcare facilities are affordable and of high quality. State inspectors who checked for compliance while it was operating on startup grant monies at the time of the site visits considered the program relatively successful. As it's supervised by the overarching, state-supported Smart Start school readiness program, it has functional business divisions and service responsibilities per Smart Start directives.

The Chowan Perquimans Smart Start Partnership is a study in adaptation, persistence, and survival. Even in the face of austere budgeting, a shortage of qualified staff, and restricted operational resources, the Partnership performs acceptably in its audits and technical assistance inspections by state Smart Start consultants.

Chowan provides a unique opportunity for study: Both it and Iredell are working on the same state policy and oversight of school readiness. Chowan is effective in its poor rural demographic. Its staff developed their Smart Start project via compliance, while Iredell, by comparison, has moved to expansion and transformation.

> **Iredell demonstrates the difference between necessary compliance and passion-fueled creativity with the attitude of "Failure is not an option."**

Iredell demonstrates the difference between necessary compliance and passion-fueled creativity with the attitude of "Failure is not an option." Chowan represents the forces that hinder advancement to true transformative capacity. Yet the idea continues to serve a need and even provides an example for how to overcome various obstacles.

For example, staff are difficult to recruit and train, as the rural multicounty surrounding area suffers a significant brain drain to adjacent areas. Nearby urban settings can pay more and offer a better lifestyle. The project also struggles with a large population in the lower socioeconomic range. Even under the best of circumstances, it's tough to make a community-wide difference among Chowan's target clients. These families face difficulties resulting from their generation-to-generation cycle of poverty. Chowan retains a strong process of advancement, which is promising.

Mediation Center of Eastern Carolina (MCEC)

The Mediation Center of Eastern Carolina is located in an historic part of New Bern, North Carolina. The town began as one of the original English settlements developed in the 18th century as a religious community commissioned by the King of England. The Mediation Center is located in an old two-story office building, just a few doors from the drugstore where Pepsi Cola was first brewed. The drugstore still evokes the era when it served the first Pepsi over 100 years ago.

The vision of The Mediation Center is:

To be recognized as the community resource for developing skills and establishing systems to improve the well-being of the community by making peaceful resolutions a way of life

Its mission is:

To help individuals in the community develop the capacity to respectfully resolve conflict

The MCEC offers a range of services, for example, general mediation and Teen Court. The latter offers proven alternatives to expensive institutional responses to juvenile delinquency. It keeps youngsters out of the criminal justice system at a critical juncture of passage to adulthood and productive citizenship.

The site visits occurred just as a new executive director was beginning to reshape the program. Previously, it had suffered from lack of leadership, used and unreplaced resources, and uninspired staff. The project had no significant place in the community. The first visit found the MCEC in the process of organizing and consolidating office space, downsizing but focusing services, developing staff and leadership, becoming part of the community, and determining how process is shaped by the inevitable passage of time. The executive director contributed greatly to every phase of planning. MCEC continues to provide expanded services.[120]

Insight into the processes, from planning to operations with attention to stabilization and expansion, brought crucial knowledge of practical details as to how each phase of the life cycle could be tackled. Extensive discussions detailed every critical feature of capacity building.

The Mediation Center of Eastern Carolina provided a unique opportunity to study how to strengthen operations, cultivate stakeholder relationships, develop a board, and especially, build capacity. Because the program was being rebuilt, it was still in the early stages of its life cycle. Thus, it provided a laboratory in which to study operations as they were being discerned and established.

Boys and Girls Club of Henderson County

The Henderson County Boys and Girls Club became a national model within the first 10 years of its incorporation. It's a stellar accomplishment driven by passion and a pervading sense of mission and their priorities:

> *To inspire and enable YOUNG PEOPLE, especially those from disadvantaged circumstances, to realize their full potential as PRODUCTIVE, RESPONSIBLE and CARING CITIZENS.*[123]

Even more impressive is their whole-person perspective on youth development:[124]

- *Mind:* Sharp Minds – Youth achieving in school and preparing for careers
- *Body:* Strong Bodies – Youth staying active and eating healthy foods
- *Soul:* True Hearts – Youth choosing positive personal actions

With these goals, children in their formative years are introduced to a philosophy for life.

Henderson County is a study in contrasts and an excellent proving ground for local service ideas. The demographics of this county are represented by both extremes of wealth and poverty, diverse ethnicities, and a large, mainly Hispanic, immigrant population.

The executive director, commenting on a unique function of place, stated that "Place is a way to break down barriers," suggesting that location is critical to success. The demographic of the county's largest target population, minorities in poverty, consists of many parents without high school education. This problem demanded action.

First, project leaders approached the local school system to offer GED classes—which they did, but to no response. It was too foreign for uneducated adults to go to a high school or even a middle school campus.

The next idea was to have local school teachers offer GED classes at the Club. The response remained unimpressive. The problem seemed to defy solution.

Finally, the executive director suggested the children's teachers, who were also Club staff, teach the adults as well in the school setting. When the Club offered this option, the outcome was positive.

It seems the barrier to formal education was the lack of connection that poorly educated minorities had with the educational establishment. The professionals in the school system didn't even know this lack of connection. However, when given an opportunity to gain a high school diploma in the same educational setting as their children, conducted by the same people who were teaching their children, parents felt comfortable enough to enroll for classes. Researchers were told that on one occasion a parent actually helped their child with homework. Pride beamed from her, staff related. What a turnaround. These "underprivileged" parents were compelled to "keep up with their children." *Place* and *attitude* were two crucial ingredients in the success of this venture.

The idea of place as an organic concept is best stated on the back of the Club's membership handbook, penned by the executive director:

The Positive Place for Kids

The Boys and Girls Club of Henderson County empowers kids to be the architects of their own lives. The #1 characteristic of successful living is a positive attitude. From a positive attitude come positive behaviors.

The Boys and Girls Club realizes kids possess the power to:
HAVE POSITIVE ATTITUDES
&
DEMONSTRATE POSITIVE BEHAVIORS IN ALL THEY DO
Thus, we expect it and we support children in achieving it.

As the executive director explained, the Club began with a vision, a determined few, and an old community center. Vision must have a home base.

Along with Iredell, The Boys and Girls Club was a refreshing oasis in this community quest for answers to dysfunctions. It added insight to the factors that make a project superior and significant. Both Henderson and Iredell demonstrate that almost any service idea can flourish when processes are engineered to work well.

> **The Club represents the power of a viable idea shaped by efficient, effective, vision-inspired process by vision-inspiring leadership.**

However, this doesn't mean a day at the Club was easy. Visits to this site over time brought into focus the urgent work of trying to hoist high needs children from the cycle of difficult circumstances.

Staff were involved in every young life. The board met onsite in the midst of the turmoil of the school day. Every element of capacity building was suffering the pains of neighborhood transformation. Consequently, staff, especially the executive director, contributed greatly to understanding the entire project life cycle. They offered particular insight into the development of resources and services and the processes of the stabilization and expansion phases of the life cycle.

The Boys and Girls Club's experience with stability and expansion then social transformation with at-risk elementary and middle school students and their families was invaluable. Few local service ideas reach the level of maturity realized by this program. The Club represents the power of a viable idea shaped by efficient, effective, vision-inspired process by vision-inspiring leadership.

We could have based this study of process entirely on either the Henderson Boys and Girls Club or the Iredell Smart Start school readiness program; they are that good. However, the addition of the other sites added pertinent and necessary variety, depth, understanding, and documentation of a proven and practical continuum of the capacity building process.

Practitioners' Insights: Keys to Understanding Project Success

Based on practitioner perspectives, Table 4.2 presents practical solutions to the following three major issues raised in the literature concerning local services delivery:

- *Government* – What is the current form of government and how can it be improved relative to services delivery, especially at the local level?

- *Implementation* – What is the nature of implementation and how can local service ideas solve the difficulties of getting beyond it to permanency?

- *Capacity Building* – What is the nature of true capacity building and its practice and focus?

Following are more specific statements and site-based practitioner perspectives regarding these issues.

Table 4.2: Practitioner Perspectives on Issues Raised in the Literature

Issues Raised in the Literature	Practitioner Explanations, Opinions, and Reflections
The public sector is stuck in govern*ment*.[125]	Local services are moving to govern*ance* based on performance and networked solutions to local needs.
Governmental leadership largely follows the top-down insular model.[126]	Local service project leadership is participatory and collaborative. The flow of information and feedback is circular, down to staff then reflection passes back to leadership for better decision making. It also continues to evolve according to the life cycle maturity of the service idea.
Government is risk-averse.[127]	Local service projects demonstrate that calculated risk is necessary for progress. The public environment is political and value laden, thus caution is necessary. However, projects progress by testing decisions with action and reflection, and carefully managing risk. Practitioners recognize that action is the only way to prove an idea works or how to adjust and abandon it if necessary.

Issues Raised in the Literature	Practitioner Explanations, Opinions, and Reflections
Government tries to satisfy too many interests.[128]	Local service practitioners target limited resources to a defined target population and location. Their philosophy is to do less, but do it well. This is crucial to stabilizing then sustaining an idea.
Government is compliance focused.[129]	Locally developed enduring services provide examples to federal, state, and local governments about how to blend necessary compliance with accountability and performance to satisfy the need for responsible (efficient and effective) use of public resources.
Government plans strategically by committee, largely as a stand alone task of leadership.[130]	Local strategic planning is a continuous process based on the collaboration of stakeholders, who combine their social capital to answer a locally-defined need. With that, stakeholders are in a better position to assess and efficiently and especially effectively employ the right available resources. A goal of continuous attention to strategy is to become socially transformative. Strategic planning is based on judgment and the science of capacity assessment, impact analysis, and process evaluation.
Government is stuck at implementation.[131]	Local service project practitioners move beyond implementation by focusing on permanency based on capacity building, the business infrastructure upon which a service depends.
Government implements (local service projects) by bureaucracy.[132]	Local service delivery provides examples for how to get beyond the difficulties of implementation and how traditional government can collaborate on networked solutions to community dysfunction. The combination of agency and networked services can be greater than the sum of the parts.

Issues Raised in the Literature	Practitioner Explanations, Opinions, and Reflections
Many times, projects are selected because they are labeled as "best practices."[133]	Because any practice must be specific to the demands of the site where it's applied, there's no such thing as a "best practice." Local service ideas are most productive when selected according to the site's capacity to deliver the idea and ability to contribute to project goals, and especially to an idea's practical effectiveness.
Government has minimal resources to provide public services.[134]	Resources are continuously modified and developed as part of an overall capacity building strategy. This reflects the lessons learned from the reality of being near the problem and its solution.
Public servants are agency specialists. [135]	Local service providers are value brokers.
Government needs to move from agency orientation toward networks and partnerships, enabling, and consensus building.[136]	Many times, local service ideas are networks comprised of multiple stakeholders, multiple streams of funding, fluid collaborations that change with assessed capacity/need, and services based on performance and flexible responses to political and practical demands. This is a direct result of local ownership of the problems and means to attack them.
Government needs a process to stabilize local service ideas.[137]	Projects should be developed according to their life cycle.

Let's consider in more detail certain areas for critique and improvement that emerged from discussions with practitioners:

- *The nature of government vs. governance* – Public bureaucracy is politically influenced and control based. Yes, traditional top-down, compliance-oriented, risk-averse, interest-driven agencies have a place in distributing goods and services; but they have (crippling) limits. Those limits can be somewhat mitigated when agencies collaborate with local service providers and practitioners to form networked/matrix solutions to local needs. With local collaboration, the constrictive rule of govern*ment* expands into a more flexible and effective govern*ance*.

- *Policy vs. process* – Governmental bureaucracies focus predominantly on policy implementation, not project development with service permanency. The latter has different goals, activities, and processes. Local performance-oriented ideas, as exemplified at Iredell and Henderson, demonstrate how to get beyond implementation, which will, in turn, improve policy effectiveness.

- *Public service vs. value brokers* – It's crucial that public servants learn, with local service providers, how to become value brokers. The process of service idea development provides a means to accomplish this transition from administrator to value broker. Ideally, the public servant moves from simply following a directive to being involved in building the business infrastructure to make it work in their community. Simply put, they know about and engage appropriate service providers who can offer the most value for the task at hand.

People in these well-functioning projects saw only possibilities and took the problems and stressors that arose in stride. This attitude is reflected in the following feature-by-feature consideration of unanticipated insights and concerns. These extend the practitioner explanations, opinions, and reflections summarized in Table 4.2.

Planning and Leadership

Of the staff at all the sites, staff at Henderson and Iredell provided the most insight about appropriate thus effective leadership. They firmly believed that *every* stakeholder group and individual has leadership potential and should be nurtured. Again, they validated the effectiveness of leaders driven by the value of individual and communal well-being.

When program initiators at the local level consider leadership, the discussion usually focuses on a board of directors, executive director, and municipal and agency officials. Usually, they volunteer. At these accomplished sites, however, equally important were appropriate stakeholder parents, students, general staff, and need-to-know stakeholders. Board members were also chosen more by what they brought to the project. A bank official for example, would obtain a board seat because he or she knows how to write a charter. A sheriff would have the most contacts in the municipality. Also, leaders of these

> The process of service idea development provides a means to accomplish this transition from administrator to value broker.

successful programs knew that feedback from students—for example, their satisfaction with the after-school programming—was vital to their success. In addition, parents were nurtured as ambassadors for their programs.

The other difference concerned the role of the board of directors. Before the field work to develop the process of capacity building, the board was most often considered an insular body in a top-down organization. It stated the vision and mission and gave directives to carry out decisions and policy.

The study sites demonstrated that, rather than a top-down directive group, a fully functioning board in the vein of value broker was a *servant* of the process. Board members were

> The study sites demonstrated that, rather than a top-down directive group, a fully functioning board in the vein of value broker was a servant of the process.

much more involved in the real work of forming the organization. For example, they developed financing or made significant donations themselves and then oversaw operations cooperatively. As a result, they got more done, and the program grew because of it. These successful sites were doing the "impossible"—closing the services-to-needs gap!

Capacity Assessment

Capacity assessment evolved. It began as a simple one-time needs assessment of local demand for a preselected service; it was terminal and narrowly focused. Observation determined it had to be a continuous process and focus more broadly on the range of services needed as determined by the target population.

Usually, capacity assessment, if done at all, is carried out when ideas are imported, many times from out of state, or sponsored by the state or a private funding entity. That is, needs assessment is completed to shoehorn the community into a suggested solution or "best practice"—the exact opposite of how it should be done.

All the study sites redefined this notion by recognizing that a need can be addressed only in terms of an array of resources, both external and internal. Stakeholders realized that regardless of a project's origins, they needed to seek a specific and unique local definition of capacity, including how to determine and develop it. This insight was an essential factor in project success and shed a bright light on the true nature of capacity building.

Scope

Practitioners didn't change the main definition of scope, which has always been about determining how much can be done. However, they added to it and changed the focus: Scope was ascertaining how much could be done *very well*. Thus, it became a matter of doing *less* and doing it properly, not more to exhaust resources and especially collective will to achieve the best results.

A second insight was how vision and mission contributed as a daily decision-making tool. Staff at the most productive sites, again Henderson and Iredell, repeatedly asked if an action fit with their mission and vision. This questioning permeated nearly every activity and discussion during the day.

> **Remember that determining scope is all about being correctly, continuously, and intimately vision-directed.**

The main issues associated with mishandling the scoping process were:

- *Assuming too much responsibility* – This is a common failing. People want very much to solve a problem that needs attention. Consequently, they define what needs to be done as broadly as possible. However, the scoping process is better served by a rigorous probing and understanding of the capacity to deliver a chosen service, with the goal of stability then long-term sustainability.

- *Choosing a "canned" intervention or service idea simply for the sake of convenience or expediency* – Many projects begin by getting funding via a grant that recommends certain "evidence-based" practices, which most likely are not appropriate to the project and especially the local one at hand. Besides that, delivering prescribed "evidence-based" practices as designed from above can be wickedly difficult. Extreme deliberation is best before adopting any service.

- *Misidentifying the primary problem because scope didn't consider capacity* – Many times, program planners simply don't define the problem correctly. The entire program must flow from a highly accurate, measurable problem statement to achieve success.

- *Not targeting limited resources to specific project populations and relevant geographic areas* – The scope must specify where, when, and especially how to direct scarce project energies and resources.

- *Not committing to performance measurement during the scoping process –* Performance considers two essential measures of process and progress. Process measurement assesses work efficiency, and progress measurement assesses effectiveness. Put another way, staff need to know if people are productive about stated purposes and thus are achieving the desired results.

Most local project staff have only a cursory understanding of scope and little appreciation of its application as an essential project-building tool. This isn't their fault, as they're usually service providers not skilled in project development; hence the need for a practical, goal-oriented capacity building process.

The obvious answer to this lack of understanding scope is to first recognize it, then become skilled in scoping as part of overall capacity building. Remember that determining scope is all about being correctly, continuously, and intimately vision-directed. In the well-functioning service project, less is actually more.

Analysis and Evaluation

Analysis and evaluation are different and need to be done in concert throughout the process of capacity building. Practitioners in the field were skilled in the art—yes, it is an art—of infusing quantitative analysis and qualitative evaluation into moment-to-moment decision making. Analysis here determines if overall goals are being achieved. Evaluation determines if staff are doing the right job the right way. Analysis and evaluation are *not* about finding things wrong; they're about determining what can be improved then improving it and pinpointing what's working well and continuing it. You know this art when you see it in processes that are efficient and effective. People are productive and pleasant about their work.

> When applied correctly, analysis and evaluation discover what's working well and reveal needed corrections as simply opportunities to make the project stronger.

Practitioners commented that the purpose of investigation is to build, not deconstruct, the project. This reverses common practice, in which an auditor or external program manager descends on a project with the purpose of finding discrepancies. This approach does much harm, the worst being that it shapes staff who need to be told precisely what to do. Therefore, that's exactly what is done, whereas staff need to have buy-in about what and how they do things. This is essential to team building, the better way—no, the only true way—to success.

Field practitioners delineated these problems with analysis and evaluation: not doing them at all; doing them separately from the other key features of capacity building; and/or conducting analysis largely to satisfy external (oversight or funding) requirements. When applied correctly, analysis and evaluation discover what's working well and reveal needed corrections as simply opportunities to make the project stronger. The aren't used punitively in any way.

Developing Reliable Funding

One of the most dramatic surprises in conceptualizing capacity building arose during the investigation of how these model sites develop funds. Usually, local public startups focus on grants as a primary source of funding. This requires continually competing for grants, the outcome of which determines the project's duration and scope. In other words, the service idea lasts as long as the grants do and accomplishes little more than what's outlined by the purpose and restrictions of those grants. These local projects resort to grants as local funds are largely functional with little discretionary monies for ideas. The work of tackling a social ill is long term and customized to the site and situation. Canned approaches aren't appropriate. In addition to their restrictions, short-term grant funds put service projects under impossible demands to produce relatively quick results, when meaningful, desired effects in the community could take years.

The forward-thinking site practitioners interviewed for this study saw the futility of this mode of terminal grants-based operation. They found ways to remove their programs from it—in some cases dramatically. Program stakeholders understand that project success is influenced by how the project is viewed in the community. A supportive community determines the success of developing resources beyond grants. Support comes from trust, and trust comes from strong relationships.

Relationships win secure funding streams such as a line item in a local municipal budget or a means of annual giving. Relationship-building takes time, and given it's critical to an idea's success, it needs to be planned.

The original line of inquiry on resources focused on developing financing. Field work revealed that development of resources is, in essence, social entrepreneurship. When you make people believe in your vision, they contribute to it. What does this say about resources development and, by extension, the entire project development process? It all needs to be concerned with building solid relationships, so people want to help and actively seek ways to become vested in the project.

Many startup project practitioners miss this point. They often treat resources development as a standalone task and not as a project-wide endeavor involving all stakeholder groups. They try to develop funds based on short-term expediency (e.g., applying or reapplying for grants) or dependency on a single or a few sources of money rather than seeing funding as streams based on goodwill. Because resources development is a critical function of capacity building, the results need to be substantial and long term. The project can't rely on stakeholders continuously applying for soft (whimsical grant) funding.

Services

When we began this study, we didn't consider services at all. We assumed that once the business infrastructure—the accounting systems, policies, and standard operating procedures—were established, services would be routinely delivered. Yet another myth of developing service ideas is dispelled!

The error became evident from the first interviews. The reason for this original lapse? Most local services start with a service in mind, which is reflected in the request for startup funding. It's tough to get local money for an "experiment." Grants are the usual target. Yes, apply for a grant, but be aware they're a pandora's box of difficulty. The biggest problem? A grant funding stream dries up eventually—and too soon for your idea to take root. Furthermore, developers often pay scant attention to vision/mission, how their idea fits into the community agency infrastructure, and how it tangibly benefits target clientele.

We noted that staff of *successful* projects that established permanency began nurturing their service(s) early in program planning. They made sure services were:

- *Performance-oriented* – Processes were efficient.

- *Evidence-based* – Project goals included measurable results, which amounted to much more than just counting numbers.

- *Part of the capacity building effort* – The service idea was formulated with permanency in mind.

Successful project staff understood that services had to result in observable behavior change in their target clients that contributed to individual, and thus community, well-being. They also understood that a service doesn't start out completely efficient. Rather, efficiency is the result of constant attention from the vision/mission-driven team. Measurable performance is a precursor to sustaining the service.

Many times, service providers—for example, counselors for at-risk youth—aren't included as part of the service acquisition process. This is a major problem. Why? Because choosing a service for emotional reasons only or because it produced "results" in another town, is a critical mistake, according to board and staff members we interviewed. It's wise, they said, to choose services dispassionately, with knowledge of what it will take to address the issues at hand. Services must match the vision and mission of the project and be able to measurably achieve the stated goals *with available resources in the considered locale.* In addition, a service must continually perform as measured by resultant changes in human behavior and ultimately benefit the community. Otherwise, it should be dropped.

North Carolina Smart Start executive directors mentioned several instances in which an idea—even one with strong support and funding—was turned down because "It wasn't what we do." In other words, the new idea didn't fit with the project's vision, mission, and scope, which is the "acid test" for *all* decisions in the well-working,

> Successful project staff understood that services had to result in observable behavior change in their target clients that contributed to individual, and thus community, well-being.

permanency-directed effort. Most project officials aren't prepared to make such difficult decisions. They haven't arrived at an intuitive sense of the scope of their program and services necessary to be self-renewing and transformative. That doesn't mean, however, that the new idea couldn't be developed by a different entity.

Staffing

Our original thinking concerning staffing didn't change during the study. We surmised that a comprehensive staff development policy would be needed. However, the most effective project staffing programs at the model sites went beyond traditional human resource development to human *capital* development. Here's the difference: The former is routinely concerned with staff *management,* and the latter is concerned with more widely *developing human potential,* both individual and especially collective. We gained insight from practitioners that, even in the smallest of projects, staff can have a comprehensive "pre-hire to post-retirement"[138] philosophy that emphasizes individual potential. This approach replaces "hiring for skills and firing for character," which is disastrously common. The approach of "hire for character and fire for skills," makes firing rare. Character development, when it's emphasized during hiring and continuously throughout employment can elevate the whole endeavor if only that people enjoy what they do together. When skills trump character, many unfortunate incidents can be traced back to lapses in moral judgment, which can have serious repercussions, including loss of career and reputation for the entire enterprise.

With this insight about human capacity development, Iredell and Henderson were able to nurture intrinsically motivated staff, who accomplished extraordinary goals with ordinary resources.

Wholistic Staff Development

First, our interviews to gather data for the critical feature of staffing for capacity building mainly dealt with hiring criteria. This quickly evolved to an effort to understand the continuum of staffing from the first job posting to the final exit interview and beyond. Interviews probed how leaders developed human resources from the perspective of encouraging staff to perform their stated duties and responsibilities, be team- and goal-oriented, and be skilled at personal and programmatic capacity building. The whole person matters. Life balance matters.

Each staff member needs to be part of a goal-oriented team. The study sites that build and strengthen transformative capacity emphasized the whole-person philosophy of staff development. This

> **Indicators of human resources difficulties are high turnover, no succession plan, and lack of a career development plan for each employee.**

approach includes formal education, relevant skills training (for example, through workshops, conferences, and certifications), and encouragement to maintain outside interests and a healthy lifestyle.

Problems arise when human capacity development is treated as separate from programmatic capacity building. Indicators of human resources difficulties are high turnover, no succession plan, and lack of a career development plan for each employee. The leadership at progressive sites considered staff the single most important determinant of program capacity and ultimate success, even over and above a steady flow of money. Simply put, if people want an idea to work and other staff and leaders appreciate their efforts along the way, the project will most likely succeed.

Practitioner insight asserts that planning never stops; it matures with the growth of the project and reaction to the realities of working in a dynamic environment. Leadership gradually proceeds from the creative process of conceptualizing and determining vision, mission, values, and perhaps creed of the service idea to working individually and collectively with staff and community to realize that vision. Project leaders evolve from idealists leading the vision to guiding hands in the background, a natural progression of working toward permanency. From their first day as a board member, they're made to understand they'll be required to commit long enough to transition from just being on the board to working on the program with assigned duties. Visioning is vital and short lived when it must be put in place.

The parenting analogy portrays how enlightened project leaders evolve. Early on, their parenting role is quite directive. It grows more supervisory, then advisory, as the child matures and stands alone. As one practitioner explained, the progressive board evolves from "inspiration to perspiration" as board members work and plan with stakeholders. Leadership at these model sites is a real working body. It's not simply a short-term assemblage of people who happen to be holding certain offices and positions at the time the service idea is proposed. Each key feature has this evolutionary nature in the capacity building, performance-driven service project. And that is the way that the future of project development should be.

Overcoming Obstacles

Building a local service project is the epitome of Variability, Uncertainty, Chaos, and Ambiguity (VUCA). The challenge is most difficult and intriguing. The philosophy is to see difficulties as opportunities to improve. This is not to encourage difficulties, of course, but to build the confidence that individually, and especially collectively, solutions are available to make the effort stronger and stronger. There's a stark difference between fearing VUCA and building strengths by overcoming it.

In spite of VUCA, some of the study sites progressed well and exemplified the life cycle concept, which encompasses the aforementioned attitude or philosophy of solutions building. Sites such as the Boys and Girls Club and school readiness at Iredell were models for the concept of building capacity and how to transform a community. The ability of these practitioners to interpret theory with practical application was impressive. For example, through practical application, program analysis grew into capacity analysis, with the further purpose of forming long-term relationships and subsequent support. Even more impressive was the fact that practitioners were exceptional theorists. Not only that, but they were *proving* this new theory of capacity building to sustain local service ideas.

Likewise, practitioners altered and certainly expanded original ideas and suppositions about project development. The thought process evolved from a background of developing community ideas with block grants, which is top-down and formulaic, to appreciating the cycle of bottom-up and back-down communication, taking a local idea to permanent reality. They redefined the nature of cooperation, collaboration, and connecting. From the stereotypical viewpoint of stakeholders being only those with leadership positions, they moved to including stakeholders based on their contribution to the long-term goal of social transformation. This meant that a board member of a post-release transitional program, for example, could be a former inmate with a previous substance abuse problem who successfully completed a program that resulted in return to the community.

We received a constant stream of insight from respondents. Clients, even children, had relevant leadership potential and much to do with the progress and growth of the project. In the vein of value-driven leadership, these practitioners demonstrated the "each one teach one" principle, to be good and do good by helping others. In fact, that's the operating motto of TROSA, Triangle Residential Options for Substance Abusers.

Operations

Among many issues concerning operations, several significant ones emerged. The executive directors at MCEC and Win-Win pointed out the wisdom of a stability to sustainability plan for each major feature. These plans then form the comprehensive plan for program endurance.

They also asserted that boards tend to be underutilized and recommended that board members function as workers with specific tasks. For example, members could be assigned to resources development, relationship and coalition building, services performance, or expansion planning.

Discussions at most of the sites brought to light the most important error of ignoring comprehensive board and (especially) staff development in favor of "more important" business.

Stability and Expansion

Originally, we thought, as most do, of the concept of "stability" as securing some sort of funding beyond initial startup monies. However, we didn't adequately consider the proper scope and detail that stabilizing a project requires. Practitioners related that the ability to endure in the community is complicated, chaotic, and continuous hard work, albeit gratifying. Why did they characterize it this way?

- *Complicated* – because each of the critical features need to be self-sustaining. These include composing a dedicated governing board of directors, understanding and employing analysis and evaluation, and hiring and developing values-oriented staff—in other words, all the key activities of Capacity Building.

- *Chaotic* – because self-sustaining stability is based on the whimsical nature of dealing with people, bureaucracies, and socio-behavioral dynamics.

- *Continuous* – because being self-sustaining must be maintained throughout the life of the idea, which should last through the life of the problem it addresses. Work has to sustain the insight that local public services are best served by building *permanent solutions to permanent problems.*

Staff at Iredell counseled not to mistake inertia for permanence in the array of community services. Here services are stuck in low-level routine rather than stretching to improve programming and achieve the stated vision and mission.

Stability is marked by a project that encompasses the following attributes:

- *Performance orientation* – It's making measurable improvement in target populations. For example, are children in afterschool programming attending school regularly and learning at or above grade level?

- *Capable staff* – The program nurtures a dynamic staff.

- *Solid relationships* – It's based on good relationships with stakeholders and the community.

- *Funding reliability* – The program has a number of reliable funding streams.

- *Analysis and evaluation* – It integrates analysis and evaluation into daily operations.

- *Sense of reasonable possibility* – The program staff holds a realistic view of what can and should be done.

Again, the revelation here was to *think small.* Tackle only what can realistically be done; pay close attention to detail; do the little things well; and target work to essential functions. Paying attention to the correct minutia is vital. This strategy will pay off in the development of reliable resources. In turn, it will lead to goal accomplishment more effectively than a large, sweeping, and perhaps dramatic effort that's short-sighted and much less controllable. Then, one success generates another one. Correctly done, Capacity Building is self-fulfilling and paves the way for the next good idea.

While vision statements are grand at successful sites, they were realized by stripping away the clutter. For example, the timid board may have a tendency to alter their purposes in an attempt to

> The timid board may have a tendency to alter their purposes in an attempt to qualify for a funding source. The bold board will simply not accept anything unless it "fits."

qualify for a funding source. The bold board will simply not accept anything unless it "fits."

Closing the service-to-needs gap isn't the result of attempting to offer more services to more people in more territory to demonstrate accomplishment. Rather than dramatic expansion, building an enduring idea involves tweaking present services and reaching just a few more people while making access easier. Establish the root and trunk of expansion before branches can sprout and flourish . . . season after season.

For example, the Iredell Partnership had been giving away car seats as part of its preschool health mandate. At-risk mothers saw it as "charity," which was off-putting. A charge of $10 made it an investment in their children, and participation in the car seat program increased noticeably. Concurrently, the playroom was also free of charge, which was also felt to be a handout. A $10 monthly fee made it a service and participation by target families accelerated. But it didn't end there. The Partnership ultimately transferred the car seat program to another agency. Its mandate for car safety then was being satisfied externally, saving in-house resources. The manpower used to procure and distribute the seats was now answering other objectives. The mission was accomplished, and the program grew stronger. Capacity building is a matter of nuances—a thousand things done just a little better . . . continuously.

Again, issues are many when considering expansion, but respondents had two overall concerns. First, project developers often tend to expand too much, too soon. Second, expansion wasn't being *planned for* early enough in the life of the project, i.e., from day one. The model programs anticipated these issues from the project's inception. Very little is left to chance in the progressive, transformative project.

Coming up, we'll look at the details of a practical process for developing and implementing a local service project. However, before examining each of the process features, it would be helpful to relate some of the initial impressions of them from the field.

Initial Impressions of the Intangibles of the Process

This brief explanation alludes to the intangibles of service project development. Intangibles are quite important because developing an idea that eventually addresses a social condition that needs improvement is much more than a plan. For example:

> **Capacity building is a matter of nuances—a thousand things done just a little better . . . continuously.**

- *Inspiration* – How does a project executive director transcend the tasks of management and leadership to inspire staff?

- *Desire* – How do project practitioners put together a successful marketing campaign that motivates people and businesses to want to contribute time and resources?

- *Participation* – How do practitioners arrive at a state of wanting to be *"part of the magic"*?

- *Actualizing* – Why do staff from one site seem to *learn more, do more, and become more* than those at another site?

The executive director at the Iredell Partnership commented that the process of idea/project nurturing boils down to three areas of focus:

- *Developing relationships* – First, delivering a service idea is based on developing relationships. Although mainly for financial support, this philosophy of relationship building extends through every aspect of project development.

- *Serving a need economically* – Second, any idea for service must serve an assessed need for financial viability. In other words, it needs to make the community measurably better at a reasonable cost. It's programmatically cost effective.

- *Constantly assessing importance to mission* – Finally, successful stakeholders constantly assess what is and especially what is not important.

These matters offer insight into important intangibles of successful capacity building. Let's briefly compare.

A Contrasting Model

The Pasquotank Drug Task Force offered a contrast to the focus on relationship building, financial capacity assessment, and mission orientation to process. The Task Force demonstrated a top-down, compliance model of service provision, which worked for the purpose at hand, which was to curtail drug traffic—but it made no attempt to address prevention of the problem. Its process was effectively narrow to accommodate traditional command and control. Leadership was agency-based in that the sheriff established county policy for drug intervention, assembled the team, gave directions, and was briefed regularly on how his directives were being carried out.

In the Capacity Building model at Iredell, leadership matured with the idea and was continuously involved in the setting, achieving, and resetting of goals. For both Iredell and Henderson, capacity assessment was an operations-wide endeavor encompassing all the critical features.

The Task Force, on the other hand, didn't need capacity assessment as the effort was determined by available county and forfeiture funds, which meant staffing remained at two investigators.

Scope at the Task Force was narrowly defined to one over-all task: drug investigations that could be prosecuted. This project required no visioning process nor detailed activity as in a capacity building process.

Relationship building was also different from site to site. The Task Force demonstrated its own manner of developing relationships within the community. The sheriff and staff made it a point to publicize the fact that illegal drug activity was being reduced in Pasquotank County. In every way, the team members were courteous and responsive to community needs and requests. As a result, the Task Force commanded respect for a job well done. This differed, in a way, from the respect earned by a service that becomes an integral part of community leadership concerned with communal problem-solving and social well-being.

Staff development was more specific with the Task Force, which focused more on investigatory competency rather than the broader professional development required in law enforcement. Still, both models of operation serve a purpose.

Generally, promising public sector governance is evolving to address locally defined problems solved by local matrices of relevant supporting services and talent.

The input to the process of project building from the Pasquotank Task Force was not as broad or in-depth as it was from the other sites, especially Iredell Smart Start and the Henderson Boys and Girls Club. However, when compared to the other sites, the Task Force demonstrated a necessary and beneficial juxtaposition of traditional govern*ment* (*what* is done) and govern*ance* (*how* it is done).

Governance is the expression of leadership in which collaboration for the greater good is the goal, not merely cooperation to get a task done. Government preserves agency services as comparatively insular silos. Governance builds individual and community well-being with the goal of a thriving neighborhood.

Regarding planning a project or program, the retired Iredell Partnership executive director stated, "No amount of planning can prepare for the education that comes from the doing of it."

In concurrence is a Renaissance great who left a lasting legacy with his nearly countless works:

> *"I have been impressed with the urgency of doing. Knowing is not enough; we must apply. Being willing is not enough; we must do."*
> – Leonardo da Vinci

Regarding the Proposed Steps in the Development Process

At the beginning of our study, we postulated certain critical steps with their associated actions as a basis for planning. Project developers and practitioners highly modified these tasks to be much more organic, dynamic, synergistic, and action-oriented as per the circumstances and demands of their projects *as they unfolded*. It is the law of experience that action determines direction. Consequently, we revised the steps and their related Effective Practices action items for each major phase of program development.

They are *not* a priority list, nor are they presented in a hierarchy; though they are *critical*. Stakeholders may see the need to do more, but neglecting any critical item is to court failure, according to respondents. In other words, one can judiciously add to the list as needed but not remove from it. (See Table 7.1: Capacity Building from the Bottom Up – A Tool for Local Public Service Practitioners on pages 203 to 205.) The exact path of actions to take must be determined by the network of stakeholders tackling the task and the unique character of each locale. Every capacity building journey has its own personality, but it needs to be performance-oriented, built on local matrix capacity, and founded on respect in and from the community.

Planning involves designing the essential operations of the project. We originally conceptualized planning based on the current workplace understanding of managerial tasks such as controlling, directing, budgeting, communicating, motivating, and organizing. However, our interviews revealed the need for much more than traditional functional tasking. That need reflected the required interaction of key functions due to the dynamic nature of the full life cycle of an idea and building the business structure of that public project. Respondents intuitively agreed with the literature that the idea must be:

- *integrated externally* with local programs and services and the community[139] and

- *integrated internally* as a responsive, flexible organization that's well fit to the community it serves.

Thus, building a service idea is trans-organizational,[140] and a local service becomes bigger than the primary supporting agency as it seeks to iteratively close the service-to-needs gap. Take, for example, any one of the sustained services we studied. The Iredell County Partnership for Young Children goes beyond local services, for example to *Dolly Parton's Imaginary Library, Parents as Teachers,* and the *United Way.*

Practitioners confirmed the importance of planning and implementation. If in planning for long-term resources, selecting services to

> **Every capacity building journey has its own personality, but it needs to be performance-oriented, built on local matrix capacity, and founded on respect in and from the community.**

benefit the community, and training stakeholders,[141] a project failed to be worthy of sustaining, it risked failure. The goal had to be endorsed in the community.

According to one project director, developing a service idea demands constantly determining "what is and is not practical" to realize the potential of the service. She asserted that a proper vision "sets boundaries" and doesn't become "lost in dreamy clouds." The project is constantly assessing the limits of structure, personnel, and resources[142] and remains resolutely within those bounds. Progress is never in question, but it's an imperfect process. Capacity building isn't a straight line, an all-encompassing foolproof checklist. The nature of experimentation results in a zigzag route. Thus, these process features are open for discussion.

Essential Questions for a Workable Process

This Capacity Building model aims to provide answers to the following questions essential to sustaining a project and improving community well-being:

- What are the major life-cycle phases, and what is the sequence (progression) of critical features (milestones) of the project development process?

- What are the most productive and practical critical action items at each phase?

- What are the most practical, effective practices for each critical action of the development process?

Answers to the above questions from experience, the field, and the literature follow.

Using the Project Life Cycle in Capacity Building

The concept, applicability, and practicality of the project life cycle is confirmed. As a concept, the life cycle graphically demonstrates the long-term, complex nature of local service delivery. It removes some of the confusion from the chaotic nature of the public service business. Furthermore, it's universally understood by explaining processes sequentially and translating them to specific productive action. It is also fungible according to your circumstances and thus accommodates your necessary actions as local circumstances define them.

This concept of the life cycle provides practitioners with a simple tool for viewing project development through then beyond the difficulties of implementation. Its focus on the local project is comprised of a bottom-up, networked matrix of services and resources aimed at resolving a defined problem. This approach is contrary to the usual top-down, controlling, and limited nature of larger public agencies and their prescribed service projects. The life cycle provides a conceptual foundation for project building based on cycles of action and reflection.

Within the life cycle, each of the process features is functional and necessary and, above all, practical as proven by successful application in the field.

The inquiry began with a checklist of 27 items and no particular conceptual framework for understanding how they might contribute to effective implementation. With the advice of a range of experts and practitioners, the unstructured list was whittled down to 10 features. Sixteen steps or actions reduced a highly complex conceptualization to something more comprehensible, communicable, and credible.

Project capacity development now is much simpler to grasp while not being made so simplistic as to be unrealistic. As described previously, a service project can be divided into three phases:

- **Phase I: Planning.** Design essential operations.
- **Phase II: Operation.** Put the plan into action.
- **Phase III: Sustain/Expand.** Realize social transformation.

Critical Features and Effective Practices

Seeing project development in terms of a long-range plan, critical features, and the most effective actions helps project staff and leadership see public service operation as a business. In fact, TROSA and LINC are based on multiple sustainable businesses with predictable, self-sustaining cash flows. No wonder these programs succeed.

Defining features and Effective Practices greatly reduces unproductive work, errors in thinking and action, and futile effort. This brings us to critical features as action statements and their relevance to capacity building in Table 4.3.

Table 4.3: Critical Features and Actions and Their Relevance to Capacity Building

Phase/Feature/Action Statement	Relevance to Capacity Building
Phase I: Planning	
Nurture and grow key leadership.	Board members' duties and responsibilities evolve as the project passes through each phase of project maturation.
Integrate capacity assessment into capacity building.	Capacity assessment seeks to understand what incremental responsibilities the program/staff can assume relative to the resources (capacity) to meet those demands.
Determine project scope.	Scope is a matter of defining what can be done well according to mission, vision, and capacity. Less is more.

Phase/Feature/Action Statement	Relevance to Capacity Building
Phase I: Planning	
Design the impact analysis and process evaluation.	Analysis determines the benefits of the project to the community (effectiveness). Evaluation determines if the processes of the project are economical and goal directed (efficiency). This picture of effectiveness and efficiency is essential to justify the project's continuation and expansion.
Nurture relationships for resources development.	Resources result from productive alliances that are based on mutual respect and credibility derived from delivering on stated (project) promises.
Develop performance-oriented services.	Services must be performance-oriented and help the organization achieve specified goals. Service providers become an integral part of the project team.
Nurture staff by a process of human capacity development.	Staff must be a major priority. It's necessary to invest in them with comprehensive, continuous human capacity development that grows their potential, personally and for the organization.
Phase II: Operation	
Plan operations with the future in mind.	Operations routinize planning, determine capacity, and set the stage for stabilization, transformation, and expansion.
Assess capacity for sustainability.	Added responsibilities or expansion of services must have the business infrastructure and capacity to support the idea.

Phase/Feature/Action Statement	Relevance to Capacity Building
Phase II: Operation	
Make scope analysis a continuous part of decision making.	Scope is how much an organization can do well; thus any additional responsibilities must be justified and proceed incrementally.
Combine process evaluation and impact analysis to optimize service delivery.	Work has to be efficient and effective in contributing to vision and mission goals.
Engage friends in strategic resource development.	Resources development, especially obtaining funding, is multifaceted. A project develops many friends in those receiving services as well as wider circles of community members. These friends may be either sources of funding or connected to potential donors.
Nurture performance-oriented service providers.	Providers who deliver the services need to understand how and how much they contribute to vision, mission, and goals.
Develop key staff for their human and social capital potential.	Staff are members of society and have influence on their communities. When people come together for the common good, society benefits.
Phase III: Stabilization/Expansion	
Stabilize operations.	Stability or sustainability happens when the idea becomes reality as a durable part of the local array of services. The program can then continue to build transformative capacity.

Phase/Feature/Action Statement	Relevance to Capacity Building
Phase III: Stabilization/Expansion	
Plot the long-range strategy and tactics for expansion.	Expansion occurs when the idea incrementally changes a social condition and promotes community health, safety, and well-being, or some combinations of these three. The idea realizes organic self-sufficiency and social transformation. It then becomes an example for wider application of the life cycle model of project development.

This table aligns the action orientation of each feature to elements of capacity building as observed by local service program practitioners. Each critical feature offers insight into its corresponding effective practice within the synergistic whole of service project development. Stability, then, is not only a state of service permanence; it's being a part of community progress and well-being. Services are often delivered as discrete tasks, each with a narrow view of what the service is meant to do. Community betterment, dare we say transformation, is attainable when all the pieces of an idea come together so the whole is much greater than the sum of its many, many parts.

The whole process is delineated in Table 7.1: Capacity Building from the Bottom Up – A Tool for Local Public Service Practitioners on pages 203 to 205. You have the entirety of your project in an easy-to-follow checklist easily tailored to your unique circumstances, capabilities, and criteria for success. Action items present a hierarchy of project-building activities in a logical continuum. Effective

> Stability, then, is not only a state of service permanence; it's being a part of community progress and well-being.

Practices logically follow and focus limited resources, especially staff time, on activities that are proven and goal directed. Staff recognize their pursuit is prescribed by the people, place, and politics of the program's municipality.

Each Effective Practice exemplifies the necessary evolution to bottom-up governance where the emphasis is properly focused on community and not agency. Public services delivery shifts from silo agencies exercising top-down control to collaborative, bottom-up synergistic matrices. The goal of public services evolves to a state of community wellness in which families can thrive.

Following is a comprehensive look at each of the three phases of the project life cycle, starting with Phase I.

PHASE I of the Project Life Cycle: Plan – Design Essential Operations

Following are descriptions of the three phases of a project life cycle with their steps and associated Effective Practices (actions). Together, they clarify how the three program life cycles contribute to building the capacity of a permanent answer to a permanent problem.

Refer to Table 7.1: Capacity Building from the Bottom Up – A Tool for Local Public Service Practitioners on pages 203 to 205 for a concise overview of the whole process.

A good place to start in Phase I, Planning, is with leadership.

1. Nurture and grow key leadership.

The interviews highlighted many of the classical descriptions of leadership observed in the field. Executive directors were getting more from people than they thought possible and didn't consider defeat an option.

We observed an unexpected twist to the readily identifiable traits and examples of leadership in that leadership was shaped by the ideas and the processes of solving problems. Capacity building project leadership is compelled and inspired by the idea of being good and doing good for others. People accomplished the "impossible" because they understood their roles. They contributed materially to the project and were committed for the long term, even when aggravated by nitpickers. Leaders didn't come to their jobs fully matured, as one might assume of board members. Leaders matured as the project matured.

Respondents recognized the leadership potential of stakeholder groups. Consequently, discussions touched on how to develop the leadership contribution of the board, senior leadership, staff, clientele, *and* the community as an entity.

Good leaders embodied principles of prioritizing long-term processes to resolve a problem over short-term procedures, which can be just getting to the end of the day. A process is the continuous, effective, inspiring work of accomplishing a program that's long term, as it needs to address a long-term problem, e.g., juvenile delinquency or reentry. Stereotypically, staff stuck in procedures dislike their job, and those who consider the overall process love doing something bigger than they are.

Capacity building is about matrices over silos of services, the common good over turfism, collaboration over cooperation, and legacy over clock-watching.

In keeping with the life-cycle concept, leaders followed the various maturational states of being observed in long-term service-project building. These states could be described as: first "apparent confusion," then "tense equilibrium," followed by "crisis containment," and finally, "stability."[143] Successful local leaders aren't distracted by the crisis of the moment and the upheaval of change. They see such situations as opportunities to strengthen and grow. Their role is to train themselves through these maturational stages to stable operations that then become a platform from which to repeat the process. Forward thinking leaders are forever coming up with the next great idea, always becoming the best they can be with their staff.

These leaders may be cautious because they're keepers of project values, but being action-oriented, they don't fear decisions. They understand how they fit into these stages of growth, how good and bad circumstances can be used to advantage, and which roles are best suited to contend with them. In fact, many nonprofit organizations are some of the best run and productive public entities, according to respondents.

Capacity building project leadership is compelled and inspired by the idea of being good and doing good for others.

Discussions on leadership largely revolved around two main points: role expectations and who should be included in the project. We witnessed this natural evolution of forward leaning program development from tasks such as grant writing and management to the perpetual work of building the idea for community betterment and well-being. These successful service delivery systems then become models for other ideas, no matter the locale. The interview instrument didn't ask specifically who comprised leadership and what their roles were, but themes emerged in the interviews at all the sites. That's the way on-site research is supposed to work.

Two leaders admitted that lead staffers were burdened with unreal expectations, especially during the formative stages of developing a local service. As public projects usually begin with little funding, the first people to be hired must do it all. Additional staff can be added only after the goal-oriented, effective processes are established, not before, as may be the case in the private sector. Respondents knew the dangers of an overburdened senior staffer feeling compelled to focus on compliance instead of the necessary transformational capacity. A project stumbles when that lead person, no matter how passionate and determined, fails to prioritize. He or she can become over-whelmed with the seeming urgencies of the moment, whereas long-term presence of the service should be the priority.

Staff at Iredell and Henderson had gone through experimenting with crisis management to arrive at the current action-reflection management style. Startup staff constantly deconstruct decisions to improve them, which was and remains highly nuanced. The Chowan Perquimans Smart Start Partnership aims to accomplish the particular action of the moment better and better. If lead staff are to survive the initial phases of project startup, it's essential to delegate lesser tasks as soon as possible without giving up responsibility.

Respondents stressed the need to include relevant people in the project devel-opment process. They termed this relationship-building, which they asserted was a major job of leadership. They further emphasized that *everyone,* even the target clientele, as well as people involved in idea development, operation, and delivery could be leaders. Thus, anyone with whom staff interacted was approached with partnering potential in mind.

Leadership is not a matter of position and title in these successful programs. Stories from satisfied clientele of all ages as well as referrals and chats between parents, relatives, and friends are key sources of new clients *and* testimonials for resource development, say practitioners. This perspective is quite different from having leadership develop collaborations mainly with prominent leaders and decision makers. Practitioners with this view fail to include people based on their potential contributions to long-term capacity.

Respondents talked about character when discussing leadership. A particular executive director had thought deeply about the roles of a leader in this hurly-burly environment of dynamic social reform. She listed the following: "champion, mentor and guide, technician and multi-tasker, networker and friend, sales representative, cheerleader, prognosticator, problem solver, and task master."

When prompted for clarification, she said the leader needs to be "confident enough not to take the safe way." He or she is "an intelligent adventurer who takes risks but does not take dumb risks and knows the value of action." This person sees himself or herself as a "vessel" carrying an idea worth doing. She mentioned "the ability to see an opportunity, the wisdom to know it's good fortune when it presents itself, then knowing how to make something of it." Many people are oblivious to daily opportunities, she observed, but the leader sees and capitalizes on them. This person believes in "signs" and has intuition that a certain decision, a certain direction, is "right." His or her intuition is a combination of nature-nurture in that some of it is an innate knowing of truths and the rest comes from years and years of experience.

New forward thinking leaders are open enough not to preclude an idea because it "can't be done," and thus they see way beyond obstacles to make the project work. These people make "chicken soup out of chicken feathers" on a daily basis—yet another description of the character-driven, visionary leader.

This was the exact case at one of the study sites. Local officials and neighborhood activists were in open revolt, objecting to an after-school program—and especially one for at-risk youngsters. All manner of protests railed against "another expensive program on top of other programs to cater to the at-risk," according to one of the program's promoters. "Too expensive," they said. "Can't be done," they determined. "We already have one in regular school," they rationalized. Despite these real obstructions, a few champions began what is now one of the best Boys and Girls Clubs *in the nation* and a model for social improvement.

The message from respondents, whether spoken or implied, is that every stakeholder group not only has project-relevant leadership potential, but it's imperative to nurture and develop this potential group by group. The four essential groups are: senior staff, general staff, the board, and community stakeholders, including clientele, partners, and collaborators. "The main job of leadership is capacity building; all else flows from that," observed a respondent.

Composing Your Board

This discussion brings us to the topic of how to approach hiring your board.

Effective Practice

Hire the board for individual expertise; nurture them for their primary, long-term capacity building roles of developing relationships and resources.

Select board members according to two criteria. First, they must bring a special talent relevant to building the business infrastructure under the intended service(s). This criterion was suggested by a practitioner who consults on how to build and manage performance-oriented boards of directors. For example, someone may be asked to serve on a board because he or she is a lawyer skilled in corporate law. That person will be responsible for writing and executing relevant legal documentation for the project, especially for its incorporation and charter. Second, hire someone according to his or her

Board participation is a long-term prospect. It demands time members often don't have but must find. Naturally, board members are required to be champions for the idea.

ability, and especially willingness, to develop relationships and resources, money being the primary resource concern.

Then teach all board members *how* to be board members. This may be considered a radical thought because it's generally assumed a board member has the skills, expertise, background, and training to be a board member. They don't, according to several project executive directors and board members.

Who will teach these board skills? Most likely it will be a senior staffer, who may even be the hiring official. And what will be taught? Board members need to learn how to conduct and work in a board meeting directed toward the unique demands of the service idea at hand. They also need to learn how to develop funds, monitor and evaluate program processes and performance, and develop relationships meaningful to the vision for and values of the service idea.

According to two executive directors, board members also need to commit to serving long after the effervescence of visioning is gone. Board participation is a long-term prospect. It demands time members often don't have but must find. Naturally, board members are required to be champions for the idea.

The board of directors or advisors needs to understand the division of responsibilities between the board and staff. The board is largely responsible for resource development, and staff are responsible for program performance, but the effort is mutual and synergistic. This operation differs from a board that's only compliance and procedure oriented rather than directed by capacity building.

One of the program directors pointed out a dilemma: Yes, the board must develop relationships that lead to resources, especially money. However, the best relationships are built on a foundation of active program performance. So, what comes first, relationships or performance? The answer is performance—for a less than obvious but essential reason. When a program performs and has a significant impact on the community, "It builds relationships with people you've never met," affirmed two practitioners. "Partners and collaborators with resources *come to you*, if the program works so the community can see it."

Stakeholder groups have something to sell. The lesson here? Any suggestion for project development must have client success and operational performance as a major concern. Practitioners must act with performance permeating every aspect of the life cycle. Planning and acting with performance in mind is a careful "dance," according to an Iredell practitioner. She pointed out that the "insane preoccupation with the next dollar obscures the essential reality of putting performance first." Board members need to make this point and help practitioners strike a balance between resource development and meaningful performance. Don't forget your secret power, your client base.

Effective Practice

Make your client base your cheerleaders.

One of the most neglected leadership groups is a project's clientele, observed practitioners. Savvy project stakeholders begin developing their clientele to sell the program, recruit other target clientele, and secure resources, which can be considerably more than money. Resources can include in-kind contributions, donations of hard goods and operational supplies, discounted services and office space, political support, expertise, and perhaps the largest resource—volunteers. Clients are taught the program's vision, mission, and goals and how they can help as they receive services. Word of mouth from satisfied clientele is a strong collective voice. It can recruit other clients and cement the project's all-important reputation in the community.

In the established local service, satisfied clients are of course the mainstay of mission accomplishment. But even a good mission with strong leadership goes nowhere without determining where to go and the means to get there. Let's look at how to use capacity assessment to build capacity.

2. Integrate capacity assessment into capacity building.

"Capacity assessment," according to senior practitioners, "is as much a matter of continuous study of appropriate data as it is a matter of knowing how to read that data and put it to productive use." Respondents noted that capacity assessment is a continuous process versus a single, scheduled event. The latter is usually the case with local public services, if it's done at all. When asked if a regularly scheduled needs assessment wouldn't be more efficient, practitioners answered with an emphatic "No." Yes, respondents recognized the important nuance that a formal capacity assessment helps build the credibility essential to gaining political and material support. However, in the end, a senior program staffer noted, the decision about how to answer a perceived need is "a guess, an emotional decision" born of study and judgment. Data is only one part of the decision; the skill to use it contextually is more important.

How much capacity assessment is enough? A senior staffer of the Boys and Girls Club responded that understanding capacity meant "doing assessment to the point of no surprises when we can almost predict results." Reasonable data collection and experientially-based intuition come together to help practitioners understand and make decisions about project development. This view correctly recognizes data is *limited* in what it can relate and *limiting* because it can unnecessarily restrict appropriate and needed action.

Respondents related four important insights about assessing the local environment:

- *Capacity assessment is critical.* Most important, staff and leadership need to realize that assessment is critical to *every* aspect of local service idea development. Often, project staff treat assessment as merely a matter of collecting data. The data most often consists only of variations on numbers of program participants to satisfy reporting requirements of funding agencies. This "assessment" is done only as a secondary or tertiary duty, and sadly, is many times dismissed as a bother. When approached this way, collecting data has little to do with understanding capacity to achieve stated goals. Sites that concentrate on building capacity understand that integrating capacity assessment is continuous (daily) and encompassing (integrated) work of foundational concern.

- *Capacity assessment builds a history of performance.* Capacity assessment is essential to building a history of performance and success, which translates to good relationships and vital support in the community. As the project grows and extends into the community, project leaders can present data on performance (constructive behavioral changes) in target populations. They can also describe what the program did and how it affected those changes.

  For example, Iredell tracked and reported on school-ready preschoolers with statements of program capability to deliver its core services with *current* levels of resources, funds, and staff. This led to statements on cost-effectiveness, which is how much *more* could be done if certain resources in certain amounts were made available. Leaders put this in terms of how much could be *saved* in local dollars by investing a dollar in a suggested new program or strengthening an existing one. Decision makers, especially those in charge of budgets, spending, and political will, understand these dollars-and-cents advantages.

True capacity assessment helps to direct programming and fund decision making rather than merely collecting numbers. Assessment in terms of cost-effectiveness and behavioral change helps the community understand how well the program is doing. As a director pointed out, such reporting is the basis of building positive relationships, which in turn, reaps vital political and funding support and resources.

- *Assessment helps ensure services with measurable impact.* The task of assessment is not one of looking for needs to satisfy. It's the ongoing understanding of capacity to deliver services with measurable impact. There is a significant difference. The former is a matter of identifying a problem in the community and addressing it with a hastily assembled answer. The latter involves looking at that same problem with a strategy to build long-term strength to confront the complex dynamic of social transformation. One is very short term; the other is long term and can be perpetual as the program gradually grows to meet demand.

- *It's vital to determine how much a project can do well.* According to a seasoned practitioner, capacity assessment should persist until project leaders have an intimate

> Capacity assessment is essential to building a history of performance and success, which translates to good relationships and vital support in the community.

and detailed knowledge about the who, what, when, where, and especially how of the intended service. It doesn't matter how few people are served, as long as their condition is measurably improved in ways that are meaningful to them and at a reasonable cost. This is an important insight that ties into the others. There would be no point in spending money on a program that doesn't accomplish real progress. Therefore, practitioners need to prove the efficiency and effectiveness of the program to the people who matter to the survival of the service, such as funders, town council members, or county commissioners.

Now, what exactly will you be assessing?

Let's consider needs Assessment vs. Capacity Assessment. Respondents reported difficulties with the usual notions of *needs* assessment being conceptualized as *capacity* assessment. Needs assessment is usually tightly focused on a community's need for a known service (vis-á-vis *best practice* or an evidence-based practice) to address a perceived problem. But this is only one component of the needs-capacity picture.

Stakeholders commonly conduct a cursory evaluation of existing services to see where their service idea might fit. This involves a one-time needs assessment to launch an idea as soon as possible without the lengthy process of understanding the service environment and what it will take to plan, operate, then sustain the service. This may be easy and look good, but it's futile. This cursory look neglects the need to deeply understand the target population and where these people are. Nor does it assess the corresponding ready resources and the organizational/community capability to attend to client-defined needs.

Building the capability/performance picture presents the dilemma of what comes first. Initial staff know that capability is important and the foundation of a secure idea, but they lack the time and expertise to do everything well themselves. Respondents suggest that capacity assessment should be one of the first priorities. Staff trained in analytical methods, data collection, and analytical automation need to be acquired, developed, and adapted to the needs of the project. This leads us to resources development.

Effective Practice

Combine capacity assessment, impact analysis, and process evaluation to justify project continuation and acquisition of resources.

Practitioners note four areas to assess: the organization, the service, the community, and the client. In other words, staff and the board must know what and how much the organization can deliver, what services are needed, what the community has to say about it all, and what target population the project will serve. Assessment includes documenting what is happening, what is not happening, and what needs to be done, then making an operational to-do list to get it done. This is an important insight about developing information that furthers understanding versus the traditional compliance-oriented capacity assessment. The latter is usually compliance data requested by funding organizations or the municipality, when those served need performance data.

Effective Practice

Use capacity assessment to assist decision making by understanding when and how the community collaboration is working.

After assessment and action, analysis determines the impact or results. Evaluation determines the efficiency and effectiveness of the processes employed. Combining analysis and evaluation with capacity assessment informs decision making. Data from capacity assessment, impact analysis, and process evaluation combine to paint a picture of competency. This proof of effectiveness justifies continuing current services and assuming further services. It's logical now to take action to determine how well your collaborations are functioning.

Effective project stakeholders aren't afraid to take action; they're prepared with assessment and not paralyzed by having to get one more piece of data. Their attitude about data and the use of it is supportive, even wholesome. They want to tell their complete story of progress and accomplishment. Furthermore, capacity assessment builds confidence in decision making, which is vital. A correct

> After assessment and action, analysis determines the impact or results. Evaluation determines the efficiency and effectiveness of the processes employed. Combining analysis and evaluation with capacity assessment informs decision making.

decision based on capacity assessment may not be the most comfortable decision, but it's the best of alternatives. Staff and leadership stay informed, thus work and direction are more goal oriented.

A practitioner pointed out the importance of basing decisions on enough data to know how to correct the situation if results of that decision go awry. Good decisions come from understanding the environment, discussing alternatives, then adjusting results as you work toward a goal. This is another practical application of the action-reflection cycle. Established service practitioners spend a lot of time course correcting. According to the staff at the Henderson Boys and Girls Club, this takes time and constant attention to how and how well the operation is working. When decision making is informed and working right, staff feel empowered and supported in their decisions and gain resolution and comfort in their actions.

When carried out continuously, noted one project leader, capacity assessment also indicates when community partnerships and political will are ready for program expansion.

Especially where pressure exists to reduce or eliminate services, data from capacity assessment, impact analysis, and process evaluation are vital for realistic decision making.

3. Determine project scope.

Part of capability is understanding project scope in terms of its original purpose (mission) and what it hopes to accomplish (vision). Originally, in this inquiry into how to build good service programs, the concept of scope meant simply how much project officials wanted to accomplish. Site visits changed this view. In keeping with the synergistic quality of each of the critical factors, practitioners at the transformative sites looked at project scope more widely. They considered it the result of continuously employing the organizational vision and mission, which need to complement each other. They didn't find this easy. Research shows a divided opinion about whether or not a vision and mission help.[144]

What's the answer? That depends on how an organization uses the vision and mission to guide its effort.[145] That observation is supported by the field interviews. The result is an effective practice suggesting that scope consider target population needs, the program's capacity to address those needs, and the benefits of its projected success.

According to one researcher,[146] "The best mission statements capture the hearts and minds of managers, front-line employees, customers, and (stake)holders."

Another researcher noted a dramatic difference in organizational interpretations of vision/mission and scope. Those with a mission that captured "hearts and minds" used it to focus on the human element; those that did not, used it to enforce compliance, much to the detriment of the project at hand.

As you will see, progressive service organizations took that lesson one step further. They integrated vision/mission and scope determination into other key features of project development right from the beginning. Then they continued to work with it as an integral, ever-present guide for their march to permanency and to closing the service-to-(assessed) needs gap in their service target population.

Synergy continues as a byword for this kind of planning. Yes, vision and mission must come first, then analysis and evaluation. Planners recognize that to work, the vision and mission must be written considering these critical functions. So when these overarching statements are being formulated, they also ask, is this measurable? Aside from adding some concreteness to the visioning process, it helps rein in impossible dreams. Success, especially myriad little successes, matter: The big dreams will then happen.

The collective effort of these mission-driven critical features and milestones then become greater than the sum of the parts. In Iredell County, for example,

> "The best mission statements capture the hearts and minds of managers, front-line employees, customers, and (stake)holders."

practitioners revisited visioning informed by current impact analysis (effectiveness) and process evaluation (efficiency). This approach painted a more compelling picture of the who, what, when, where, why, and how of service idea development. Together these variables became a powerful decision-making tool. Obviously, the content of an effective vision/mission statement matters.

Again, with the purpose of understanding their organization, any investigation must lead to the how. *How* is the only question that leads to action, and action is the only way to determine that leadership, staff, and program are on track for success. Let us reiterate that success is not client numbers required of a grant, for instance. Success is if the project survives and then thrives.

Determining appropriate scope is a matter of reaching out, judicially, to those who are affected by the project and can influence its course. These people include the major stakeholders, clients, decision makers, partners (those who bring resources), and collaborators (those who bring expertise). Pause and think about the difference between these key external entities and how you will approach and enlist each. Local practitioners stated that the task is one of coaxing necessary partners out of their agency and municipal silos and involving them in the strategic planning process as well as in mapping resources. Of course, it highlights sharing the success of a project worth doing and how these partners and collaborators are significantly helping.

Track the changes (preferably behavioral) in the target population and the benefit to the community. Then translate the data into descriptions that appeal to the various stakeholder views and needs. Cost effectiveness works best. In other words, compute how a dollar invested returns that dollar and much more.

For example, businessmen and women, elected officials, and agency heads may like to see the cost benefit as they're sensitive to budgetary justification. Don't stop there. After you have the cost benefit, compute the cost effectiveness of agency investment in this (their) idea. Funding agencies want to know that the project is accomplishing its stated goals in terms of the numbers served and/or improvements in target populations. They want, rather need, to be associated with a winner.

This knowledge of accomplishment and of the resources *required* to achieve the defined scope can be compared to *available* resources to uncover the services gap. Such information can be used for project management, decision making, and especially project justification. Determining scope is tied to all the critical features, especially capacity assessment and impact analysis.

More always needs to be done, but according to practitioners, biting off more than you can chew predicts failure. This truism can become apparent during the heady days of startup overreach and is a common mistake of implementation, especially in the public sector.

Other practitioners pointed out that another danger of taking on more than you can deliver is being seen as a fraud. They said many local nonprofits have a tendency to promise more than they can do to cater to funding agencies, or any oversight body for that matter. This never serves the project well. Naysayers can hardly wait for a promise unkept. Accurate, meaningful scope relies on resources matching promises.

According to a senior staffer, "No decision is made without referring to vision/mission and scope, which must be stated so that it will be understood in thirty seconds." Respondents observed that vision/mission and scope do not begin fully formed. Also, there must be a continuity of long-term activities involving the use and refinement of vision/mission and scope. The development of long-term activities is not a one-time compilation of a wishful "to-do" list. It takes time for a mission to become potent. Determining vision/mission and scope is an encompassing, continuous process that must begin at idea inception and last as long as the service organization does. They should be reasonably revisited regularly to make sure they are relevant and potent *and* that they are integral to daily operations as well as long-term accomplishment.

Contrast this with the Pasquotank Drug Task Force at the time of this formal study. Although this particular program is apparently no longer operating, it had another take on the scoping process. The Task Force scope was the product of a model built on and requiring compliance, a top-down defined local service reflected in its base of operation. It was also a manifestation of a narrowly defined purpose, the prosecution of illicit drug traffickers, especially juveniles. Their operational plant was an abandoned public maintenance garage, which belied the level of expertise and effectiveness of the narcotics team. The team had regular contact with the sheriff's office for the purposes of administration, filing reports, processing cases, and briefing the sheriff as the need arose. The sheriff was in firm control. Duties and responsibilities were defined and followed to facilitate the investigation and conviction of local drug offenders. It worked if the sheriff secured local funding.

The contrast between the Task Force and other services based on capacity building provided more information as to how scope should shape and be

> Determining vision/mission and scope is an encompassing, continuous process that must begin at idea inception and last as long as the service organization does.

shaped by the idea to further goal accomplishment. For example, scope for the Task Force considered assessing trafficking hot spots and the number of convictions, while school readiness scope considers need by target populations, community-wide impact, capacity, and process efficiency and effectiveness. Notice how the former monitored immediate, convenient numbers, while the latter considered project and community well-being. Each serves a purpose, only one eyes capacity building for permanency. This leads to scope that's not about how *much* you can do and risk overreach but about how *little* you can do well—very well.

Effective Practice

Develop project scope by mapping clientele and community resources.

A successful program leader observed that an understanding of scope comes with constant analysis of it, the understanding of ground truths about it, the maturity of the organization, and the continuous application of it.

Vision/mission and scope flow from the work done for capacity building, which should compose a picture that captures:

- the target population,
- their location(s),
- resources,
- gaps in service,
- how much of that gap can be serviced according to available resources, and
- especially the local political will to support the evolution toward assuming more responsibilities.

It is quite helpful to precisely map where target populations are clustered in relation to available resources so that gaps in service begin to emerge. The more pictures, graphics, and bullet summaries the better. They are elements of the picture of persuasion to make the case for existing and further services.

When all this is done right, it actually portrays a telling, interesting, even compelling story.

The extent of such an exercise "is the art of combining experience and data. In the end, it's a feeling [about a decision to assume more responsibility or program-

> **Delivery estimates that are too aggressive and too early court unnecessary risks. Too late and an imperative may be missed.**

ming] that prevails," observed another executive director. She further noted that scoping is about "building a history of outcomes and results," which can be used to justify current programming and assuming additional work.

This leads to another point about the nature of local service delivery. Early in the evolution of a public project, stakeholders—especially political and financial backers—expect, even demand, results. This expectation presents another unrealistic dilemma. Should promises be made to curry support from resource and interest groups, or should the expense of determining scope be borne before a commitment to provide services is made?

Site respondents promise only what can be delivered, meaning that analysis comes *first,* then project staff can make the case for *what* can be competently delivered and, more importantly, estimate *when* it can be delivered. Delivery estimates that are too aggressive and too early court unnecessary risks. Too late and an imperative may be missed. Obviously, informed timing matters. This removes some of the pressure for unrealistic immediate results. Social difficulties take decades to manifest; good solutions thankfully won't take that long. When project staff deliver what they say they will deliver, to borrow from Mark Twain, they will pleasantly surprise most of the people and astonish the rest. Once these elements all come together, workflow, team effort, correct decisions, and successful solutions will most likely follow.

Once staff have considered scope—at least initially—they need to analyze their results and the methods they used to achieve them.

4. Design the impact analysis and process evaluation.

Executive staff at the Iredell Partnership and the Boys and Girls Club observe that determining efficiency and effectiveness is a matter of *how* a metric is used, not necessarily *which* one is used. In the end, decision making is being clear headed with decisions that are "politically astute and value laden."[148] Staff gradually learn when and how to adjust methods of inquiry, goals, objectives, and programming, while becoming more proficient at it over time. All work off the same data. Perspective matters. But first let's consider a vital distinction in assessing how well you are doing: the Evidence Based Practice, EBP.

Considering capacity building, an evidence-based practice is a service within a program, such as a therapeutic modality with a scientific basis for a positive, measurable effect that contributes to goal accomplishment. It can be hard justification for your program or expand it to meet the need your stakeholders want. (Please refer to the Glossary, page 217, for a full definition of EBP within Capacity Building.)

To help determine if an evidence-based practice needs to be added, the executive director continually gets better at asking, "So what!?"

For example: This elementary school has a rate of 74 percent school-ready kindergartners, and that school has 82 percent of its youngsters school ready. "So what?" How can we improve both, because our goal for next year is to have 95 percent of the incoming class school ready?

Our community has preschool facilities for only 54 percent of its children and *that* community has 100 percent of its children in preschool. "So what?" How do we improve the percentage for *our* community?

This jurisdiction in our county has dental screening for 42 percent of its children and that one has 87 percent of its preschoolers screened. "So what?" How can we improve the numbers for both, especially the first jurisdiction, because our goal is 100 percent dental screening for our preschoolers?

This approach implies a structure to the inquiry process, and the answer is usually another question, which begins with "How."

Key people hired for their analytical skills are a necessary addition to essential staff.[149] However, study site inquiry programs needed to ensure that *all* staff had essential investigatory skills. Skilled leaders cannot function without agents to execute policy, techniques, and action.

Inquiry is mechanized and made routine at the Iredell and Henderson sites by:

- policy,
- written duties and responsibilities,
- formal reporting,
- written standards,
- regular meetings,
- the hardware and software to make it all happen, and
- the people motivated and skilled to tell your success stories … by the numbers.

This structure makes evaluation and analysis almost a moment-to-moment part of *daily* operations. Data is entered when it happens! Everyone understands how and how well they as a unit are doing *and* how each individual contributes to efficiency and effectiveness. Evaluation and analysis are meant to be a positive, constructive part of the day. Notice the difference in intention from traditional forms of determining if processes are as prescribed and the project is fulfilling intentions.

Analysis and evaluation focused and equipped to build the business under the idea is another departure from convention. It differs, for example, from the traditional external audit, which has punitive overtones. The auditor is charged with finding something *wrong* even in the best run programs. Data seems self-defeating, so why do it, or worse, why not fudge a little? Punitive analysis corrupts.

The successful programs studied were self-regulating. They didn't need oversight, even though they had it. The philosophy of investigation adopted at the progressive, transformative sites was to view investigation as a tool for

> **The philosophy of investigation adopted at the progressive, transformative sites was to view investigation as a tool for strengthening the organization.**

strengthening the organization. The best sites celebrated an employee who found something essential to improve, defined how to do it, then did it. That is empowering.

The sites in this capacity building model use appropriate quantitative and especially qualitative methods to inform a participatory action-reflection-action process. For example, school readiness indicators are combined with client satisfaction surveys and testimonials. These sources help determine the effectiveness of services and *how* programming might benefit from lessons learned.

Another unique take from the field on project scrutiny is that it's opportunistic and flexible. Relevant data can come from just about *any* source. For example, Iredell used waiting lists at day care centers to determine targeted need for preschool services by geographic location within the county.

Data gathering and analysis was kept on track by constantly asking if an action was goal directed and accomplished the intended vision and mission. Throughout the evolution of the project, staff and stakeholders were trained in analytical skills and their use. This is another example of the "teaching to knit" philosophy versus "doing the knitting" for people. That empowerment approach permeates the critical features of capacity building. The results can be striking.

For example, the Iredell Smart Start project demonstrated performance in dramatic fashion. At the time of this writing, a recent kindergarten class was *100 percent* school ready according to local school district third-party tests. Unheard of. This is a good example of establishing a project with a single purpose, achieving it, then reflecting that success back to stakeholders. It makes excellent monetary sense to municipal budgetary officials that the Partnership is a profitable use of tax revenues. The program helps a child get ready for school rather than have that child begin school and possibly drop out. If that were to happen, it would involve expensive social services or, worse yet, the criminal justice system. Plus, success in primary and secondary school bodes well for success in life with a career that sustains a family.

This irrefutable progress indicator of school readiness was fed into every other critical feature to continuously strengthen the project as an entity and its standing in the community. For example, leadership understood how this goal was achieved and subsequently continued targeted effective practices to maintain the positive trend of school readiness. Stakeholders acquired knowledge then *applied* lessons learned.

Telling the data-based success story built a huge store of credibility, even beyond stakeholders. That credibility was channeled into courting friends, new and old, who had more incentive to contribute money, supplies, resources, and all-important volunteer hours. Respondents commented that when they visited potential supporters, it was not uncommon for supporters to be ready with the checkbook. Fundraising, which can be tedious, became a pleasant experience.

The resources required to prepare a class of kindergartners for school were fully understood. Moving to the next level of service delivery was a matter of matching increments of more responsibility to the available capacity. This would not be possible if understanding process and performance were detached and part-time, maybe sometime efforts.

Effective Practice

Combine methods of inquiry to strengthen operations, build capacity, and justify support.

How does this then fit into gathering a range of necessary support?

All critical planning features are continuous and cyclical, but analysis (performance) and evaluation (efficiency) should be done in concert. Impact analysis should provide a running commentary on what the project is accomplishing, according to a practitioner. For example, progress toward stated goals may be measured as effectiveness.

Continuous process analysis provides feedback to keep the operation running efficiently—a measurement of efficiency. Thus, staff may flowchart tasks to eliminate duplications, contract or outsource work, and automate and prioritize tasking, for example. "Every primary motivation of every stakeholder group, staff, board, contributors, and clients must be considered to the point where there are no surprises from [survey] results," observed a senior staffer.

This is a good rule of thumb for determining the symphony, synergy, and essences of efficiency and effectiveness in concert, according to a board member. Together, they tell a much better story of accomplishments. Practitioners arrived at this connection after first focusing on effectiveness to the exclusion of efficiencies. They did this because of the ever-present pressure from decision makers and funding officials to so quickly report results that they were unrealistic. However, experience demonstrates that transformative results cannot be realized unless operations are efficient.

So that answers one chicken-or-the-egg conundrum. Efficient processes must be a foremost consideration *before* a project can be expected to *perform* significantly and thus succeed. Yes, the vision, mission, and goals are in place, but they mean little if staff are not "with the program."

When the onsite interview on analysis and evaluation began with the executive director at the Henderson Boys and Girls Club, he pulled out his battered and dog-eared three-ring binder on analysis, a real testament to policy and process in action. He began his overview of project capacity development by saying that seeking to understand why and how to improve things should arrive at the "next best step." He went on to explain that progress is not a great leap of a few policy statements. It is a matter of iterations accomplished by many decisions throughout the *day* over *years*.

Each of these stable projects had similar programs: The Iredell Partnership and the Henderson Boys and Girls Club serve as examples. These programs are based on practitioner-proven activities. In the case of the Boys and Girls Club, introspection and improvement have their roots in the years immediately after the American Civil War, when Boys and Girls Clubs began(!). Consequently, the policy of a constructive critique at Henderson is formalized from years of experimentation and adjustment in scores of environments and conditions over the decades.

Gradually, the following processes were developed to enhance success.

- *Plan training for all key stakeholders.* – Regular participation in workshops and professional development augment training programs for staff and board members. It's best to have a career progression plan, which suggests a progression of development offerings.

- *Conduct needs assessment.* – Staff conduct a thorough assessment of needs relative to the capacity to fulfill those needs.

- *Establish benchmarking.* – Project leaders and practitioners set project-supportive targets and are in regular communication with people who represent backing, especially financial. For example, contributors receive a flyer explaining what their money is doing, in terms they can understand.

- *Outline and open communication channels.* – Staff give county commissioners regular briefings before budgetary meetings.

- *Keep clientele informed.* – Staff also keep clientele informed about programming and project successes. All successes matter, especially the small, everyday ones.

- *Understand efficiency and effect.* – Leaders and staff put into place concomitant process evaluation and impact analyses. They present these as a simple picture, only a few measures mattered, that tells a story of real successes and growing potential that the listener can understand and act upon.

- *Offer performance-oriented services.* – The program accepts services only after proving they're based on performance. Stakeholders, especially staff, receive the results from performance data during regular meetings.

- *Use data-based decision making.* – Qualitative pre- and post-service questionnaires from target populations confirm process efficiencies, production numbers, rates of change, cost-effectiveness, and eventually tradeoff [150] numbers. These can analyze behavioral change and client satisfaction. Decisions are made accordingly.

- *Conduct regular progress meetings.* – Staff hold formalized, regular status and progress meetings—weekly, monthly, and quarterly. These culminate with an annual report to the board and perhaps wider dissemination via mail-outs or electronic media.

- *Time the annual report.* – Note that the annual report to the Boys and Girls Club board is given *months* in advance of community budgetary meetings. Arguments, especially the tradeoff statement, are formulated or updated according to progress.

This is the epitome of the action-reflection-action cycle that builds service delivery infrastructure. Imagine: This way of thinking and building services was initiated during our Civil War and is still evolving—because it can and it must.

The connection of activities to results is continuous. For example, the Iredell Partnership concerned itself with learning about school readiness effects on school misbehavior and dropout rates. More disciplined behavior in school translates to improved graduation rates and placement in technical and post-secondary education. The Boys and Girls Club became interested in alumni graduating from college or going into the trades or the military. This is an important point. These progressive programs plan for long-range measurement of project effect on the community *from the inception* of the project. Now, people and resources are starting to come to these programs unsolicited because the Henderson Boys and Girls Club is a proven, contributing member of the community. People want to be part of winning. As program leaders point out, when well done, analysis/evaluation makes sense in the community, in the wallet, and in the heart.

> The history of regular individual giving becomes the holy grail of funding as, over time, it becomes *predictable.*

The leaders also say that understanding how well the organization is operating is probably the critical success factor most neglected. Practitioners in the Iredell Partnership constantly put an account of progress in front of stakeholders, who need to be informed as to how their investment in money, resources, and time is doing. Determining impact and making operations run smoothly and effectively figure prominently in the vital necessity to nurture local support. Analysis "builds the history of results," according to one practitioner, and results are the heart of building relationships that lead to support.

A program leader summarized her analysis process by commenting that it was constructed to be "thorough, descriptive, upfront, nonbiased, and locally determined." This philosophy of analysis is a combination of the theoretic and scientific while emphasizing the utilitarian. It's a mechanized process tempered by judgment and practicality. By being part of a bigger vision of what needs to be accomplished, it's comprehensive, building on measurable performance and success.

Let's turn now to another way of developing a range of resources—through good working relationships and even friendships.

5. Nurture relationships for resources development.

Mature, enduring, stable service ideas as exemplified by Smart Start Partnerships and Boys and Girls Clubs need a range of financial resources. Dependency on a few sources of funding is risky. Any one of them can fail, even dramatically. How about a promised grant that fails to materialize as "the money ran out"? The development of communal resources evolves into the pursuit of wider and varied funding sources, such as support from national nonprofits. Successful program staff see that developing resources involves way more than finding funding. Let's consider how these model programs support themselves.

While many project staff are adept at writing winning proposals to foundations and governmental granting agencies, they recognize the collective power of smaller corporate or individual donations. The leverage of these small donations is that they are *regular* and cumulative. The annual $500 gift is much more powerful than the one-time grant. Services can then be planned with the predictability of an established line item for funding in a local budget. The history of regular individual giving becomes the holy grail of funding as, over time, it becomes *predictable*. Thus you can budget operations. If you can budget accurately, you can get mission critical actions done. Other sources round out primary project funding.

The major funding sources used by local services are budgetary allotments from their municipal governments, grants, corporate giving, individual giving, and volunteers, whose time is counted in terms of dollars. To a lesser extent, stakeholders may try fees for services, a share of taxes, procuring goods and services, discounted resources, matching and in-kind dollars, fundraisers, or legislated funding. Let's get more creative.

The more mature programs, with years of experience in making their communities better, enter into estate planning to build endowments. This is true of the Iredell and Henderson Partnerships and transitional post-release programs such as the Durham, North Carolina-based Triangle Residential Options for Substance Abusers (TROSA) and the Wilmington, North Carolina-based Leading Into New Communities (LINC). Most projects dismiss this possibility out of hand because of its exotic and long-term nature. The remarkable thing is that this highly sophisticated means of planned estate giving was part of the strategic plan for these programs *from the beginning!* Now *that* is resources development.[151]

This reality has implications. Developing reliable funding is not a standalone, iffy job, like writing a grant and moving on. Funding streams flow from the partners who are inspired by a dream that proposes and delivers lofty endeavors compelling participation. This strategic decision to build funding streams directs and determines how leadership and staff conduct themselves. It determines project scope and how capacity is developed from understanding services capacity and a good analysis/evaluation process. The interconnectedness of how a well-working program conducts daily business is most evident in putting together long-term, reliable operational resources.

The bottom line, then, is that the project must be a good, "profitable" business, meaning it yields a dollars-and-cents return on investment. All the features must be well planned and integrated. However, it's tough to determine where one begins and another ends. This is why respondents collectively suggested setting up a commitment center that focuses each component on relationship-building, a great departure from assigning someone to write a few grant proposals during the year.

Effective Practice

Establish a Commitment Center to gain (financial) commitments from targeted stakeholder groups.

A Commitment Center assembles the talent and wherewithal to focus on the job of developing resources by gaining commitments from targeted stakeholder groups. The name "Commitment Center" says much about the philosophy of establishing long-term, mutually beneficial relationships. It does this by communicating the *worth* of the project, which inspires investing in the "dream" and a winning team. The school readiness program in Iredell County and the after-school program in Henderson County serve as models for how to compose and conduct a resource development Commitment Center.[152]

You may be thinking, "But I am the only staffer for my small service idea; my day is already ten hours long; how can *I* be a Commitment Center?"[149]

Answer: A fully functioning Commitment Center somewhat depends on the purpose, size, and maturity of the organization. However, what matters are the why and especially the *how* of this development concept. These large service ideas started with one or just a few people. The lessons they learned and now share apply to *any* size of operation.

The ideal development effort is a *way of thinking,* not necessarily an entity; it is the combined effort of a group of stakeholders who share purpose, resources, and staff. First, the board forms a development committee, the job of which is to ensure project accountability and build relationships that lead to funding streams. Why is accountability important to money? Again, accountability, performance, and delivering on promises are the basis of credibility, then respect, then friendship, then money, *in that order*. The core resources development team is composed of staff, board members, community stakeholders, and most important, clients. There are two overarching purposes for the commitment center:

- *Be accountable to stakeholders.* – Ensure the organization is accountable to all stakeholders, especially the beneficiaries of the service.

- *Engage the public.* – Help the public realize the importance and value of the project.

From these main purposes emerge the tactics for approaching each donor or donor agency for their regular gift, because the actual request has to be tailored to the needs of the particular donor. For example, a local bank executive expected to donate about the same time every year, before taxes were filed. He had an interest in keeping children in school to ready them for the working world. So, the staff highlighted graduation rates for him.

Again, start small; a gift of a few dollars has the tendency to grow over the years. Remember, almost every donor has the potential for planned giving via estate planning.

The Boys and Girls Club ensures accountability via a series of analysis and monitoring tools. They apply a well-tested accreditation matrix, which specifies performance indicators for critical functions that largely follow the critical features in the project life cycle. Take for example, the accreditation standard for the charitable fund development function: "The organization's fund development practices are consistent with its mission, founded on truthfulness, respect, and responsible stewardship, and compatible with organizational capacity." Notice this doesn't mention compliance with foundation or grantor requirements. Yet it speaks solidly to potential donors. It says, "Come and be part of this."

Then, the first of six indicators must be met: "The organization's solicitation, promotional materials, and grant applications are accurate, ethical, and clearly identify the organization's mission and the intended use of the solicited funds."

Furthermore, these organizations have a standard for weaning the project from soft monies by establishing indicators. These indicators specify the project will move from having no more than 40 percent of operational funds from soft sources to no more than 15 percent within a specified period of time. Each of the critical functions, which amount to a combination of leadership and business practices, is subjected to standards that embody the qualities of truth, respect, stewardship, inclusion, performance, responsibility, high expectations, equality of opportunity, and capacity. These enduring model projects have managed the impossible. They have quantified and embodied a concept—integrity—which leads to successful fundraising. This philosophy applies to any size service and a commitment center that may be staffed by only one person for a nascent or small project.

This is the expression and heart of character-based leadership that will lead delivery of public sector services now and far into the future.

A Henderson County couple that began the Boys and Girls Club endowment with a large gift commented on the passion they have as founding members of the Club. Their sentiments capture the symbiotic spirit of project and funds development:

> *One* – If you do the right things for the right reasons, somehow, someway, things always work out.

> *Two* – If we can't make a difference in this little community, then the entire world is in trouble.

> *Three* – To reach our objectives for the disadvantaged youth in this community, the entire community must take ownership.

These are much more than beautiful sentiments. They inspire action, meaningful participation, and *very* long-term commitment.

Of course, services, without which all this is moot, must also perform. They are the tip of the spear.

> These enduring model projects have managed the impossible. They have quantified and embodied a concept—integrity—which leads to successful fundraising.

6. Develop performance-oriented services.

Whether delivered by project staff or project-sponsored providers, services continue the theme of building via collaboration toward a motivational purpose, if not inspiring vision. The success of services is dependent on "the determination of passionate local people," according to a Win-Win board member. "It's a process of building on strengths, expectations of excellence, and the common belief in a dream," offered another.

Services are acquired and developed in a methodical way by:

- planning each service according to overall purposes,
- developing the service environment,
- implementing the idea correctly (with a view to long-term capacity),
- measuring progress,
- making improvements, and
- continuing to rise to service-needs tempered by available capacity.

The success of services requires expectations for staff, providers, and surprisingly, program clientele. An example from Iredell serves to illustrate what good service looks like.

The Early Learning Resource Center (ELRC) at a highly successful Smart Start site is a working laboratory for researching, making, and loaning out age- and purpose-appropriate learning resources. Two jam-packed but quite neat rooms are bursting with thousands of items all organized by purpose, function, and type. Hundreds of bags of manipulative learning toys, all organized by age and sequential number, hang on clothing trees ready for checkout. Of course the clothing trees were donated from a local clothing outlet. A first-class computer stands ready for research, whether by a mom or an early childhood development student from the local college. The ELRC even has a table of learning toys made from recycled materials, cast-offs from local businesses. One such toy is a discarded plastic soft drink bottle that contains a cotton ball soaked in vanilla. Infants are fascinated by its movement and their control of it. While they learn motor movements, they can savor the vanilla aroma. Who thinks of things like this?! Naturally, the ELRC is open after hours and Saturdays to suit families and childcare professionals, not necessarily partnership staff. Notice how project constituents are recognized and prioritized by matching program intent and services to them.

Operational and service ideas must compete with other supported services and be worth the tradeoff expenses of sacrificed functions and services that can't be done.

Two board members stressed the point that sponsored services must have a real return on investment. They must continuously demonstrate that return or risk having their service cancelled for nonperformance. No friends of the family doing "make work" jobs. In the well-functioning project, service providers know the standards of performance from the outset, as expectations are set before a contract is signed. Thus, they work doubly hard to meet them. While this is not difficult to do, it is not the case with many public service ideas where a provider is hired because they are convenient—so they manage conveniently. They continue with "business as usual" or even dictate policy and procedures to project leadership and staff, even though they can be at cross purposes with the goals of the project.

Developing services with high expectations can't be done if there's a counter-productive or emotional attachment to the service. Therefore, project stakeholders choose services with a research basis that document performance whenever possible. The latest fad or "best practice" or "evidence-based practice" is *never* accepted without being modified to the resources and philosophy of the project and needs of the community. All the while, service fidelity is maintained. That is, the proposed service is delivered as originally designed and intended and continues daily under the watchful eye of all staff.

Once the policy, procedures, and especially the stated measures for service performance are understood and regularly measured, services are usually self-regulating. Good work is the norm. The environment of mutual struggle and accomplishment of something worthy quickly moves service providers from independent contractors to members of the transformational team.

Effective Practice

Plan for performance-oriented services and providers.

Program leaders set high expectations before developing a service or hiring a service provider. For example, during solicitation for service providers, the request for proposals specifies:

- goals,
- measures,
- modes of service delivery,
- reporting requirements,
- consequences for failure to achieve expectations, and
- a brief history of experience in the RFP area.

A rigorous vetting process winnows the field even *before* providers apply. What a time-saver that is. What disappointments and wasted effort are avoided by good procedure and policy. Furthermore, these criteria also stand for staff members who are also service providers. *All* team members are held to measurable standards of performance tied to overall program goals. The program includes much time training and developing staff according to stated measures. Performance standards are mutually agreed upon and continuously enforced. Expectations are put forth from the moment the service provider is contacted to avoid misunderstandings, and progress toward goals begins the moment the service provider reports to work. It was a genuinely soul-warming experience to see this in action at the sites.

How these expectations are accomplished is another element that exemplified a high-performing service project. A service provider knows when he or she is not meeting expectations well in advance of being dismissed. Every advantage, courtesy, and example is given to a struggling provider. Only after an honest attempt from all parties is a relationship with a provider severed. The policy becomes self-enforcing and is congruent with the ideals and purposes of a superior, evidence-based, performance-oriented project.

This is also an example of another positive theme in successful service project development. Many times, public agencies have a punitive, negative working environment because the primary purpose is compliance. Progressive sites work very hard to turn their operations into places of mutual accomplishment and respect, hard and rewarding work, and actualization. When an organization gets essential operations working based on efficiency, effectiveness, and *intrinsic* motivation, people smile . . . a lot.

Good programs appreciate and reward their staff by offering opportunities to develop and grow.

7. Nurture staff by a process of human capacity development.

Many leaders of public agencies say, "Our people are our most important asset." And those with stable, enduring local services mean it! Developing personnel at the local level of government is normally difficult because of staff turnover, poor training and development opportunities, and an environment of frequent personal burnout. However, leaders at these model sites find ways to make human capital development a vital part of staff development rather than the standard human resources work.[153]

First and foremost, staff are respected as the adults they are. They're given the responsibility for a job and the authority to do it, and they're recognized as talented, creative, hard-working folk. While performance monitoring is constant, it's in the spirit of cooperation, collaboration, collegiality, and common cause.

Hiring begins by attracting genuinely special people who gravitate to this difficult public service work. Beyond the standard qualifications of education, experience, and training, executive directors look for people with *tough skin* to be able to take constructive criticism and learn. These individuals become engaged in productive change. According to one leader, "The projects that get further have people who can tuck away their egos." They are people who like to "play hard and accept their limits." They can anticipate where they need to be to get the job done. While equitable pay and benefits always lag behind those of the private market and other career fields, progressive boards and executive directors are always working to raise them. They also recognize that, up to a point, people stay on the job for more than money. What evolves with this mentality of mutual accomplishment is a three-part policy of recruitment, retention, and retirement (transition). This trifecta builds real team capabilities where more is accomplished than expected.[154]

Enduring sites persist as local conditions dictate; the Chowan Smart Start project serves as an example of working past staffing obstacles. Chowan and Perquimans Counties are poor, rural counties with no national childcare outlets. All childcare originates from small home or church-based operations. Yet the Partnership has succeeded in increasing the quality and number of their childcare facilities. Recruiting staff is difficult, but they have managed to hire staff that are qualified and motivated.

The executive director offered an example of the problems with recruitment. One posting produced a highly educated, experienced, and qualified applicant. However, the recruit had to commute 40 minutes one way. Every concession was made to attract this person, including offering flexible hours, telecommuting, and a better than usual salary. In other words, this person could construct the job entirely to suit her situation.

> **While performance monitoring is constant, it's in the spirit of cooperation, collaboration, collegiality, and common cause.**

In the end, she refused the job for an offer of one "just a few miles up the road." They persisted and were eventually able to hire a graduate from a nearby college. This person was trained and mentored to the needs of the project, and the work at Chowan continued.

Effective Practice

Draft a comprehensive process of human capacity development based on individualized career development plans.

Hiring the right people is only the beginning. "They have to be continuously molded into a team," nearly minute by minute, according to two practitioners. Passion is the number one intangible qualification mentioned. An executive director saw that her primary duty relative to staff was to train everyone, especially new hires, to "skate to where the puck is going to be" (paraphrasing the father of the hockey great, Wayne Gretzky). This means staff needed to *anticipate* the next decision or action, *not react* to the environment. This thinking about staff (human capacity) development takes understanding how people can develop their social capital and willingly, collectively work toward a transformative goal. It's not all drudgery; fun figures in this equation.

The people policy of an effective project should be based on individual character and seek to continually strengthen everyone to benefit the purposes of the organization. This way you break the common cycle of "Hire for skills, and fire for character." According to respondents, progressive staff development considers each of the following phases:

- *Recruitment* – The basic tool of recruitment is a detailed job description. The interview process will clarify the intangibles of achieving high expectations in a frenetic environment. An effective approach is to consider assessing character before hiring. Consider employing a unique personality assessment to determine Emotional Quotient, character, and suitability for the job. Many good assessments are available, and they keep improving. Try before you buy, if you can. Not all will fit the "personality" of your organizational purposes. If over time one doesn't fit, test and employ another.

- *Retention* – The tools of retention are a career development plan, based on a matrix of specific education, training, and professional development tailored to the individual. Wellness and well-being training also figure in the process to develop the character and health of the new team member.

    You'll want to provide ongoing feedback and an annual personal performance review. This keeps the individual challenged and contributing to organizational goals and purposes while growing as a team member *and* as an individual.

Assigning premier staff as mentors is remarkably effective. Many benefits accrue beyond increasingly better job satisfaction. For example, people are productive much, much faster, develop as good collaborators, and confirm the job is worthy, hence they stay for more than the money. Progressive leaders see they are not taking a senior staffer away from the job; they are molding a vital part of a well-oiled machine. This is how staff, the sterile reference to employees, become human, vital, and part of the project family.

Note that forward thinking leadership of a successful service program never fear losing a well-qualified staffer to a better job or a headhunter, because staff who are nurtured and challenged tend to stay. Even if they do move on, it's a good message to recruits. They see they're about to become part of an organization that has promotion potential and challenges to keep them stimulated.

- *Retirement* – When a staffer transitions from the organization, it should be on good terms and without a disruption to daily production. Ideally, retirements involve an exit interview, a succession plan, and perhaps even a cake and a poignant farewell "roast." Staff can be prepared to view retirement not as the end but a new beginning.

By developing employees for increased responsibility and perhaps another job or career out of the organization, they become mature, stable stakeholders who stick around. Consequently, turnover reduces. People stay in this business because they are appreciated, nurtured, encouraged, even loved.

After a policy of human capital development is documented and recruits accept it, the lion's share of the work is character and career development. Character is developed with career-long education and development in ethics, character, and well-being.

Career development is facilitated by a tool that outlines the individual's qualifications and accomplishments in education, training, and professional development relative to those he or she

Character development teaches how to live well by continuously becoming more just, wise, courageous, and temperate.

will need to become fully qualified and fully functioning within the organization. Note also that the ideal career development plan is never completed. The realization of an originally targeted level of competency becomes a platform from which to tackle the next level. The purpose of career development is to train and qualify people for continuous advancement. Character development is a wise addition.

Character development teaches how to live well by continuously becoming more just, wise, courageous, and temperate. Yes, there's more than a little classical philosophy in getting the organization headed rightly.

An often ignored and essential part of human capital development is preparing for staff transition within the organization by promotion. Another often ignored aspect is career broadening with added challenges.

Respondents comment that succession planning is necessary. Every individual should document how they perform their jobs. Getting things done is much more than what's reflected in a job description and an operating procedure. Documentation can be as simple as keeping a notebook of what you do.

With this, staff should also be cross-trained into and routinely participate in critical functions wherever possible. A staff member pointed out that this ensures a continuation of smooth operations during turnover, turmoil, or transition. Short-sighted organizations don't develop their staff for fear that added qualifications will enable staff to leave for better jobs and that staff development detracts from "production." The opposite is the reality. Successful youth-oriented sites, such as Iredell and Henderson and post-release programs such as TROSA, LINC, and the Durham County Criminal Justice Center in Durham, North Carolina, experience greater retention with this holistic philosophy of human capital development. The approach taps intrinsic motivation and multiplies organizational social capital, the stuff of good, hard work.

Let's move on now to Phase II, which describes operation, or putting the plan into action. This is where all the preparations and training are put to the test.

PHASE II of the Project Life Cycle: Operation – Putting the Plan into Action

Operation is the action part of the planning phase that involves moving slowly enough to anticipate problems, correct them, and continue to build friendships, respect, capacity, and a history of accomplishment. It doesn't begin with a cannon blast; it's a gradual flowering of the idea. That said . . .

Even if you're on the right track, you'll get run over if you just sit there.

– Will Rogers

The thoroughness of the planning phase determines the success of this and the next phase of the project life cycle. Let me reiterate: While you may tend to give planning a lick and a promise, *don't do that*. Furthermore, what you may have learned in business school or a workshop is only an introduction to making ideas work. Much success lies in the school of hard knocks. Remember again, each application of an idea is unique by the place, people, policies, and politics.

Practitioners stress that operations are a blend of science and art, with the emphasis on art, coupled with a double dose of hard work. When planning progresses to action, you may find yourself making lots of educated guesses. Some operations may even have to begin while planning is still in progress. There's no easy way out. You must do the work. But you'll find it's well worth the effort to produce good results.

Consider the following suggestions from practitioners to aid the success of your operations.

- *Action evolves through repetition, needing leadership by intent.* – Conceptually, implementation of the plan is routine. However, each feature of planning is treated again from the perspective of active operations. Effective practices evolve from speculation about how to do things to realization of the optimal way as tempered by the real world.

  Respondents agreed that the elements of planning are not "one and done" because of the organic and flexible nature of project development. For most public service projects, operations usually begin the moment first funding is available. Thus, a plan, and especially operational procedures, are usually cobbled together as needs or crises arise. People actually love a crisis as they can wrestle it to the ground and feel accomplished—even though the walls are tumbling down. This is management by crisis instead of leadership with intent.

  Obviously, this is not the way to go about building a stable idea. In fact, all of the ideas herein are points of departure. Shape them as you will, as your idea meets the reality of the road and as it matures to meet your service-to-needs gap.

  Methodical, comprehensive planning assures that when the project is in full operation, it's fixed on transformative goal accomplishment. This insight reflects practitioners' evolution from experience. They go from the all-too-common crisis-oriented operation to a sense of community, one for all and all for one, from doing something meaningful in a learning environment that's challenging, rewarding, and goal-oriented. Each essential element of planning continues in these latter phases of project development but is altered by the growth of the organization and the project as they synergistically mature in comradery, sophistication, and impact.

- *Skillful and artful staff run with the idea and prepare the board members.* – Good staff, well prepared and mentored, should be hired as quickly as possible to do routine tasks such as fiscal accounting, payroll, and scheduling to lessen the burden on the project director who is quickly overwhelmed. The crisis of the moment disallows their focus on a hierarchy of priorities, and one of the highest is the training and development of the board. When staff take the burdens of daily tasks, even a crisis or two, then he or she can oncentrate on project building activities, the main one being continuous relationship-building and maintenance.

> The goal of senior staff, usually the executive director,regarding board members is to "get *them* to believe."

Another suggestion for the operational phase is that the board of directors—as a body and especially individually—must mature from speculating about how things should be done to making them happen. With any luck, you avoid the serial visioneers who are all too happy to list *their* big ideas for *you* to do so they can bask in the glow of creativity, many times impractical, and quickly move on. The board must be a working board.

The goal of senior staff, usually the executive director, regarding board members is to "get *them* to believe," according to a seasoned practitioner. Appointed members want to serve, but they don't know how. Plus, they certainly don't come to the job with a complete understanding of the vision and mission. How is a sense of purpose for an undertaking taught? By assigning specific duties and responsibilities and requiring material work from board members. Those who aren't committed usually self-eliminate or never accept the job in the first place when they understand they're expected to do a mountain of work regularly.

This is an about-face from the usual assumption that board members are qualified by their positions in the community. In public programs, senior staff exercise certain leadership *over* the board, such as orienting and training them. Board members are used to being in charge and may bridle at a role reversal.

Senior staff must artfully fulfill their roles of hiring, mentoring, training, and motivating board members. Many times they are ex officio and are not fully aware nor skilled at their roles relative to Capacity Building. Senior staff can then get true collaboration from good board members who are willing to listen and *work* to make their ideas work.

- *Constant communication is key.* – One practitioner respondent emphasized "getting insight from hindsight" via constant communication with stakeholders. Both mechanical and nonmechanical ways to encourage the sharing of information must be built in. For example, depending on each stakeholder group's needs, you need to hold regular, *purpose-driven* meetings between staff, the board, and the community. Informally, you can have communication via email, public service announcements via radio, TV, or streaming, news articles, and mail-outs.

  Practitioners make the point that the process of running a service operation is very much about continually staying informed about what has and is happening. You need to understand the on-the-ground truths of your program. This demonstrates a clear departure from the usual regularly scheduled meetings that disseminate top-down information and directives. It's heartwarming to observe this in action—it *can* be done. It *is* being done.

Senior staff concurred about the following three critical dynamics of operating a local service.

8. *Plan operations with the future in mind.*

For sustainability, project leaders need to consider structure, expectations, and reliability.

- *Establish structure.* – Have a clear structure of schedules and procedures, which allows stakeholders and clients to ask and answer questions such as, "Where am I supposed to be and what should I be doing at 11:15 a.m. on Tuesday?"

- *Set expectations.* – Establish high expectations for staff, stakeholders, and clientele.

- *Hire reliability.* – Hire and develop reliable people who show up and get the job, the right job, done.

The measure of a successful, cohesive operation according to a leading practitioner is that "You won't have to wait for the community to tell you that you're doing well; they will tell you with compliments and dollars."

Planning must translate to something actionable. A Boys and Girls Club senior staffer observed that, "Some of our most important lessons came from screw-ups." Adequate planning enables a mistake to become an opportunity to adjust and move on. "There has never been a plan written that can anticipate everything reality throws at you," said another staffer. So reflective action is what matters in operations. Note that these successful staffers knew the absolute necessity to act with just enough preparation to notice the opportunity in a mistake.

Effective Practice
Develop leadership with compassion, empathy, and intelligence.

The most effective leaders realize their major job is to serve the people delivering the service, who are next to those served and actually determine success. The top-down narrative becomes bottom up and *then* top down and cyclically back again. The whole organization becomes more informed in an ever improving continuous cycle, up and down but ever tracking upward. In fact, this continuous feedback loop is self-fulfilling. The more the information flows, the better the individuals and the organization get. That is the definition of success. Let's dissect this a bit.

The executive director must be "the biggest cheerleader and the toughest critic," says a practitioner. He or she assumes responsibility for at least:

- operations,
- personnel and fiscal management,
- community outreach and public relations,
- resources development,
- staff and board development,
- program (services) development, and
- implementation.

All of the above is vision, mission, and performance driven based on continuously developing and motivating staff. Then there are the "other duties as assigned," which essentially means the director has responsibility for *all* of the features and activities in this process. He or she *needs to be* informed by front-line staff.

From the outset of the service idea, senior staff caution to be wary of and resolve turf issues and plan for succession.

The board is actually the extension of the executive director. Board members, too, are better served by the bottom-up top-down model.

> **After asking "why" and "why not," the most important question to ask is "*How*"—THE essential question.**

During operations, the board progresses from *thinking* about the work to *doing* the work of service delivery, *but from an oversight perspective.* Involvement treads a fine, yet definite line of being materially involved for the betterment of the organization while not "bothering" staff. This according to a board member at the Mediation Center of Eastern Carolina.

A board member must make time to be trained in board functions and project operations, especially in determining performance. This training period is when a board member becomes a *team* member and a believer, keeper, and symbol of the vision. Each member must help to manage the decision-making process by asking the "why?" and "why not?" questions, usually together, while internalizing a moral responsibility for the oversight role. After asking "why" and "why not," the most important question to ask is "How"—THE essential question. They have to conduct regular reviews of executive staff, be accessible to staff, and support them when necessary. As much as possible, they must develop an unerring moral compass. They must continually remind themselves that any action, activity, or decision must facilitate goal attainment. One great fact remains.

The board must *always* represent the idea, vision, and mission of the program. Being a board member is largely perspiration once the inspiration is in place. They need to internalize this before they accept an appointment. Thus, the executive director should have specific roles and tasks for the prospective member to seriously consider before they take a seat in the board room.

It is not coincidental that leadership, especially that of the executive director, becomes authentic.[155] According to one respondent, these leaders are quite comfortable with who they are, don't crave adulation, point people in a worthy direction, and create value. In fact, they are the ultimate value brokers. The leaders and staff of the study sites are goal directed and "no obstacles" oriented. They have created meaning and purpose from an idea by embodying the following:

- *The passionate pursuit of their collective purposes* – Thus they impassion those with whom they work or who are influenced by them.

- *Personal values* – Developing values and inspiring others to do the same is a lifetime process. Living in an exemplary way with character matters. Thus each one teaches one, teaches the many.

- *Leadership with compassion, empathy, and intelligence* – This is being firm, fair, insightful, and smart. Ego, conceit, and heaven forbid, narcissism have no place in these leaders.

- *Meaningful personal and professional relationships* – This is essential. Authentic leaders intuitively understand the potential of social capital and the power of the collective whole.

- *Self-discipline and personal growth* – Along the way to accomplishment, authentic leaders continually become better people themselves.[156]

Effective Practice

Refocus the senior staffer from internal operations to external relationship-building and resources development as soon as possible.

An executive director comes to the job several ways. He or she may come up with an idea and assume the job, may be hired to get a service idea going, or may be asked to rescue a failing one. That person is more important than the governing board, according to respondents.

An active director reflected on the responsibility of this person as she experienced it. This person needs to develop each stakeholder group according to their duties and responsibilities. He or she must work and act as if to make their position redundant. This champion senior staffer best serves by being a teacher/mentor to every stakeholder and accomplishes the myriad tasks of running a local service until that work can and must be delegated. Hence a critical talent of the executive director is delegation. It's an art to know who can be trusted to take on additional, especially essential, tasks. The hardest task of all is to let people do their jobs with only an occasional, helpful guiding hand.

However, the hubbub of supervision and management can crowd out vital leadership. The trap for the senior staffer is to remain internally focused on the daily operations critical to managing the chaos of service provision. The crisis of the moment can draw the executive's attention away from the vital realities of developing relationships and justifying the very existence of the project.

Naturally, this senior staffer feels he or she is the "only one" who can do these things and often can't seem to delegate. These senior people must learn to let go and let their properly trained, led, and motivated staff handle the hubbub. They can do this by delegating first then hiring an assistant to handle internal operations. The board may object to hiring more staff because present staff always manage to get the job done and it's expensive to hire more. The program may then stutter to a stop—continuously implementing, never building to self-sufficiency. Thus, as soon as possible, the director needs to hire an assistant for internal operations or delegate such authority, while maintaining responsibility for that person. It's called leadership. Trust the trustworthy and be pleasantly surprised when they say, "Sure, I can do that"—and actually do it better than you could have imagined.

Effective Practice

Redirect board functions to include operational and oversight duties.

The board is well advised to assume or modify certain duties that come with the growth of operations. The Iredell Partnership outlines those essential duties, which can be delegated, at least in part.

- Personnel duties concern board administration, executive director collaboration, volunteer management and development, and legal accountability.

- Planning is widespread, but at the operations stage of the life cycle, it focuses more on long-range planning for stability and enduring capacity. Concurrently, planning must ensure services and operational efficiency and performance as guided by the vision and mission.

- Financial discipline belongs primarily to the board. They ensure that funds are managed according to the standards of the accounting industry.

- Board operation is a privilege and a job. Board members are also responsible for their own efficient and effective operation as a body. Thus, they must be self-disciplining with bylaws, administrative policy, and legal responsibility.

- Public relationship building also belongs to the board in concert with the executive director. They are the keepers of the organizational image in the community. It is a board's primary responsibility to ensure that the community continues to hold the project in high esteem. Thus, board members need to retain old friends and partners while making new ones, a responsibility many times neglected.

A well-functioning board is not automatic. A respondent commented it had been a lot of work to assemble the Mediation Center board so members understood and believed in the mission *and* understood and acted upon its responsibilities. By comparison, at another program, only three of 15 board members attended the quarterly meeting, even after receiving reminder calls, pleading really, from the executive director. Staff conducted most of the business. The meeting lacked the obvious energy and focus of the Mediation Center advisory committee. However, at the Boys and Girls Club, a long-standing board member left a sick bed with a very painful back to attend an impromptu lunch meeting. Think about this. How did this stark difference manifest? Then do what works.

9. Assess capacity for sustainability.

Capacity assessment, when properly planned, is most effective when it's a continuous part of daily operations. It's fed by information and data from each of the critical functions, informing decision making and problem solving. It's also the basis of the action-reflection cycle. It becomes more and more critical as the project matures and begins to affect the community. Aside from providing a daily picture of goal accomplishment, capacity assessment should also focus on the sustainability plan.

Effective Practice

Build capacity assessment into organizational processes.

Both internal and external capacity assessment need to be built into daily operations. Assess internal operations using a proven assessment instrument such as the Marguerite Casey Foundation Capacity Assessment Tool.[157] Soon after that assessment is in place, staff should plan and execute external capacity assessment. External assessment involves understanding the clients—where they are, who they are, their needs and, crucially, the state of local resources to answer their needs. Then both should be worked into a picture of the necessary capacity to address targeted

Translating qualitative changes into monetary statements strengthens support for the idea.

clients in specific areas. It doesn't matter how much is done, if it is the right thing done well. "Think; we are excellence," emphasized program leaders.

Leadership is vital. This suggests demands that staff consider leadership development. The philosophy should be to use strengths by understanding weaknesses. With that in mind, the board should be organized into subcommittees according to goal accomplishment and capacity building tasks. Senior practitioners recommend, at least, committees on performance, capacity building assessment, and resources development.

A combination of both quantitative and qualitative data is most powerful, compelling, and productive. The quantitative data is from existing sources and self-generated from surveys and focus groups, for example. Once the data is combined, it's worthwhile to develop, analyze, and disseminate it for the gain it produces—most importantly, to justify the existence of your idea. Let's add a reminder here. Virtually anyone, any entity is a "partner" who has interest in your success and can help. Practitioners wisely observe that your clients are your best partners and "sales staff," so keep them informed.

Qualitative vignettes are still relevant, but only to emphasize a point in the data picture. Gone are the days when emotional appeal alone swings a political nod, secures a line item in a budget, or obtains a donation. These days, compelling numbers best demonstrate the efficient, and especially effective, use of dollars. Study respondents referred in private-sector terms to the *profit* they were making for the community. By this, they meant the lives they were changing for the better, which translated to cash savings for the municipality. Translating qualitative changes into monetary statements strengthens support for the idea. Fiscal responsibility is a large part of program and individual accountability. All of this describes the picture of your service program performance.

Effective Practice

Develop and implement a sustainability plan based on performance.

Program leaders noted that work during the operational phase should focus on permanency based on performance and improvements to the general good. Thus, it needs to consider the following:

- *Sustainability assessment* – This uses a tool, perhaps a questionnaire or checklist, to assess readiness to assume more services, considering available resources, community support, and political will. If your core people in and out of your program are lackluster about the vision, retrench. Make them believers.

- *Financing* – This is an estimation of financial assets, details of corresponding expenditures, and a listing of funding requirements. The strategy is then "tested" by its fit with organizational vision, mission, and values.

- *Development* – This is a plan to maintain current funding streams and court new ones. Be creative. Even a bake sale by a supportive community is worthy. At the other end, mature projects get into estate planning, where large gifts come from a will.

- *Performance* – Program endurance depends on goal attainment that makes a material improvement in the community. You need a written strategy with tactics on how to continuously enhance the circumstances of the target population and the municipality. Pick one or two of the most meaningful measures along the continuum of measures from initial improvements to intermediate betterment to ultimate well-being. Remember, every measure tallied has an incremental cost in monitoring and producing it.

These components of stability planning double as suggestions for board sub-committees representing the providers addressing the project's focus. In this case, that focus is school readiness and success in primary/secondary school. Consider having sustainability, finance/development, and performance subcommittees. When a project is operating well, all aspects work together. Project staff at this study site observe you will know when it happens.

One goal of a stability plan is to develop at least a half year of reserves for operational expenses. A project leader suggests that a strong sustainability plan should consider developing an endowment from planned giving. This may seem an otherworldly consideration in the hand-to-mouth environment of the local municipality. However, it is *exactly* what forward-thinking, transformative organizations such as the Henderson Boys and Girls Club are doing. In many ways, such as building an endowment and being based on performance and relationships, projects like the Henderson and Iredell Partnerships embody the successful public agency of the future of sustainable service ideas. It can be done.

10. *Make scope analysis a continuous part of decision making.*

When considering scope, the job of leadership is to always question how a service is doing on two fronts: goal accomplishment and closing the services-to-needs gaps. Adjusting project scope begins with a good capacity assessment, augmented by client input via surveys and focus groups, if possible. This enables the board to determine when to increase or decrease commitments. Scope analysis is done with science, quantitative and qualitative analyses, as a beginning for the ultimate decision: a feeling that it's time to "Fish or cut bait."

Please note that scoping can be a trap. Defining how much to do, especially initially, is unrealistic. The impetus to do more and more is always pressing. Resist it. A failure is deadly. Again, scoping is a matter of doing less and doing it well.

Effective Practice

Develop scope analysis as part of comprehensive, continuous decision making.

As with the work of capacity building, practitioners say that vision, mission, and scope continuously inform the decision-making process. Respondents discussed the process in detail and how project assessment is composed of a lot of imperfect pieces. First of all, data must be collected to satisfy short-term funding agency requirements. This may not always be directed to long-term project purposes, but taken together, they become an indispensable part of every decision. Why? Because collectively they relate progress, or lack of it, toward goals and inform the action forward.

Measures of success are by nature, quite crude. They attempt to capture subjective and subtle long-term behavioral changes meant to demonstrate a return on investment of effort and scarce, insecure public dollars. Analytical instruments, for example, may be pre- and post-tests from service recipients on how they feel about the service and how they may be more capable since experiencing the service.

Alone, these so called "smile sheets" may not say much. However, they can do so when combined with *standards of excellence* measures. For example, Boys and Girls Clubs combined them with goals for reducing school expulsions and discipline infractions. Then, these tests and measurements coalesced into a strong indicator of how well the defined scope was being handled. As with any goal-oriented procedure, the worth of this approach increased with the practice of it, which happened at all the model study sites.

Staff at Iredell "painted a picture" of needs versus capacity—the scoping process. They tracked live births in the county to project school readiness programming needs. If all

Successful programs exude creativity, ingenuity, and effectiveness.

those children needed the services of a school readiness program, the Partnership would require 70 *more* staff just for Parents as Teachers (PAT) training and assistance. This fact was then combined with intimate knowledge of target client family needs and where the major client concentrations were relative to available resources. In turn, this provided an adequate (though not perfect) statement about how much service they could deliver, while making a measurable difference. The live birth data alone is almost meaningless, yet it was a good point of departure. Leaders used it to justify the staff of three PAT specialists, while still making a statement about those children who should and could be served when they could hire more staff. Furthermore, the professionally conducted process gained the Partnership added respect, which strengthened community and stakeholder bonds. This is a great example of combining quantitative and qualitative data conveniently lying around to create a vibrant picture of need versus capacity—and get the dollars. Successful programs exude creativity, ingenuity, and effectiveness.

11. Combine process evaluation and impact analysis to optimize service delivery.

Researchers Rao and Woolcock suggest that qualitative methods "improve, complement, and supplement" quantitative inquiry.[158] Respondents agree that the usefulness of a project inquiry process is determined by two factors. The first is how well it's grounded in fact and the second how well the numbers help interpret an almost entirely behavioral, thus subjective, landscape. Exemplary programs demonstrate a happy blend of experiential wisdom and science. This is an important point because theory guided science is not usually given its due in the crush of developing and delivering a service. Yet, the capacity building model sites found ways to do so. They deftly used automation and blended the numbers into even the most mundane decision affecting every critical feature. Everyone at a progressive site is most comfortable with both the numbers (quantitative) and pragmatic (qualitative) aspects of decision making.

In the case of the inquiry process, stakeholders must be willing and able to participate.[159] The twist in the field is that senior staff accurately assume that people, especially staff, don't know the first thing about analysis and evaluation. Therefore, the skills of inquiry are taught to each stakeholder, expecting they will be used for important management and decisions. As an aside, it also helps build team cohesiveness when everyone is meaningfully involved in management and goal accomplishment.

Again, practice the ever-present practical wisdom: Start small. It takes quite a while to put the tools, people, and practices in place. Ideally, project building should be a teaching, learning environment and experience. The process becomes a great teacher as it gradually falls into place. It's a matter of following at least one meaningful measure through the processes of defining the measure, collecting data, analyzing it, and above all, using it to make decisions. Please don't generate numbers just to collect numbers.

Likewise, with a capacity building process it's as simple as asking questions about efficiencies at first. Executive directors at study sites have an expectation of performance that's written into board and staff job descriptions and specifications. The important message to the project inquiry team is that analysis and evaluation are part of the larger strategy to understand and continuously improve service delivery. Remember, ask "how" continually. The theme of synergy emerges again.

Effective Practice

Set up automation systems to help integrate process monitoring and compliance and performance analysis into daily operations.

Automation workstations can be built to facilitate monitoring, audits, and analysis, which respectively provide data on efficiency, compliance, and effectiveness. The director of administration at Iredell described her computer as the latest and most powerful that the budget would allow. The Partnership was also networked within the project and to the internet. Software is off-the-shelf whenever possible.

Custom applications are expensive and difficult to maintain, and they present connectivity problems. The larger sites had a collection of commercial applications for data and information processing. They also had applications for operational duties such as financial and personnel management, managing a client database, and managing funding streams and donors. Low-level internet technological maintenance is handled by staff. Heavy systems maintenance was done professionally by the firm that originally built the network. While the systems at Iredell and Henderson are large compared to

> **A complete plan for resources development needs to consider three essential areas: place, staff, and money.**

a one- or two-person service, the same capabilities apply; it is only a matter of scale.

Don't discount Artificial Intelligence. Begin using it now and increase its use as it grows in relevance and sophistication. Buy the best you can afford.

Another neglected and easily tapped resource is your growing stable of friends. They can help you develop further sources of aid for your program.

12. Engage friends in strategic resource development.

A revelation about developing money and support emerged in discussions about operating the plan. These discussions illuminated how good relationships and goodwill in the community are an overarching concern for forward-thinking stakeholders. They know that all else flows from these connections. This was a change from the original thinking that development of resources meant simply the pursuit of grants. The effective practice of establishing a commitment center captures this philosophy of making friends first and last.

A complete plan for resources development needs to consider three essential areas: place, staff, and money. These essentials compose the key infrastructure of supporting a service, according to an experienced resources developer.

- *Place* – You need to procure, operate, supply, and maintain a place to work that will be the base of operations early in program planning. To start with, it could be one room for the executive director and a receptionist. As the money grows so can the number of rooms.

- *Staff* – Development requires staff who are constantly being cultivated, with a hire-to-retire mentality.

- *Money* – As mentioned, you need to develop money in reliable streams, according to the source category. Reliability is established over time. The goal for a funding stream is that it establishes a predictable stream. This predictability can then be used to justify further support and plan spending. Respondents who have learned from successful, stabilized service projects say that individual donors are likely one of the best sources of money. Donations year after year establish a relatively predictable funding stream as opposed to terminal, capricious, and austere discretionary (government) funding. Here, again, is a departure from the standard opinion at most local service sites. Many rarely look to small donations as a predictable source of funds. Even an annual bake sale and car wash establishes cash flow.

Effective Practice

Continue to operate a funding commitment center based on a public engagement strategic plan.

Developing resources is a matter of recognizing gold dust here and there, which adds up to a gold mine. The Iredell Partnership, for example, had *40* sources of monetary and tangible asset support. Their main sources are from grants, direct mail, business and general solicitations, in-kind donations, cost sharing, and insurance. In addition, at the time of this study, they were working on an endowment via planned giving. Imagine that! Who would think a relatively small local service provider would consider endowments? This resource is usually dismissed as the purview of large institutions such as Harvard or a billionaire's foundation.

Suggest to your donors that they can become philanthropists. Private Donor Advised Funds grant billions of dollars yearly. The advantages are compelling. Once a tax deductible donation is made, interest accrues tax free! Then the magic of compounding takes over. It's a way to pass personal values to heirs, and the trend is accelerating, especially with the retirement of baby boomers. Anyone can begin a DAF with a few thousand dollars and make an automatic annual donation to your program. Considerations like this help support these programs long term and improve thousands of lives over the years. Let's look at how you can develop this and other exemplary ideas to sustain capital for your program.

Every contact with anyone, be it written, electronic, personal, or via a second party (clientele), contains an "ask" for support. Every stakeholder, top-to-bottom and bottom-to-top, internally and externally is involved in development. Board members and the executive director, for example, stay in regular and continuous contact with leading business figures so an appropriate and regular gift is expected and willingly offered. One program official tells the story of his regular visit to a banker. As the program officer enters, his contact reaches for his checkbook. No doubt that circumstance reflects years of building a great program, respect, and trust. Now *that* is development!

At the other end of the giving spectrum, walk-in visitors are given a flyer that explains the Partnership *and* how a range of donations would help. Every potential donor knows what their appropriate gift is *and* what that gift

> **Developing resources is a matter of recognizing gold dust here and there, which adds up to a gold mine.**

will do. Hence it becomes an investment, and the donor is made to feel they are participating in something for the greater good—which, of course, they are.

The flyer, for example, specifies what donations of $5, $10, $20, and $50 will make possible. The donor is drawn into the vision and mission by enabling a *specific* outcome with a *real* entity, whether their donation helps with programming or provides an item of furniture. Likewise, the corporate executive knows the business sense of a four- or five-figure "investment." These suggestions are presented repeatedly, via every form of communication and available media. People are gently, tactfully, but inexorably steered toward a suitable donation. Spending can be planned when streams develop a predictable amount over time. That spending can be based on how the dollar will perform and achieve stated purposes.

Let's see how Iredell defines the Commitment Center concept by outlining the specifics of how they will build relationships with stakeholders via their Public Engagement action plan. What began as a lecture on strategies for working together[160] ended as a highly detailed, multi-year strategy and plan of action to bring people into the Partnership.

It begins with vision, mission, and core beliefs that communicate universally to stakeholder groups. Beliefs that inspire. Next, it defines audiences by recognizing that *any* contact is an occasion for influence. Finally, it outlines six specific objectives and corresponding detailed activities:

- *Increase sharing the idea.* – This is based mainly on strategies to build capacity by reaching out to groups. These may consist of the media, the religious community, businesses, and educators, to mention a few Iredell Partnership friends.

- *Ensure all stakeholders understand that quality childcare, for example, is good for economic, community, and workforce development.* – School readiness makes economic sense to everyone in the community, and especially for the youngster on a path to a career that will support a family.

- *Promote public appreciation for child health and safety.* – This elevates a partnership priority to a holistic community priority.

- *Increase donations by 15 percent.* – This is a realistic benchmark tempered by the exigencies of the community and giving environment. Again, donations are only one source in a comprehensive strategy.

- *Mobilize stakeholders to become politically involved in the issues of young children.* – Advocacy is essential in moving a countywide service idea such as school readiness forward.

- *Honor and celebrate ethnic, cultural, linguistic, economic, and geographic diversity.* – Henderson County is a remarkable socioeconomic melting pot. Each of many groups has a unique culture that influences development strategy and tactics.

As the organization becomes more and more accountable and as more and more people are drawn into its successes, each major funding source is pursued methodically. For example, the Iredell Partnership wrote a goal and activity to contact every possible major donor *seven times a year* by a variety of means, which increased willing donations. Iredell *really* understands how giving works. Contacts included a social event, a public announcement, the website, a flyer, a visit, or multiples of these contact methods. The "ask" for funds then became a rewarding, welcomed, and anticipated experience by the donor. What a contrast with having to make a typical cold call or missing out because someone was just not open to another rather questionable request for money.

13. Nurture performance-oriented service providers.

The old way of a service being predefined by the funding proposal, the qualifications of staff as providers, or contract providers has been usurped by governance thinking.

Operating a service became much more involved as the service providers were seen as *vital partners* in the pursuit of project goals and community betterment.

> **Begin by hiring, educating, and developing service providers for character and performance, and that is what you'll get.**

The people responsible for working with clientele were steeped in the vision/mission of the project, emphasizing performance orientation. Consequently, service providers were mentored to participate in decision making. This was well beyond the usual expectation of meeting clientele for a specified number of hours and contacts, for example. Developing performance-oriented services is a matter of changing the culture of service delivery. It moves from a compliance orientation to changing behaviors in specific, beneficial ways to all allies, especially those served.

While this sounds difficult to accomplish, it's relatively easy to provide service professionals with the tools and imbue them with the motivation to be performance oriented. Begin by hiring, educating, and developing service providers for character and performance, and that is what you'll get. Accomplishing this lies in making performance part of the provider's contract then demonstrating and measuring performance and the provider's part in it as the service progresses.

"Choose services that meaningfully change behavior and improve the neighborhood," counsel model site senior staff. Be mindful of employing a service idea that may duplicate or supplant another carried out by a different agency. Rather, partner with this agency. In other words, if another organization can be persuaded to provide a service that achieves the purposes of the program, engage it. For example, the Iredell Partnership includes dental screening as part of comprehensive school readiness. The health department does dental screening, so the Partnership shifted the full responsibility for dental screening to the agency primarily responsible for this mandate. Partnership resources were freed to provide other services.

Another criterion for acquiring a service is a fairly firm projection of funding to take the service to stability.

Effective Practice

Develop career paths for your performance-oriented service providers.

Model study sites use essentially four steps to achieve effective, high-performing services: setting expectations, establishing standards of performance, assessment and monitoring, and mentoring and management.

- *Setting expectations* – Service providers know even before they're hired what their performance and team expectations are and how to get there. They're shown they can contribute to something bigger than they are—even noble. Thus, your service provider team is both externally and internally motivated. Setting expectations sifts the hiring pool, resulting in the best candidates. It's win, win, win, especially for the youngsters of Iredell early in their developmental years.

- *Establishing standards of performance* – Standards of performance are exemplified by the *Early Childhood Environment Rating Scale: Revised Edition* for preschool.[161] Seven primary areas and 43 subscales comprise preschool services. Each primary area is rated from one (poor) to seven (excellent), and each subscale is weighted to combine for a total measure of performance. This total score strengthens the assessment tool by allowing program-to-program comparisons and rating on a 100-point scale.

  The process of scoring services presents opportunities for provider self-correction as well as ideas for staff to improve the service. Notice how it forces, in a good way, in-depth participation in the process. Also, this system of assessment allows an objective way to understand how different services compare to each other as to overall goal accomplishment. Scores associated with a performance statement and an action statement leave little doubt as to how to increase a score.

- *Assessing and monitoring* – Once standards and subsequent measures are set and agreed upon, assessment and monitoring begin. Monitoring is a combination of analyzing the numbers, technical assistance and training, and reporting. If services are remote, site visits and regular observation of how the service is being delivered are frequent. Iredell keeps only a skeleton crew at the main office throughout the day because service staff are where they should be, in the field preparing children for school.

  Training is continuously delivered via the teachable moment and formal classroom or workshop instruction. Staff hold regular meetings to discuss how the operation is working. They record client data before and after service delivery.

  Likewise, reporting is regular and routine. Reporting begins with the daily or frequent tally of services delivered to target groups and the number of recipients of that service. Assessments are completed. Staff hold weekly meetings and quarterly and annual meetings with the board. These meetings are devoted to ensuring that services perform according to realistic but challenging measures.

Iredell board members are compelled to *know their knitting*. For example, *all* are required to do an annual onsite service assessment. This keeps them intimately involved in how well they are all delivering services and accomplishing their goals. While a collective collegiality of involvement exists, so does a division of labor.

When all these things come together, it's obvious. I observed staff counseling a young Hispanic family on Iredell Partnership services. The briefing was done in fluent Spanish by a Latina staffer. The young parents asked a river of questions and smiled a lot while, at their feet, their children played with educational toys. A palpable sense of rightness about the program manifested in their smiles.

- *Mentoring and managing* – Assessment and monitoring work seamlessly with mentoring and managing. The process of assessment and monitoring provides accurate and regular performance status *before* service quality is threatened. Staff immediately deal with any deviation from standards or lack of progress toward a goal. They extend every effort to help the service correct any slip in performance. This process exemplifies the leadership, bottom up again, necessary to guide the project.

  As a senior staffer observed, mentoring and managing combine, looking for strengths to capitalize on, recognizing weaknesses to improve, and holding a strong expectation of challenging but realistic results. The process is an artful line between good oversight (while not micro-managing) and collaboration to achieve a high level of operation. With this system of service development, adjustments are minor, routine, and constructive. This approach usually avoids situations that fester into crises.

  The philosophy is to treat adults as responsible, in which case, they respond in kind. Service professionals are regarded as part of the team, not just paid help. Rather than imposing external controls on duties, responsibilities, and standards, the emphasis is on the more powerful intrinsic motivation.

14. Develop key staff for their human and social capital potential.

Every exemplary organization visited stressed the importance of staff. Many times, this sentiment of the primacy of staff is just a slogan. What was different here? It was how these stakeholders put this vital ingredient of intrinsically motivated staff into action. People at these sites evolved from being employees to being self- and organizational-actualizing team members on a mission. This was accomplished by viewing the human resources (HR) function as one of developing the capacity of staff to transform a local social condition. Leaders expect and engender excellence in all staff.

For example, the executive director from Win-Win defines her staff as authentic leaders,[162] whom she seeks and develops via her comprehensive staff development program. She looks for people with a willingness to find, assume, and accomplish whatever it takes to get the job done well. She chooses people with passion and harnesses that passion to organizational needs, rewarding performance. Furthermore, she and her staff have *fun*. Oh yes, high intensity comes with working in difficult circumstances with high needs clientele. However, this was coupled with the enjoyment that comes from doing a professional, well-done job with communal purpose. The hiring of these professionals begins with the job posting, which sets the stage for human capacity development.

Effective Practice

Nurture staff with a "hire-to-retire" process of human capacity development.

One program leader characterized her staff development as, "True graduate school, where we teach what is not taught in the classroom." Her point is to create a "culture of cooperation, collaboration, and mutual support." Her process is to imbue employees with ownership in the organization, where they have a constant say in what and how things are done. The buy-in is palpable. This is a far cry from Human Resources that's administrative and meant to manage change and people.

When applied correctly, human capacity development results in employees who are prepared for and intuitively make correct, goal-oriented decisions. They occupy their days productively as a matter of course. Effective staff development starts with recruitment and moves to retention, training, and evaluation, then to transition out of the organization with respect, gratitude, and smiles.

- *Recruiting* – Respondents recommended obtaining, if possible, a deep pool of prospective employees based on a performance-oriented job description. The job posting describes the work environment, lists duties and responsibilities, and sets the stage for high expectations and challenging but rewarding work. The interview ensures prospects understand what is expected.

Interviewers give prospects ample time to explain their thoughts on how they would contribute and fit in and do a lot of listening. *Before* any offer is made, the intended employee knows his or her place in the organizational scheme of accomplishing goals and specific performance expectations. In fact, the interviewer has far less to say than the prospective employee. The official realizes that one or even a series of interviews is a desperately short time to get to know someone with whom you may spend years.

- *Retention and Training* – Once a prospect accepts the offer, the comprehensive and constant retention phase begins. The orientation ensures the new hire knows where and how they fit into the organization. It's highly recommended that a new staff member have a mentor. A leader or mentor formally or informally explains the career development plan and schedules any initial training.

> **Effective staff development starts with recruitment and moves to retention, training, and evaluation, then to transition out of the organization with respect, gratitude, and smiles.**

The ideal career development plan outlines, in matrix form, expectations for education, training, and professional development. Completion of any development is according to the need and availability of the particular development experience.

The Henderson Boys and Girls Club makes it a point to have biannual training, for which the Club is shut down for everything except training. They actually stop doing the work of the day to get better at it. Only a high-performing operation would see the value of this and take the bold step to actually close the doors for a day or two. They also make every effort to send employees to off-site training. Yes, it's much more expensive to do things away from the work site, but the message is much more important. Staff are vital to the operation, and management is willing to spend precious dollars on helping them be as good as they can be!

Training and mentoring as exemplified at Iredell and Henderson are continuous—formal and informal, personal, and communal. Training progresses according to an individual's career development plan. If the plan works well, the employee will never finish career development but will continuously progress. People are trained for ever increasing responsibilities and more demanding jobs. A promotion out of the organization is not feared because an organization with such career progression attracts more and better people. The new brand of leadership sees its primary role as supporting and listening to line staff from the bottom up.

On the informal side of career development, senior and lead staff are constantly teaching. I observed one executive director conduct endless "on-the-fly teaching conversations," as he called them. He did it in an appropriately fatherly way and on the basis of many years of experience. In turn, his employees saw him constantly learning and taking in information from *them*. In the first hour and a half of the day, he had 10 such conversations with his staff.

Another senior leader would regularly accompany staff in the field. Her sole purpose was to instruct and mentor them during the many teachable moments of delivering a service or doing the business of the Partnership. These executive directors embody what on-the-job training can and must be. This is leadership in action.

- *Evaluation* – Career development includes a personal evaluation program. This, in turn, involves reviewing the past year's training and scheduling the next year's training.

  Upon evaluation, if all is going well, employees may take on an additional duty that helps the organization do the minor but necessary tasks that don't require a full-time employee. Employees receive cross-training for several purposes. It helps when they understand how the organization functions and can fill in when necessary. As at Henderson, they may be organized into teams or subcommittees to mirror and work with the board. This enables them to cover critical but encompassing functions such as accountability or resources development.

- *Transition* – The final phase of human capacity development is to have a procedure to transition staff out of the organization with as little disruption as possible. Successful sites managed this with a succession plan, one of the solutions to the plague of turnover. Senior staff at established sites train their own replacement. They hire good people without fear of attracting people better than they are and develop people who have the potential to succeed beyond their accomplishments. And so it is with successful succession planning.

  Detailed job descriptions are backed by defined duties and responsibilities. The focus is not so much on what needs to be done as how it should be done.

Standard operating procedures (SOPs) outline how critical functions are performed to further the vision, mission, goals, and organizational cohesion. Critical staff may augment SOPs by more explicitly documenting how they do their jobs. These progressive sites require staff to make personal notes in the SOPs, detailing the idiosyncrasies of a job. Staff are cross-trained in critical tasking or smaller jobs as much as possible. This also ensures a high level of attention to detail because even the smallest of tasks has a responsible party. Cross-training not only supports succession planning, but it adds to the depth of organizational capability.

Staff naturally empathize with fellow staff and occasionally work another job. This has the added benefit of providing variety to the routine of assigned duties and responsibilities.

The succession policy also establishes how a farewell is done to include an exit interview. The people conducting the interview listen carefully to what the exiting party has to say and learn from it.

Ideally, when a staffer, especially a seasoned one, moves on or retires, operations should hardly hesitate—except for a little cake, ice cream, a plaque, a gag gift, and a hug or two.

The Henderson Partnership has managed to capture much of what a comprehensive human capacity development process should do. Even in their frenetic environment of providing out-of-school services to at-risk students, they've had only three staff leave in the preceding *nine years* at the time of this inquiry. One left for marriage, another returned to graduate school, and one left for other personal reasons. This is a remarkable record for a nonprofit organization working in an exceptionally demanding environment for relatively low wages. The Partnership enjoys the multiple fruits of collective corporate effort fueled by focused social capital, high expectations, and passion.

The first stage of project maturity, Phase I: Planning, lays out a strategy of essential operational functions. Through it, people understand what the purpose

> **Cross-training not only supports succession planning, but it adds to the depth of organizational capability.**

of the project is and what they're to do to reach those goals. Phase II: Operation, is a transition from planning to delivering the service. Phase III: Stability and Expansion, continues the life cycle evolution of the service idea. In this phase, the idea becomes self-sustaining, gradually meeting the true need in the community. Ideally, this is when the service realizes its capability of transformation.

> **The primary difficulty of operating with grant money is it provides little motivation to prove that the service is actually doing what it needs to do.**

PHASE III of the Project Life Cycle: Sustainability and Expansion – Realizing Social Transformation

This stage was difficult to investigate because few projects reach the point where they're stable, enduring, *and* transformative. To be able to do that, they need to have *self-sustaining* operational resources. As previously mentioned, many projects are fully or largely supported by soft money—undependable, usually terminal, grant money. This soft support is problematic for many reasons beyond its whimsical nature. The primary difficulty of operating with grant money is it provides little motivation to prove that the service is actually doing what it needs to do. Oh, these projects may show "results" galore, but they are shallow, even on superficial inspection. What the government giveth the government can easily taketh away, and summarily at that. This type of programming is structural. What can be done?

Programs that develop capacity building for self-sustaining operational resources and have a passion to do measurable good in their communities show us every day. Fortunately, for the purposes of this study, sites such as the Henderson Boys and Girls Club, the Iredell Partnership, and beyond to TROSA, LINC, The Durham County Justice Resource Center, and Dismas Charities have achieved a state of transformative capacity. They are as stout and persistent as the social dysfunction they tackle. They offer many examples of how to provide local services—building permanent solutions to permanent problems. There is hope.

To summarize, the lesson is that sustainability must be *planned* from the beginning.[163] Planning needs to consider:

- *The proper way to build an idea* – Build your service program from the bottom-up so that staff's technical expertise and cohesiveness are nurtured.

- *The proper way to build capacity* – Build organizational capacity from the top-down, then the bottom-up.

- *The proper way to partner* – Include partnerships where local stakeholders join the effort.

- *The proper way to empower stakeholders* – Keep an egalitarian eye to empowering the community.[164]

When all is working well, a capacity-built matrix solution to a local problem is an enviable, unending virtuous cycle. A stable project has the potential to benefit the wider community, become institutionalized, and be focused on capacity building.[165] Project design is proven to help the idea overcome potential problems of implementation. The number one problem of getting a good idea going—implementation—is solved. When a project is a matrix solution, planned for permanency, and well-executed, project participants can collectively ask, "Now, how can we make a real difference?"

The Henderson site illustrates this state of transformative capability. On the initial visit to Henderson, the administrative assistant introduced me to the executive director. Before I could begin introducing my purpose for the visit, the lead executive said, "Let's tour the campus." He later explained that many visitors are content with a visit confined to his office and a few pieces of paper. He tries *never* to let this happen. Any visit inevitably begins with letting all the senses experience what is going on. It was clear he was proud of what they had done over the past hard years and especially wanted to dream with anyone about what will come to be.

He gave me Monday's detailed, hour-by-hour schedule of classes and activities as we walked from frugally appointed room to room with age appropriate classes in session. One class was Passport to Manhood, which gives boys probably their first exposure about how to act responsibly, be mannerly with a girl, show respect for authority, and personally set a curfew. Notice how these topics were tailored to the needs of the student, not designed by a detached committee. What was even more telling? The director entered a room to immediate greeting from students whom he addressed by name as if addressing his own children. Further, he immediately interacted with the students, one of whom spontaneously dedicated a song they were practicing to *him*. The children not only respected him; they *revered* him. This reverence was felt not only by the children but by his board, his staff, the parents, and the wider community. How did he make this happen?

> **When all is working well, a capacity-built matrix solution to a local problem is an enviable, unending virtuous cycle.**

The tour progressed to the center of the campus of about five buildings, where he paused to describe the site. The neighborhood was known for poverty, drugs, prostitution, serious crimes, and broken homes in the cycle of poverty. It was also known for undisciplined juveniles, school and social dropouts, gambling, and generally widespread personal, communal, and socially retrograde behaviors. Everything screamed disappointment and struggle. He pointed to two houses just across the street and described them as active crack houses, adding, "This is the perfect place for us!" How many others could see a nexus to drug trafficking and intergenerational failure as the "perfect place" for a boys and girls club?

His day revolves and evolves around the children. Every interaction with a child is seen as a teachable moment. The teaching, mentoring, and care form one continuous stream. Everyone from the board to the volunteers works as one. It's beyond heartwarming to observe and feel the energy of youth with hope. Staff really understand what they can do and do it well. Their vision, mission, goals, and credo are the pulse of daily work. Dollars flow in even though they are hard fought and won. The program is well justified, and work happens smoothly if not joyfully. How refreshing! The staff are admired and respected in the community and a model for those who care to ask for guidance, which they give willingly. Work continues sunup to sundown, and they still make time for a visitor! Everything they do, every service they offer, contributes measurably to stated purposes. Are these not the things that determine success and social transformation? Do they not describe an idea that's a permanent solution to a permanent problem? I think so.

> The director entered a room to immediate greeting from students whom he addressed by name as if addressing his own children. Further, he immediately interacted with the students, one of whom spontaneously dedicated a song they were practicing to *him*. The children not only respected him; they revered *him*.

15. Sustain operations.

Now we return to this major theme because achieving local service project stability is at once difficult, unusual (in the public sector), and essential. It's essential to *making a difference* in individual and communal quality of life—*especially* if a project is located among crack houses! A project must be stable before it can begin to meaningfully attack local community dysfunction. Senior staff and board members of the Henderson project commented that becoming permanent and closing the gap between existing and needed services is the stage sought by all service projects. However, they admitted sustainability is difficult to attain because most projects get caught in an endless loop of implementation, with only wistful dreams of expansion.

The Capacity Building Pyramid

This mindset of capacity building is also the current bent of philanthropy. From the early 1990s, foundations began the demonstrable shift from "knitting" *for* people to teaching *them* to knit. The Capacity Assessment Grid[166] conceptualizes this Capacity Building model by seeing the organization as a pyramid. It establishes the context for and priorities of organizational improvement at this third stage of operational maturity. (See more about Capacity Assessment in Chapter 5 and in the Explanatory Glossary.) At this stage, the services-to-needs gaps are closed, and the project begins to measurably transform its target community.

The foundation of the pyramid is based on human resources, systems and infrastructure, and organizational structure that includes organizational skills, strategies, and aspirations, in that order. It's a vision-bound collaborative culture that transcends cooperation on a task to get to the end of the day. Everyone rows in the same direction, even if it's upstream, in which case they just pull harder. Practitioners at these model sites are realizing that everything is based on a culture that inspires by combining values and performance.[167]

Stabilization

Stabilization is a heady time for stakeholders and a real pleasure to observe. Leadership, mainly the board and the executive director, know how to build respect, ensure performance, and develop resources. Capacity assessment allows stakeholders to thoroughly understand their organization, their programming, and their community. The vision/mission statement inspires and is internalized such that it guides even mundane daily activities and decisions.

Thinking excellence and doing things *incrementally* and *well* are the tactics of building scope. Any local public service project needs to internalize this immutable law.

Analysis of results and evaluation of process work together to justify the project. They paint a picture of vision-driven performance and productivity guided by inspirational leadership.

- *Applying the science of inquiry* – Stakeholders are adept at the science of inquiry and use it as one of many decision-making tools.

- *Developing reliable friends* – Resource development is based on ever-widening networks of friends of the project and great respect in the community.

- *Acquiring funding streams* – Various streams of funding are stable enough to support budgetary decisions.

- *Expecting paramount performance* – Contract or developed services are based on the expectation of performance.

- *Inspiring stakeholders* – Stakeholders, especially organizational staff, realize that the project rises or falls on them. Hence, they are shaped to the needs of the organization by comprehensive development designed to nurture staff.

In other words, the capacity for social transformation is in place. The mutual respect from program staff and the community is palpable. It can be done!

Effective Practice

Adjust and sustain operations via a self-accreditation process.

Self-Accreditation

Leading staff provide suggestions. It pays, they say, to make a regular, comprehensive, and in-depth inquiry into how operations can be made as solid as possible. This is not unlike an accreditation inspection. It can be in conjunction with an audit or a certification process. A possible approach is to assemble inspection checklists from the duties and responsibilities of the major functions; then combine those with generic inspection checklists tailored to the organization and community. Such an inspection needs to be constructive, with positive suggestions to improve. A punitive inspection, internal or external, destroys motivation and morale.

What is traditionally looked at as a discrepancy list, or a "gotcha" list, becomes an *opportunity* list. It's characterized in some positive way as a tool for betterment, with follow up until all shortcomings are corrected or answered. No acrimony, no finger pointing, no shaming. Any shortcoming is corrected on the spot or rectified by assigning it to a responsible party. The conduct of the inspection is collegial, open, candid, and rewarding. Everyone enjoys the growth. What matters is that stakeholders take time to strengthen the business that supports project services *before* additional responsibilities are assumed.

Vision, mission, and goals, which are *aspirations,* must be aligned with *strategy* and integrated into *infrastructure.* Reliable funding streams must continuously improve staff and operational systems. All come together to spark the *inspiration* that makes the difference between coasting and soaring.

Such an inspection needs to be constructive, with positive suggestions to improve.

It's most advisable that staff be developed and educated on the essentials of character-based leadership, humility, and introspection. They must ensure the project is integrated functionally and by work groups for temporary need or critical tasking, such as ensuring performance, resources development, or capacity assessment.

In short, self-inspection should ensure all project components come together to build long-term value to those served and thus the community as a whole.

When to Expand

A measure of when to expand is when the project has the capacity, usually the manpower and support, to continuously deliver the service reliably and well. Staff observe science and data have less to do with expansion than experience and intuition. For example, the Boys and Girls Club expanded services as enrollments increased. However, they also knew when to hold enrollments with a waiting list, which was another measure of need. Hiring decisions also had to consider need.

Staff response to this reality of need exemplified their creative problem-solving. They monitored overtime religiously. When overtime equaled a full-time staffer, the need for a new hire was justified with a statement of what operational goals were not being accomplished by the lack of personnel *and* what that was costing the community. They combined this with a cost-effectiveness statement about how much this new position would return on the "investment."

In short, self-inspection should ensure all project components come together to build long-term value to those served and thus the community as a whole.

Quite brilliant as it justifies more help in terms decision makers understand.

Usually, a proposal to add staff is seen as a difficult decision because of the expense, which delays the decision beyond when help is needed. When made as a rational proposition that will save the municipality money, the decision is so much easier. Insightful and smart practitioners always make a tradeoff argument about what *not* hiring a new person will cost.

Most projects approach funding as a terminal task, usually grant writing or a budget proposal, a practice these study sites initially adopted. Site officials, especially at Iredell and Henderson, saw early in the evolution of their projects that stability depends on funding streams they must continually develop. Thus, this development threaded through everything they did and was a major factor in deciding when and if to expand.

First, they made every effort to satisfy the client and family. This formed the basis for building credibility and respect with direct stakeholders and in the wider community. They even gave clients brochures about vision and mission and how they fit within the overall scheme of the project. Thus a request to increase a budget became a rational argument to improve the community.

> Thinking excellence and doing things *incrementally* and *well* are the tactics of building scope. Any local public service project needs to internalize this immutable law.

Staff recognized that satisfied customers not only network to potential clientele but tell the story of their successes. This face-to-face precursor to networking via social media continues to be a potent tool of community work. Goodwill aids the effort to develop donations.

Second, staff evolved to understand resources development as a fluid process. Such a process considers how to fund anticipated needs and confront the vicissitudes of austere and unpredictable funding. Resources development in that mode is the antithesis of crisis management. Anticipating need is vital and another indicator of a strong project. Many projects seek funding simply for survival, and consequently, that's what they do—merely exist. Practitioners at a maturing, impactful service site see the future and make the case to reach for it.

That said, experienced senior staff also know when not to expand. Again, less is more when it's done well. This vital insight is as important as knowing when to assume more responsibility. Success causes pressure from the community to do more. Voters even make the case for your services.

Eagerly grabbing for more responsibility takes many forms. When a glimmer of progress appears, the tendency is to reach more clientele, cover more territory, take on more services, or perhaps look at more measures of success. However, overreach can be as deathly as *not* doing well.

The Iredell Smart Start and the Henderson Boys and Girls

> The reward for staying mission focused and within the means of the project ultimately pays off in being able to expand judiciously—the goal all along.

Club were constantly asked to do more or open a satellite. Both held the line for several good reasons. Primarily, their mission would not allow it. A sense of mission told them that their primary purpose would suffer if more work were assumed. Second, they knew the absolute limits of their capability and never violated them—because they were measuring capacity daily. For example, the Club agreed to expansion but only if it were guaranteed a campus with commensurate operational funds. Their experience told them that building a facility is relatively easy—relative, that is, to generating necessary operating funds for the life of the added infrastructure and responsibilities.

Besides understanding how to build a steady flow of funds and successfully satisfying clients, a third consideration in the expansion scenario is building reputation. According to practitioners, reputation is hard fought and won. Expansion presents the reality that startup woes would affect the mother operation, which could ruin years of work and building reputation. "Sometimes," they agreed, "it is just better to stick with your knitting, no matter how tempting it is to do a little more." The reward for staying mission focused and within the means of the project ultimately pays off in being able to expand judiciously—the goal all along.

16. Plot the long-range strategy and tactics for expansion.

At all the model study sites, I noticed urgency about and discomfort with the current level of work and service. It was a collective sense that more could be and had to be done. The status quo just does not gather purchase with projects that transform.

When considering future moves, a project leader commented that, "The most important thing we can do is listen," meaning pay attention. *Pay attention* to growing waiting lists at focus groups, *pay attention* to the analyses, *listen* to stakeholders, *pay attention* to client pre- and post-tests, *note* trends in the field, and especially *listen* to your intuition. It all figures into the judgment and decision of how much more can be done and when to do it.

To listen and then act, a senior staffer began attending community meetings—uninvited but tactfully—until she was invited to speak to people who had become friends. She recruited these new friends from the business community to bring books and read to children in the Partnership's programs. She also encouraged them to start a recycling program in which business castoffs were brought to the Partnership to be reborn and repurposed. This represents a natural evolution of finding answers to needs. Most times they are small needs, but collectively, they're vital. Minutia, but the correct minutia, matter.

The willing involvement of businessmen and women in the reading program made them believers in the project. In turn, they shared their resources, connections, political will, expertise, and financial support. Why? They became part of something worthwhile that was even bigger than they were and responded to the basic need to improve communal well-being.

There is no defining moment when project staff conclude they're ready to expand. According to senior staff and board members, that opportunity is built on a development strategy that matures with the service. It's more of a feeling, they say, or an educated, artful guess that's not as scientific as the pundits would wish. Routinizing evaluation and analysis provides a steady stream of subjective comments and quantitative data about capacity to staff and especially decision makers.

Note that the transformative sites moved away from the usual top-down reaction-compliance management style. They adopted the preferred participatory bottom-up leadership mode of action-reflection-planning-action, even though they had no formal training in the method. They used theory and science, but only to a degree. In the end, weighty decisions are quite human—so decide we must.

The strategy for project development and especially expansion must be vision-mission driven. As mentioned, you need to ensure operational funding as much as possible. It bears repeating, your board and staff better serve the idea if they are especially inspired by the mission. Furthermore, local support for the program needs to be solid. If your communities, neighbors, businesses, and politicians aren't fully behind you, work on getting them there. You likely won't be respected by all, so target those who are amenable to the idea.

Again, don't assume board members come to the job ready to go. All the dynamics are new. This is their first time in this situation, with these people, in this community, with this purpose. Even the most qualified need training in the program and how they can work as a cohesive unit. Many schools or workshops train board members. Stanford has *Board Governance Training* online

> The willing involvement of businessmen and women in the reading program made them believers in the project. In turn, they shared their resources, connections, political will, expertise, and financial support.

or on campus. Notice the sophistication of the title. They train in governance, the *how* of getting things done. They get it.

When all that's in place and a service is added or a current one expanded, it's better to embed that service in the existing array of services rather than have it stand alone. Then it won't trigger the thought of, "Oh, no, not something else;" nor will it be considered a burden on limited supporting resources and flagging political will.

Therefore, as quickly as possible, establish a history of performance and social transformation. Make your idea continuously prove itself by meaningfully improving the lot of its target population(s) and making a measurable positive difference in the community.

Effective Practice

Form a community transition team to assess current needs and suggest ways to continue closing the service-to-needs gap.

The Iredell staff and board had a strategic goal to regularly assess community needs relative to their program purposes. They participated in a municipal focus group formed to address expansion and other strategic duties and desires.

Another way to address capacity assessment and begin closing the service-to-needs gap is to delegate the responsibility to a board subcommittee. This networked body of stakeholders can design project strategies to expand the organization and programming, in one-, two-, five- and ten-year increments, for example.

An experienced project leader suggested using a readiness template on which to base the feasibility of expansion. Simple inquiries with yes or no answers can determine what has been done or needs to be done. By assessing the entire life cycle of a service or project idea, decision makers are much better informed and prepared for strategic and tactical action.

This senior staffer had more advice. She said whatever method you choose to close your gap should be composed of appropriate stakeholders—people with a stake in increasingly good outcomes. These stakeholders will be mandated to track the dynamics of target populations and the resources to satisfy equally dynamic needs within the scope of the project.

> Conceptualizing the process in terms of its life cycle is a new way to look at community service development. It resonates. It rewires how things are done—and it's replicable.

As the rounds of interviews closed at the Boys and Girls Club and we considered the research project and its implications, the program executive director provided one of his many insights: "We must not, *cannot,* depend on government to make our communities whole and wholesome. Good communities are the responsibility of their citizens." He pointed out that the future presents a remarkable and genuine opportunity to realize this kind of neighborhood citizen ownership.

The executive director observed, at the time of this research, that over $3 trillion in personal wealth from baby boomers has already begun changing hands—and at an accelerating pace. With solid programs built on good principles and a reliable business model, a significant amount of that money will likely be willingly passed to worthy, proven ideas. His solid and proven Boys and Girls Club is the justification for the planned giving endowment that his club is building. Such regular financing will help that service idea continue expanding to ever more children—*continuously,* providing *a permanent answer to a permanent problem.*

Overall, respondents agreed with the process of capacity building outlined in Table 7.1 on pages 203 to 205. Conceptualizing the process in terms of its life cycle is a new way to look at community service development. It resonates. It rewires how things are done—and it's replicable.

This model captures the necessary long-term, complex yet achievable nature of working on local service durability. As expected, practitioners expanded the theory of building project capacity from the bottom-up with perception, perspective, and practicality. Their insight, for example, captured the fact that resource

> "We must not, *cannot,* depend on government to make our communities whole and wholesome. Good communities are the responsibility of their citizens."

development is based on establishing a history of delivering on promises and making friendships. Field-level perspective shaped this theory of local capacity development by explaining that service providers are part of the problem-solving social capital of the project, not merely subcontractors.

Primarily respondents made this theory of capacity building practical, applicable, and useful. They confirmed that the process will work and is transferable to similar development applications. They have shown that working in a bottom-up mode improves communities.

Summary

Chapter 4 explained every detail of the Capacity Building approach and process, along with examples and practitioner input from successful sites. It described the three phases of the life cycle of program development and explained the importance of each step. With an example of a contrasting top-down model, it clarified the advantages of the Capacity Building approach and what's needed to sustain this type of program so it can transform a community.

The next chapter explains how this process fits into the implementation debate. It reflects on capacity building's place and future in the evolution of community public services and governance.

Chapter 5

THE BUSINESS BENEATH THE BUSINESS

Chapter 5

THE BUSINESS BENEATH
THE BUSINESS

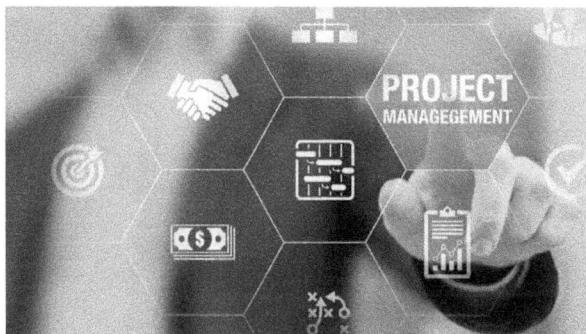

Everything should be made as simple as possible, but not simpler.

– Albert Einstein

At every study site, I observed many binders filled with suggestions of what should be done to make a project work. In fact, I observed this at scores of sites over my 25 years of looking at projects in all stages of succeeding . . . or not. But the *what* wasn't enough. A project became successful when stakeholders figured out *how* things needed to be put together, *how* they should be done, and especially *how much* of something needed to be done to realize measurable, positive results. Capacity building is the *how*—the business beneath the business of the social program.

Staff at these projects answered the classic struggles of implementation[168] and, thankfully, were most willing to share their hard-won and practical perceptions, wisdom, and lessons learned. However, a practitioner-based process is not a guarantee of smooth sailing; mistakes are unavoidable.

Using a process that guides practitioners through the usual mistakes, mishaps, and misjudgments needs to be unique to the circumstances at hand, with negative effects minimized and positive effects upon which to capitalize. Stuff happens—that's the substance of progress. A useful, proven process in project development via capacity building has an organic nature because it's shaped by the dynamics of change over time. It must evolve continuously becoming better and better—from the bottom up.

Capacity Building for Social Transformation – Unconventional Wisdom

This in-depth probe into extraordinary local service projects confirms the expectations[169] that local service projects, especially those for keeping people away from dependency on public resources and out of prison and jails, have difficulties getting beyond implementation. The way to progress is via a capacity building process, as explained in Chapter 4.[170]

Prior to this book's take on capacity building, no clear path was offered to enhance the chances of reliably sustaining a service idea. Reducing the chaos to a generally applicable checklist has a significant impact on services building and delivery. Practitioners can see what they need to do and when. The goal of building a permanent answer to a local permanent problem becomes realistic. All stakeholders, including the community at large, develop a sense of a wider, bigger purpose. People are made better, and thus communities are made better.

The site visits verified the economic sense of strengthening local service projects that focus on keeping people out of prisons and jails, especially our youngest children.[171] Thus the Iredell County Partnership for Young Children and the Henderson Boys and Girls Club are real standouts.

> *Let's figure out ways of keeping our children out of the juvenile justice system and in the classroom so they'll thrive.* – Valerie Jarrett

Referring also to projects beyond the study sites, such as TROSA, LINC, Dismas Charities, the Durham County Criminal Justice Resource Center, we see proof of success. We can note how that success was accomplished with a depth of understanding that previously has not been documented. Chaos is diminished, even bows to, an applicable, practical checklist of project building from conception to permanence.

Yes, many projects survive for years because of factors other than capacity, such as a powerful sponsor or a perpetual grant; but that survival is usually at a level much below their potential. Services are usually agency based and thus limited by definition and the confines of the host. Much, much more can be accomplished with true agency-to-agency matrix collaboration specifically chosen for the task at hand to craft community well-being. Every successful project I visited exemplified this fact, and these practitioners willingly shared how they were doing it. In the spirit of the new bottom-up, inspired and inspiring leader, successful project staff continuously improve, both individually and collectively.

Practitioners at the model sites spent considerable time explaining how to move local service ideas beyond imple- mentation. They exuded humility and

> **Leadership is less the imposition of will on the project than willingness to become servants of a worthy idea to enhance the greater good.**

pride in their accomplishments. The hope for this approach is that, over time, one good, inspired idea at a time will create permanent improvement. From one can then come many.

Following is a review of significant practitioner contributions and insights by phase and feature.

Leadership

Key people mature with the project. Roles progress, cohesiveness cements, the group is other driven. Project development is more art than methods such as applying financial and management rules and conventions. Virtuous, character-based living with ethics and morals shines through. Ideas realized for common betterment result in a strong business organization.

> *Leaders do not form the service idea; it shapes them.*

Out of all that's been written on leadership roles, study respondents kept returning to two: the coach and the technician.[172] Even these two primary leadership roles are shaped by the service idea, *not the other way around*. The field work confirmed that, as a coach, the local leader needs to be a networker, the keeper of the vision, the builder of relationships, a salesperson, a mentor, and the center of energy.[173] As a technician, he or she needs to master the technical aspects of the business of service delivery, the most important of which is process evaluation and impact analysis.[174]

Key staff at TROSA, LINC, the Durham County Resource Center, Dismas Inc., the Iredell County Partnership for Young Children, and the Henderson Boys and Girls Club observe that these roles are shaped by the 16 major milestones/tasks of service growth. These tasks include capacity building and staff development. Any role assumed by project leadership is a product of the particular environment of the developing service idea. Leadership is less the imposition of will on the project than willingness to become servants of a worthy idea to enhance the greater good.

This altered view of leadership as the vehicle of an idea, not the reverse, is reflected in the vision. First comes clarity of imagination, purpose, and commitment—usually all three at once—*then* comes vision.[175] Frequently, it's stated in the opposite order.

Site observations, interviews, research, and especially experience suggest that the imagining of new realities, of new possibilities, needs to come before commitment to a vision statement. Then leadership moves the organization in a unified direction.[176] While many tangible technical talents of leadership are important, each exemplary site illuminated the *critical intangibles* of leadership: *judgment and intuition*.

Capacity Assessment

Capacity assessment is much more than needs assessment. Interviews probed how simple, easy-to-process numbers became continuous capacity assessment, informing daily micro- and strategic macro-decision making. This insight led to this critical factor evolving from needs assessment into capacity assessment. The seemingly small change in perspective and tactics resulted in profound effects on the selection and shaping of a service idea, especially an evidence-based one. The change helped the idea endure with continuous impact.

Capacity assessment is the task of building toward permanency.

If capacity assessment is done at all, it's usually a one-and-done thing, which is a real problem for this reason: *Continuously* understanding what and how much you can deliver is the difference between success and fizzling out. The best remedy is conceptualizing project development in terms of life-cycle processes. Unfortunately, current methods and tools, such as the McKinsey Capacity Assessment Grid and the Marguerite Casey Foundation Capacity Assessment Tool, imply that assessment can be done at a certain point as a terminal activity. Experience advises against this temptation. Rather, assessment should be a priority during planning then done *continuously*. Staff need to monitor daily work processes with the intent of improving efficiency and effectiveness and keeping processes goal oriented.

Assessment, internal and external, should be one of the first priorities as it contributes to the chain of planning, operations, stability, and expansion. Ultimately, it contributes to successfully answering the social dysfunction it was founded to address in the first place.

Capacity assessment is one of the most productive uses of resources, yet it's one of the most neglected aspects of service development. Capacity assessment should, as observed in the field:

- *Stimulate discussion.* – Target it to either the task at hand or solving problems that lead to program growth.

- *Set priorities and expectations.* – Any work or decision is best served by testing it against vision, mission, and goals.

- *Form extended relationships.* – Identify your stakeholders and develop them into partners.

- *Build capacity to deliver.* – Gradually, according to resources and political support, close the service-to-needs gap.

So many good ideas rarely get past discussion, and many needs assessments are concocted to force the community to fit a service idea. This is contradictory and backwards. The idea must evolve to meet the demands and environment of each unique community that contemplates that idea for service. Yes, the overall goal of improving individual and community betterment is still primary. But, if the idea is not subjected to the process of capacity assessment, problems will ensue. The gathering, understanding, internalizing, and use of vital information *will* be neglected, and the idea will never nestle snugly into the community.

> *Continuously* understanding what and how much you can deliver is the difference between success and fizzling out.

Scope

Scope is about thinking and acting within manageable guidelines. Yes, vision and mission shape the project overall but fail if staff don't determine what and critically *how much* a project should tackle. First do something well, then ever so judiciously build on that. It's a limiting mechanism as much as it is a dream of what can be. It's better to do one thing well than assume more responsibilities with questionable outcomes and all the attendant frustrations, not the least of which is pulling the plug.

Scope is a narrowing of project grasp to fit capability.

Focus is the key. Staff cannot focus on a vision that's too grand. A good vision/mission needs to be inspirational and transformational but possible. It can be possible by not trying to do too much and by being practical for the long-term.

The literature makes another point, which investigation confirmed: Vision/mission and scope potency are determined by *how* they are achieved and *how* they are applied.[177] They must be actionable by direct daily work, not just will-o'-the-wisp dreamy statements. Let's be clear: The essential requirement for vision/mission and scope is to facilitate community relationships and project capacity to improve the lot of target clientele. In turn, the project improves the community.

Process Evaluation and Impact Analysis

Evaluation of process efficiency and analysis of impact effectiveness are not discrete processes but synergistic. However, process evaluation needs to be a priority because an operation must run efficiently, that is work well, before it can have a lasting and positive impact. This is another reversal of common practice in local project development. Usually, results come first, no matter how flimsy they are. However, with true Capacity Building they must be made to work together, because all other critical features are built upon evaluation and analysis. For example, no matter how inspired leaders are, their decisions must be based on understanding how decisions affect project function and outcomes.

> **Changes are clarified by viewing the project from a new vantage point after the modified road just traveled. This describes the learning organization.**

Process evaluation and impact analysis are different.
The project benefits when they work in tandem.

The process of evaluation/analysis follows the life-cycle concept.[178] Analysis/evaluation activities, according to practitioners, should have five phases:

1. Pre-project *planning*
2. Start-up that begins with baselines, or target *measures*
3. *Implementation* and adjustment based on ground-level, realistic intelligence
4. Improving *maintenance* and strengthening project *stability*
5. Enacting policy from what is *learned*

To this, site staff add that the process should be contiguous and continuous, but framed as a new beginning rather than repeating a bothersome job. This philosophy of cyclical investigation–planning–action–investigation is based on continuous improvement. Changes are clarified by viewing the project from a new vantage point after the modified road just traveled. This describes the learning organization.

Resources Development

Resources are much more than winning the next round of funds. They're multifaceted and multidimensional.

Resources are more than money.

Resources can be in-kind volunteer labor or donated supplies and secondhand equipment. A resource may even be an abandoned jail bought from the county for a dollar a year. Yes, LINC, North Carolina, did this then got a development loan, which it repaid in a few years with sustainable enterprises. This happened in a very economically challenged part of town. I must say, the founder is inspired and inspiring. What an example for us all that capacity building for well-being works. Thus, an abandoned building was transformed into a sparkling halfway house for adults returning to the community as productive members of society.

Resources can be a defined giving program or winning a line item in the local budget. They're limited only by the imagination and the necessary yet rewarding work of turning them into reliable streams. Resources come from people; thus they are based on relationships.

Developing resources links directly to establishing then improving credibility, which is done through relationships. Indeed, relationships are the key to increasing capacity and project impact. Resource development must be flexible, rational, and systematic.[179] But what comes first for practitioners—the laying hen or the egg?

Do project staff build relationships to garner many small donations, reliable over time, or go after larger grants, which are less dependent on relationships and terminal? Do staff ask for money for more services or construct the organization first? The goal of establishing relationships is a neighborly state of affairs in which everyone knows you, you know them, and you all know what can be done together. *That* is the answer to the first dilemma: Relationships come first, before the money.

Nevertheless, opposition to this observation is commonly expressed as, "We need money now! It takes time to make friends." In fact, the enduring sites managed to prioritize relationship-building that promotes developing funds particularly with respect to winning important seed money and vital resources for stability and growth. Several executive directors from the study sites recognized that a strong image compels buy-in. Thus, streams of resources are planned *with* people, not *for* them. Recognizing this, forward-thinking stakeholders conduct development only if the organization can accomplish stated goals. They must have the ability to deliver; a promise to do so is sacrosanct.

Should a fledgling organization accept easy and "necessary" money that may diverge from the mission—or say no? The courageous, vision-directed leaders say no and thrive. A well-functioning organization grows *with* resources, not behind them. Easy money is not the best money, as it usually comes with unrealistic demands. Any resources *must* contribute to project stability, goal accomplishment, and community betterment and well-being. Under this philosophy, donors not only expect to be asked for money, but they also readily proffer the appropriate donation because it makes business sense first as well as heartfelt sense. They have been groomed as friends to make a certain donation and they are ready to do so. The "ask" is therefore a most pleasant transaction. Making friends by establishing integrity and credibility first makes resources development much easier and reliable. And when resources development becomes part of the overall process, not an end in itself, stakeholders can focus on the more important work of community betterment. Practitioners observe what happens when relationships are a first priority followed by resources development. It establishes a positive virtuous cycle in which promises are kept and the friends made bring in more friends, whereby resource streams gradually grow. The program can then structure and justify good budgets. They can then realize their aspirational yet reasonable goals.

Key Staff

Staff spent many hours understanding how to hire people for their character, enthusiasm, and potential. They then had to nurture new hires to become an integral part of a dynamic, driven team that accomplishes more than stakeholders thought possible. This dramatically departs from what occurs in the public sector, where staffing is a routine and terminal task meant to comply with the legalities of fairness and transparency. I've observed many job interviews in which the interviewer did nearly all the talking, and the things that mattered remained a mystery to the new hire.

Hire and develop passion in a "hire to retire," nurturing environment.

The thriving study sites have sound and effective human capacity development policies and procedures. Their overall strategy is to hire good staff, align their talents to the needs of the organization, train them well and diligently, monitor them, and continuously improve their performance.[180] Staffing development evolves with the maturity of the project into a "pre-hire to post-retirement" philosophy and process that begins in the planning phase. Even before hiring begins, forward-thinking staff know whom they will hire and how they will develop them as teammates. They continuously develop a pool of qualified potential hires. First and foremost, the best recruiting tool is a respected, well-led, fun to work at, rewarding program. Public services delivery is about more than money. Good people will transform themselves and their positions if they're inspired and well prepared for the job.

While these sites don't initially have the resources to incorporate a comprehensive human resources development program, stakeholders still incrementally make it a work in progress. The growth of the individual is as important at these progressive sites as his or her production is to a transformative organization.

Services

Staff must adopt a single-minded pursuit of performance, especially with reference to chosen services. They choose services for reasons of convenience or, horrors, political necessity. Leaders need to nurture service providers to become performance-oriented or not hire them on. This obviates carrying dead weight as it's remarkably tough to jettison a weak performer. If potential partners understand this from the start, they will be more likely to work up to expectations.

> *Services must either be performance-based and contribute to goal accomplishment or be cut.*

The development of good services is a two-pronged process: (1) hiring and nurturing the providers to be part of the goal-oriented team and (2) establishing a process to ensure quality service delivery. First adopt the mantra *"Hire for character and fire for skills."* It's usually the reverse and, not surprising, more people are let go for lapses in character. Both hiring for character and establishing good services delivery are motivated and guided by very high expectations that are challenging and perhaps just a little out of reach. If character is demanded from the outset, there's rarely, if ever, the need to fire.

> Public services delivery is about more than money. Good people will transform themselves and their positions if they're inspired and well prepared for the job.

Service providers, according to practitioners, should have the following specific qualifications:

- Knowledge, skills, and abilities as expressed by *experience*
- *Factual knowledge* in the service field
- Post-secondary *education, certification, or licensing,* if applicable
- Appropriate administrative and professional *skills*
- The *personality* for the task at hand
- *Character* qualities that make the difference between merely "making the numbers" and mutual goal accomplishment

Service providers need to be good role models with backbone who make the right client-oriented decisions at the right moments, without being under the gaze of someone else. It's about continuously doing the right thing, even when no one is looking, over and over again until doing what is right becomes second nature.

They should be:

- organized,
- empathetic as they relate to clientele,
- adaptable from client to client,
- dedicated and professional in appearance and comportment, and
- knowledgeable about the science of measuring and producing performance.

A well selected, nurtured, and motivated service provider will become part of the project team and tend to overcome the usual barriers to service provision. Such barriers may be lack of funding, complacency in the community, and other inevitable obstructions.

Operation

The transition to operation has subtleties beyond the maturation of all the critical features. Every effort must contribute by being linked to the realistic yet reasonably challenging project vision and mission. Staff do this by tracking processes and measuring results in the chain of outcomes toward accomplishing the vision. Operations should induce an atmosphere of "whatever it takes." Staff and service providers in the transforming projects maintain mutual responsibility for one another and the mission.

Beliefs, vision, and mission guide all decisions to support project goals.

Being on site for days at a time revealed to me that transformative projects are based on work that is efficient, effective, and goal-oriented at *all* times. This is facilitated by a functional organizational design that's bottom-up and back again, improving with each iteration. While the program may be traditionally organized, it's well served to be flexible in response to ground realities. Leaders and staff need to be aware of what the delivery services know about what's going on. For example, there may be (political) pressure to offer another or additional services to "meet demand." However, if the "boots on the ground" relate that the timing isn't right, then it's best to let well enough alone for the time being.

Finally, a challenging goal achieved together builds esprit de corps. Make sure everyone, including staff, those served, and the community, shares in the little victories along the way to transformation.

Stabilization and Sustainability

A major purpose of planning and operations is to arrive at a permanent, respected position in the municipal community, which is sustainability. This is where the gap between the service and the need begins to close. Stabilization, when considering Capacity Building, is when operations become routinized, even though they aren't expanding to meet the assessed need. This is a good stage, but it doesn't serve the intent of rising to potential.

Whereas *stabilization* is routinizing operations, *sustainability* is building capacity to meet demand. This stage means operations and resources have become self-sustaining and are thus growing to meet assessed need. Sustainability is the stage at which the targeted community realizes the effects of your program. Your idea remains strong, vital, and potent as long as the problem it addresses persists. At that point, the program can claim social transformation.

> A service must improve social behavior to a degree that's meaningful to the individual and the community.

While the idea is closer to reaching its potential during stabilization, it's a world away from sustainability, where the community needs it to be. From a position of sustainability, an idea can *begin* to reduce the service-to-needs gap in a way felt in a neighborhood and realized in overall community well-being. Any other project goal, such as delivering a certain number of training classes, is short-sighted. Why?

Because just reaching certain numbers, while good, misses the point that a service must improve social behavior to a degree that's meaningful to the individual and the community.

Stability is the first milestone to enabling expansion, which happens with sustainability. Individual, then communal, well-being needs to be the focus of local service projects: It's the necessary long view over the horizon. Most important, it must be part of planning! *And* in the vision, mission, goals, and statement of beliefs!

> *Sustainability means a project endures beyond the long term and leads to social transformation.*

Inquiry revealed that at the ultimate point of reducing the service-to-needs gap, the project can judiciously take on more responsibility, and expansion may be possible. Next, staff must guide it to permanence, a state of self-renewal, by generating steady operational resources. Paramount is nurturing staff to be a team in which the whole is greater than the sum of the parts. Only *then* should it move to planned growth.

Leadership is crucial to the development of the business. Leaders need to thoroughly understand what marginal capacity is required to tackle additional tasks.

When it all comes together in sustainability, services continually change lives and contribute to community well-being. Stable staff are competent, confident, collegial, and *inspired*. Thus, they actualize their collective reach for tough, meaningful goals.

Expansion and Transformation

Political will to grow an idea is a result of officials maturing with the idea as it progresses through the project life cycle. Transformational project practitioners know when the conditions and timing can support more responsibilities because it "feels right." This feeling is not arrived at lightly. Expansion is a deliberate and cautious undertaking. With miscalculation, a project might expand to the point of dissolution. According to the field experts, established infrastructure and systems can strain and break under ill-advised loads. At that point, the capacity to provide stabilized levels of service deteriorates. In worst cases, "victory" is declared by simply not accepting the reality of defeat to justify not moving on.

Even with years of experience in the project, practitioners can be too optimistic. Projects must be guided by well selected measurable goals. The fewer hard targets the better. This anticipates chaos and minimizes the effects when it happens.

*Expansion needs to be timed according to assessed capability and,
more importantly, political will.
It must result in measurably improved lives and communities.*

Documenting a process of capacity building beyond the difficulties of implementation is the first step to building a transformational idea. It's the *business beneath the business* of delivering a good idea. Each experiment in service delivery with the capacity building process will greatly expand the effective practices checklist. It was meant to be fluid. Every location and idea brought to fruition will apply the process differently. Likewise, the process needs to consider the unique perspectives of federal and state decision makers and those agency-level officials concerned with the wider universe of community development. Every community tackling a project will discover better ways to implement new ideas for permanence. Each will tweak and document the process over the years, honing it with the friction of real-world experience.

Expansion is a deliberate and cautious undertaking. With miscalculation, a project might expand to the point of dissolution.

Summary

Chapter 5 built on the previous chapter to more fully explain the business aspects of capacity building. It described what the board and staff need to consider for success when assembling and conducting each critical feature of the program. However, recommendations acknowledge that the answers to what lie beyond implementation will be as unique as each idea that seeks to be socially transformative.

The following chapter presents more practitioner insights to help you avoid mistakes and enhance your progress.

Chapter 6

LESSONS LEARNED –
PRACTITIONER INSIGHTS

Chapter 6

LESSONS LEARNED – PRACTITIONER INSIGHTS

Beyond the fact that it's quite realistic to tame the chaos of service project implementation, practitioners had further insights to share. First, let's consider their general insights stemming from the public struggle to understand implementation.

- *Public risk aversion* – The short-term focus and risk aversion of the public sector can be ameliorated by changing the focus from *what* the stakeholders may or may not be doing to *how* the project itself is doing. No one gets a feather ruffled. In other words, capacity building takes the personalities out of project building and focuses people on processes.

- *Private business orientation* – Another insight from the field is that enduring service ideas are more business oriented than public administration oriented. Practitioners intuitively adopt good private enterprise practices. These practices are more creative and action-oriented than public administrative duties and responsibilities, which may be largely top-down directives and compliance oriented. The latter approaches are ripe for morale-deadening critique.

- *Maverick practices* – Observations about maverick business practices, things done differently to shake things up, fit the prosperous local service idea as exemplified by the model reform programs.[181] Mavericks see things others can't, take careful risks, and anticipate the resistance with logic and passion. For example, calculated risk is good; service is about values; collective intelligence is greater than the sum of its parts; and employees are truly most important.[182] This environment takes calculated risks into a bit of the unknown, resulting in some attendant mistakes. However, risk for the sake of the program is okay, providing it's not foolish. This environment is also where mistakes of good conscience and character are seen as opportunities for a course correction, improving staff and processes, and progressing.

- *Partners and team members* – Further, the efficient, effective municipal service idea based on capacity building is slightly unorthodox in its path to permanency. Stakeholders are constantly learning from other people who have plowed the ground of idea development already. Plus, they are constantly mentoring the next generation of service businesspeople and providers. Employees are more than these models' most important assets; they are *partners—team members*. The whole process concerns much more than the silos of effort we're used to seeing.

> **Wise practitioners confirmed that starting with a proven, practical, planning process focused on critical activities can be the most important part of project development.**

- *Consensus planning* – Since project implementation is a social phenomenon, it becomes the work of consensus. The difficulties of arriving at a common purpose are lessened by making regular performance-oriented meetings for consensus building mandatory. In most cases, people involved with a project quite naturally and immediately move to survival mode under the crush of immediate demands. But rule by crises is not planning. It's ineffectual. A sequence of practitioner-based milestones and activities provides a rational and less contentious path through the crisis nature of current project development.

- *Delineated roles* – Duties, roles, and responsibilities are initially muddled, according to respondents at every study site. Focused discourse and planning based on who does what when, and especially how, clarifies and harmonizes.

   This approach supports a more collegial atmosphere. It focuses the human part of service delivery on process and goal attainment rather than natural human frailties such as turfism. The environment becomes much less confrontational, individually isolating, and political than in traditional hierarchical operations. It's a pleasure watching these teams of friends at work.

- *Initial planning* – Failure of implementation is often caused by jumping the gun and giving planning short shrift. Stakeholders tend to immediately begin delivering a service when winning startup funds, usually via a capricious public grant. Wise practitioners confirmed that starting with a proven, practical, planning process focused on critical activities can be the most important part of project development.

  Unfortunately, services planning in the lion's share of municipalities is usually incidental, distracted by minutiae, or both. Thus, the project is marginalized or doomed from the outset. Also, services delivery is often considered a soft priority compared to municipal responsibilities such as paying for administration, fire, police, and recreation, for example. This frailty of services programming, though arguably vital, is problematic. It not only represents the less than optimal allocation of limited public dollars but a loss of opportunity for the failed but worthy service idea—*and* for further ideas that won't be attempted after a disappointing initial experience. A failure reverberates for years, hindering who knows how many good ideas. The status quo plows on.

These problems reflect the lack of a practitioner-based process that anticipates these difficulties. Thinking about process tends to force a thorough planning phase that emphasizes the building blocks of permanence. These building blocks are Capacity Building, focus on performance, and relationship-building in that order.

Now let's review the practical contributions of practitioners in the trenches.

Summary of Wisdom from Practitioners Getting the Job Done

We've covered a great deal of information and advice from staff at the successful study sites, the literature, and my years of experience working in the public sector. Following is a summary of lessons successful practitioners have learned.

- *How is much more important than what.* Focus on process. Minimize hoarding information and protecting turf. Form your organization with networks, matrices of select people and services specifically targeted to solve problems. Make data development foundational. Become evidence based. Build permanency.

- *Less is more when considering all aspects of service development.* Do only what can be done with available resources according to measurable results. Remember, those measures need to be relevant to the target population first, *then* to benefactors and especially granting agencies. It's better to do less and do it well than to do that little extra and fail. This lesson was hard learned. Wisely stated: "You get what you measure."

- *A local service idea is first a business and then a service.* A service is only as strong as the service delivery systems—the business infrastructures—that support it. Smart Start, the Boys and Girls Club, TROSA, LINC, The Durham County CJRC, and Crisis Intervention Teams all had a thorough, proven business model in place *before* services begin. Note again that it took TROSA, wildly successful by any measure, 30 years to open a satellite. The model had to be solidly strengthened before they assumed more responsibility. Every one of these projects has learned this the hard way. It would be a shame for other hopeful practitioners to have to relearn this lesson when there's a process to avoid it.

- *The whole is greater than the sum of the parts.* The parts of Capacity Building create synergies that enable stakeholders to resolve problems, strive, survive, then flourish. They can rise above barriers and obstructions, attack the difficult, and *succeed* where others fail. The critical features of project development work best when combined from the beginning during planning. Even in an industry where salaries are notoriously low, sites that endure, such as TROSA, Dismas Charities, and Smart Start, hire passionate people fueled by a common worthy purpose. People want meaning, but they also thrive on tactful recognition at work, so make sure they have plenty of it.

- *Process matters, but it must continuously evolve.* Project operation should be designed to continuously evolve as it's tested by the realities of action on the ground. Checklists work only so far. The Henderson County Boys and Girls Club board is intimately involved in the operations of the Club. Board members even carry out regular process assessments themselves. They do this for the express purpose of making adjustments that can only be done with intimate knowledge of how systems are working.

- *Critical milestones and activities are continuous.* Capacity assessment and determining scope, for example, are not one-time tasks or short-term activities to be done and quickly dismissed. They're continuous and should be woven into activities of the moment. Project staff are always working on the milestones that began in the pre-operational planning phase.

> **The critical features of project development work best when combined from the beginning during planning.**

What makes these successful practitioners unique? They recognize the connectedness of each capacity building milestone and how these milestones evolve as the project and community mature and change.

- *People matter most.* Prosperous site leaders intuitively recognize that everyone is a leader and a potential partner. The Iredell County school readiness project begins from the outset to train *the wider community* as service assessors, recruiters, and public relations agents.

  TROSA is largely staffed by former graduates. TROSA staff know that if anyone can be enticed to visit the campus, they'll be "hooked" on what the project is doing. Passionate stakeholders, especially staff and service recipients, can make just about any idea prosper when they're meaningfully engaged and have a stake in its success. Imagine the sense of pride and great accomplishment at TROSA when senior program clients, not staff, conduct intakes, training, and mentoring of incoming participants. Imagine how incoming TROSA clients must feel when they can see the results of the program in their comrades who are reclaiming their lives. Clients epitomize the program's motto: "Each one teach one."

> *Education breeds confidence. Confidence breeds hope.*
> *Hope breeds peace.* – Confucius

- *Combine impact analysis and process evaluation with capacity assessment* to paint a picture of program performance and justification. Successful sites recognize that numbers matter. Gone are the days when simply an emotional appeal makes the case for programming or justifies a decision. The data need to make sense and reliably inform stakeholders that expenditures in money and time are making a difference. Preferably it's a monetary difference that reflects in better lives. Draw your audience in to your project as participants in this success.

- *Planning is essential, but it must lead to calculated, proper action.* And act you must. Over-dependence on gathering information and data is the enemy of progress if not good. Amassing additional or perfect information can lead to paralysis. Experienced board members stressed the importance of making decisions that put the program's gears into motion. Staff must analyze, deliberate, decide, and determine what needs to be done next—then do it. Never go for 100 percent analysis and information gathering because you will never get there. Eighty percent of the research works nicely. Better yet, analyze enough so the collective mind of program practitioners feels right about making a certain decision.

  Progressive sites continually take rational action even though it has an element of risk. They recognize that a decision is ultimately intuitive but based on extensive experience. Action will tell you if you're right or need to modify, or give you the rationale to abandon a failed idea. And that's okay! Successful leaders embrace risk for what it is—the chance to prosper and grow.

Do or do not. There is no try. – Yoda

- *Problems are opportunities.* At the risk of stating the obvious, social problem solving is some of the toughest and most rewarding work there is. The founding champions of the Henderson Boys and Girls Club noticed that at-risk youth "disappeared" from school and the community just prior to high school. Finding those children then organizing a program to retain them resulted in a national model for after-school programming. It makes a difference in an intractable problem—school dropouts. How can one program do this and so many others struggle to do so? Capacity Building is an answer.

He who opens a school door, closes a prison. – Victor Hugo

- *Difficulties frequently present as unpleasant either-or dilemmas, but they're not.* The easy solution to a problem usually cripples progress. For example, employing additional staff is an expensive organizational decision; therefore, the initial impulse is to retain the status quo and staffing levels. However, the largest determining factor of increasing service capability is to justifiably add more staff. Progressive sites begin by understanding needs and the capacity

Practitioners must adjust the expectations of those clamoring for big changes too soon in the life of the project.

to satisfy those needs, especially with regard to appropriate staffing. When it's time to add personnel, they've already made the case to funding or budgetary bodies. Usually, they couch it in terms of a cost-effective return on investment (*not* cost-benefit). In other words, facts in these arguments represent the incremental savings to the municipality for each dollar of investment in your service idea. This is a poignant interpretation of public "profit" that effectively communicates to people making budgetary decisions. The dilemma of constant program inertia is turned into an opportunity to justify more staffing. Action matters. Throughout, risks are opportunities if only they're seen as such.

- *Persistence matters.* Win-Win Resolutions endures because of the founding director. She weathered the startup phase with no salary, 80-hour work weeks, and the collapse of resources. However, this successful director only sees her service idea as expanding and being fulfilled. Thus, so do project stakeholders. All else falls away. Every one of these fruitful sites has a similar story of persisting beyond endurance.

- *All effort must be guided by living the vision/mission, understanding scope, being goal-oriented, and staying on process.* Stakeholders at permanent services internalize what it is they want. The values of vision and the sense of mission guide *all* decisions and activities from the mundane to the grand. There's little misdirected or frivolous work in the productive, goal-oriented local service organization that focuses on Capacity Building.

- *Closing the service-to-needs gap is subtle, iterative, and very long-term work.* A sad fact of this work is the overwhelming pressure to show "results" way too soon. Early results are detached from goals and not very meaningful. Again, the numbers of people taking a course or being in a program has little to do with whether they learned anything. Nor does it mean they are doing anything with it.

Practitioners must adjust the expectations of those clamoring for big changes too soon in the life of the project. It's enough, for example, to expect a young aftercare client to clean his or her room first. Getting these young clients to attend group sessions *and* pay attention is the next step. For them to make better life decisions and stay out of jail, away from drugs, is a distant result over mountains.

- *Program stability precedes the permanence that leads to social transformation.* Stability and permanence are quite different. Arriving at program *stability* means acting from planning then ironing out the plan according to the realities of operations. In fact, stability is just another state of operations. It's an interim condition in which the project is *poised* to make a measurable difference in community well-being. A state of stability doesn't mean the project is a success; it may even be doing the *wrong* thing or at least not doing the most productive things. Stability must be marked by sustained transformative capacity. *Program permanence,* or endurance, is marked by having self-sustaining operational resources and making material improvements in individual thriving and community well-being.

- *Transformative ideas develop from a process of action-reflection.* The sites that make a positive change in their communities are constantly attempting to understand *what* they're doing and especially *how* they're doing it—then acting on those insights. In fact, these dynamic sites are always in a state of evolution.

- *It's all about the matrix.* Any community, your community, has a true wealth of services you need. Partner with them guided by your vision and your plan for Capacity Building. This is part of the philosophy of the whole becoming greater than the sum of the parts.

- *Your service idea is YOURS.* No matter where you got your idea, it's yours. You can learn mightily from successful programs and practitioners, but your people, your place, your politics are unique. Your idea then has to have your stamp for sustainability and making a difference.

Any local idea can work when it becomes a local idea solved with local people and resources. That is the ultimate buy in. Program stakeholders know that imported ideas that worked in another community aren't guaranteed to work in theirs. Again, there's no such thing as a "best practice." But good ideas can work when tailored to unique municipal circumstances. What matters is that people own *their* idea and go about it methodically, purposefully, even courageously.

> *Program permanence,* or endurance, is marked by having self-sustaining operational resources and making material improvements in individual thriving and community well-being.

Summary

Chapter 6 summarized the wisdom gained from the staff and directors of the successful study sites. It gave many examples of how and why certain things worked or didn't from the perspectives of those in the trenches. Such experience and knowledge are invaluable when creating your own social program with goals of sustainability and transformation.

The following chapter features Table 7.1, which hones the entire process of building a successful social service project to permanence into a to-do checklist to use as a tool to keep you on track.

Chapter 7

THE CAPACITY BUILDING TOOL

Chapter 7

THE CAPACITY BUILDING TOOL

A step-by-step outline of Capacity Building is presented in Table 7.1, illustrating how a local service idea gets beyond implementation. You can use it as a check-list of actions for success.

This table includes the major phases in a project's life cycle, the main features of each phase, and the associated effective practices for each feature. Yes, it's summative and simplified, and the process takes years—but this action checklist does work.

As a researcher, it's my job, my responsibility, to make things simple but not simplistic. A chart facilitates understanding of critical parts of the process, hopefully in a way that generates proper action and helps realize a great idea.

A highly important aspect of this Capacity Building tool is that project stake-holders can "see" their program taking shape. They have a palpable sense that it's all possible. This table demonstrates that effective services can be *planned to* be socially transformative, which is only a beginning and worthy of pursuit. May your success be only the first.

Capacity Building from the Bottom Up - A Tool for Local Public Service Practitioners

This plan of implementation is only a point of departure for ideas that can work and make a big, big difference. The greatest complement you can give Capacity Building is if you make your own Capacity Building plan of action from this one. These Effective Practices for project development are *yours* and meant to be modified as you see fit.

These suggestions are born of hard-won experiences, and thus they're a good—no great!—start. The main purpose of Capacity Building is to be the structure for an initial idea to succeed to permanency. From that comes another, then two, and off you go.

I recommend you edit a master copy with your experiences, successes, and yes, wonderful failures, which teach so much. Keep the checklist in a binder as a table of contents for explanatory documents and experiences, lessons learned, and advice for those that follow.

Keep it action-oriented, rooted in measured improvements in your town. This checklist then helps you to "Be Good and Do Good for the Common Good." Then tackle your next idea. Better yet, collaborate with the adjoining municipality and improve your part of the world even more.

Successful Capacity Building is an intergenerational legacy. Note also that your path to successful services is your history, which, paraphrasing Churchill, doesn't happen unless it is written. This is about:

Building Permanent Solutions to Permanent Problems

Table 7.1
The Capacity Building Process from the Bottom Up and Back: PHASES I-III, with Key Action Items and Effective Practices

PHASE I of the Project Life Cycle: Plan – *Design Essential Operations.*
1. **Key Action Item:** Nurture and grow key leadership.
Effective Practice (EP): Hire the board for individual expertise; nurture them for their primary, long-term capacity building roles of developing relationships and resources.
EP: Make your client base your cheerleaders.
2. Integrate capacity assessment into capacity building.
EP: Use capacity assessment to assist decision making by understanding when and how the community collaboration is working.
3. Determine project scope.
EP: Develop project scope by mapping clientele and community resources.
4. Design the impact analysis and process evaluation.
EP: Combine methods of inquiry to strengthen operations, build capacity, and justify support.
5. Nurture relationships for resources development.
EP: Establish a Commitment Center to gain (financial) commitments from targeted stakeholder groups.
6. Develop performance-oriented services.
EP: Plan for performance-oriented services and providers.
7. Nurture staff by a process of human capacity development.
EP: Draft a comprehensive process of human capacity development based on individualized career development plans.

The Capacity Building Process from the Bottom Up and Back: PHASES I-III, with Key Action Items and Effective Practices
PHASE II of the Project Life Cycle: Operation – *Putting the Plan into Action*
8. Plan operations with the future in mind.
EP: Develop leadership with compassion, empathy, and intelligence.
EP: Refocus the senior staffer from internal operations to external relationship-building and resources development as soon as possible.
EP: Redirect board functions to include operational and oversight duties.
9. Assess capacity for sustainability.
EP: Build capacity assessment into organizational processes.
EP: Develop and implement a sustainability plan based on performance.
10. Make scope analysis a continuous part of decision making.
EP: Develop scope analysis as part of comprehensive, continuous decision making.
11. Combine process evaluation and impact analysis to optimize service delivery.
EP: Set up automation systems to help integrate process monitoring and compliance and performance analysis into daily operations.
12. Engage friends in strategic resource development.
EP: Continue to operate a funding commitment center based on a public engagement strategic plan.
13. Nurture performance-oriented service providers.
EP: Develop career paths for your performance-oriented service partners.
14. Develop key staff for their human and social capital potential.
EP: Nurture staff with a 'hire to retire' process of human capacity development.

<table>
<tr><td colspan="1">

The Capacity Building Process from the Bottom Up and Back: PHASES I-III, with Key Action Items and Effective Practices

</td></tr>
<tr><td>

PHASE III of the Project Life Cycle: *Sustainability and Expansion – Realizing Social Transformation*

</td></tr>
<tr><td>

15. Sustain operations.

</td></tr>
<tr><td>

    EP: Adjust and sustain operations via a self-accreditation process.

</td></tr>
<tr><td>

16. Plot the long-range strategy and tactics for expansion.

</td></tr>
<tr><td>

    EP: Form a community transition team to assess current needs and suggest ways to begin closing the service-to-needs gap.

</td></tr>
</table>

Practitioners involved in a local service project of their *own* design are a study of tension between passion and restraint. They offer encouragement with caution as they employ their effective practices. Frequently, seasoned staff stress that assessment must guide every aspect of operations, even insisting it must become part of daily business. Real need must be the basis for any decision, expenditure, or action, because a single mistaken policy decision or series of incorrect decisions will spoil the best of service ideas—and paralyze the next good idea.

Prioritization of activities is the logical extension of determining need. Action must be parsimonious, practical, on process, and performance-oriented. The difference between projects that struggle to an early demise and those that eventually endure is that successful project staff understand that relatively few crucial items matter. They aren't distracted by the crisis of the moment.

Is leadership more important than resources . . . than staff . . . than partners? No. Equal weight should be given to these critical factors. All are essentials and must be "juggled" effectively with as few wasted resources, especially time, as possible. "Know your knitting," staffers reiterate.

As government transitions from silo agency services to services being delivered by networks, or matrices, of people and services, they will need practical advice on how to organize themselves and their work. Hopefully, the Capacity Building process will be used for programs to benefit the formerly incarcerated who want to return home, mental health consumers who are ill-served by the criminal justice system, and our youngest citizens who need to stay in school. Social transformation will become more evident as more great ideas survive to effective permanency.

> **Real need must be the basis for any decision, expenditure, or action, because a single mistaken policy decision or series of incorrect decisions will spoil the best of service ideas— and paralyze the next good idea.**

Summary

Capacity Building is ready for application. It represents the culmination of nearly two decades of thought about the difficulties of implementing a service idea to its concomitant social transformation.

Chapter 7 provided a step-by-step checklist of features and Effective Practices you can follow for your own local project development. Chapter 8 gives an overview of how to use the Capacity Building model and contribute to a reform movement that brings about transformation for thriving communities.

The highest compliment that can be paid to this work is that it is used and, by that use, is made even more practical and more widely applicable.

Chapter 8

HOW TO USE THIS CAPACITY BUILDING PROCESS

HOW TO USE THIS CAPACITY BUILDING PROCESS

T his model's potential for communities taking responsibility for their own destiny is considerable—to put it mildly. By using Capacity Building, concerned, creative, and collaborative citizens will make great strides in going about the job of realizing their ideas. One success will lead to two, to four and so on. The multiplier effect of just one flourishing local idea to improve a community is staggering.

The Model

This model is a living document in that practitioners can craft it to the ground realities of various service ideas in any community. They can monitor their progress with the model and the tool, which they can also use to structure their process of action-reflection-action. This process and the Capacity Building tool in Table 7.1 will greatly facilitate knowledge acquisition and the attendant development of problem-solving actions.

The Process

Until this investigation, any action away from top-down, rules-bound project development was relatively stagnant, with endemic public project failure.[183] More was accomplished by this investigation beyond simply documenting a practical, credible process to take practitioners beyond implementation to permanency, where good ideas go to burgeon. It also clearly showed the advantages of collaborative work among people of high character with a passion for the common good.

The Project Life Cycle

The project life cycle is simple enough for all to grasp and then communicate goal-directed action. It's suitable to building service projects because it's of, by, and for locals to define a problem and see the realistic vision of its solution. It's suitable as it can be applied to any locale by any group of citizens motivated to work hard but effectively on solving their communal problems.

The Capacity Building Checklist

The Capacity Building checklist in Table 7.1 is proof that an idea can take form and make a difference. It delineates a rational process and practical advice from people who have figured out what it takes to be successful. In addition, it can be tailored to your unique locale, resources, circumstances, and personalities. Build a new idea or strengthen an old one. This tells you how step by step.

The Strength of Community

Any community can put the process to work on its problems and benefit from the strength of grassroots social problem-solving capital, energy, creativity, and resources. One seasoned senior staffer commented, "If it's a question of money, there's no problem." The problem before has been no suggested path through the maze of the startup. Now, thanks to the participants in this study, there is!

> It isn't about overhauling our public systems but rather making them work more productively to conserve public resources.

The task of further research is to continue the understanding of how a project becomes socially transformative in various contexts and environments.

Parting Thoughts: Capacity Building – The Reform Movement

Beginning local service projects that challenge the status quo of top-down agency control of services will lead to reform. The result will be authentic collaboration between our public institutions and agencies and local communities—from the bottom up. The people closest to our most vexing problems and their solutions will be involved in the process of delivering services. It isn't about overhauling our public systems but rather making them work more productively to conserve public resources.

This collaboration signals hope for some of our most needy citizens, such as troubled youth, those struggling with mental health issues, those returning home from incarceration, and those who struggle with substance abuse. Most of them want to change. They only need a practical, workable way to alter their circumstances and encouragement to do the work of returning to productivity and a place called home.

Now, there is a way.

Thank you for reading this seminal book in the Capacity Building series. It's my fond hope you will take its invitation seriously to develop a program that enhances your community's well-being by *Building Permanent Solutions to Permanent Problems.*

GLOSSARY

REFERENCES

ABOUT THE AUTHOR

ENDNOTES

GLOSSARY

Capacity building

Capacity building in this model of local project development refers to building the infrastructure and resources to resolve a locally defined social concern. This infrastructure is a matrix of those resources and services specifically chosen for their long-term commitment to resolving the local problem. These supports are both internal (organizational) and external (private, community, state, and federal). In short, capacity building involves amassing whatever it takes to build, support, and sustain the work of delivering a local service. This includes a combination of:

- *Political will* – The collective means and determination to see the project through to sustainability
- *Human capacity* – Staff developed for their wholistic contribution to building the service idea
- *Leadership* – An executive director and board chosen for the will to succeed
- *Dedicated matrices of local services* – A team of local entities chosen for their applicability and dedication to the program
- *Facilities* – Including equipment and supplies, with funds for replenishment, operation, and measured expansions
- *Capability* – Operational capability such as financial management and training
- *Funding* – Separate streams/sources of financial support for program development, maintenance, and expansion
- *Processes* – A measurably effective means of service delivery; the efficient and effective daily work of the project
- *Measured effectiveness* – Analyses in place to measure effectiveness in improving target population and develop the "picture" of success for program justification

The primary concern is to support local service ideas that promote community well-being (a systemic, wholistic approach) instead of simply complying to the more narrow wishes of, say, the town council, or a grantor. According to the McKinsey Capacity Assessment Grid, seven dimensions of internal capacity are involved.[184] These include:

- aspirations,
- strategy,
- organizational skills,
- human resources,
- systems and infrastructure,
- organizational structure, and
- culture.

The Marguerite Casey Foundation Capacity Tool simplifies these seven dimensions into four:[185]

- *Leadership* capacity needs to be understood according to its strengths and weaknesses with the purpose of developing values-oriented leadership and bottom-up management.

- *Adaptive* capacity is the organizational capability to assess its performance and impact and adjust accordingly.

- *Management* capacity is the administrative ability to work efficiently and particularly effectively.

- *Operational* capacity is the ability to successfully implement project functions to reach program sustainability.

Collectively, these dimensions comprise the project's ability to effect measurable social change, preferably as long as the social condition of focus exists. For example, need for a reentry strategy will always exist in every community, from the mega-metropolises to the one-stop country towns. Measurement must also develop the performance picture by making cost-effectiveness statements ("profit") and tradeoff statements (what can and cannot be done with or without the project).

Effective practice

This is an action that's been proven by application and experience by successful practitioners to be practicable and productive, and to lead to a measurable good effect. However, it's *not* a "best" practice, because what's best is uniquely individual to a project, determined by myriad variables, and *not* easily replicable. What's effective in one locale has relevance to another only when properly implemented via Capacity Building and proven to work in that locale. Effective practices are the *essential* activities that can be applied in whole or part to other service development projects.

The goal is to build program sustainability to eventually facilitate incremental expansion to close the service-to-needs gap. Although myriad practices exist across all local projects, "effective practices" form the *basis* of what project developers need to learn and do to perpetuate program efficiencies, effectiveness, and sustainability.

Evidence-Based Practice (EBP)

Simply, an EBP is a practice proven to be efficient and effective by practical application over time. It's the careful use of the best evidence in making decisions or taking action.[186] Understanding this concept is fundamental to delivering an idea that makes meaningful and cost-effective improvements. In other words, a project must make a good argument for spending public dollars. Further, you can argue for unintended benefits and tradeoffs. Simply put, "Pay now or pay later" by *not* developing this idea. Figuring cost benefit from the beginning is fundamental to Capacity Building—starting a project and sustaining it until it makes real communal impact.

An EBP contributes significantly to sustainability.

Its research basis determines that, under certain conditions, the practice can have—must have—a measurable, positive result or results—usually a favorable change in the behavior of a target population. More important, the way an EBP is conducted is continually informed by meaningful data. A few performance measures will do to tell the story of program progress and effect. And they must be quantified in dollars to be cost effective. Data is collected, analyzed, and used in some cases on an hourly basis. However, stating a practice is evidence based is only the beginning of making such a practice work from location to location.

Pennsylvania's Juvenile Justice System Enhancement Strategy says it best:

> "Evidence-based practice" simply means applying what we know
> in terms of research to what we do in our work with youth, their
> families, and communities in which we live. It is the progressive,
> organizational use of direct, current scientific evidence to guide
> and inform the (delivery of) efficient and effective services."[187]

Relative to capacity building to deliver local public services, sometimes the term "evidence-based practice" is misconstrued as the label for the entire task of building capacity or the program itself. An EBP is part of and essential to capacity building. If you can't prove an action is first cost effective then makes a difference, the project dwindles and fades away. It's usually a service or procedure within the wider work of building the supporting infrastructure for that service or procedure.

For a better understanding of an EBP, consider the hierarchy of the chain of outcomes:

- *Inputs* – These are the resources for doing the work such as people, supplies, offices, furniture, vans, etc. These resources are important to an evidence-based practice because the resources need to be frugally obtained and effectively put to work doing something that matters to those served.

- *Activities* – Activities must be vision-, mission- and goal-targeted to enable measurement of progress.

- *Outputs* – Outputs are whatever the organization does or produces, epitomized by its people, who must be doing the right things in efficient and effective ways that can be measured.

- *Outcome* – Here the program begins to show behavioral changes in the target group and community as a whole.

- *Impact* – This is the long-term, quantifiable contribution to the community. Data paint the picture of program accomplishments, especially in monetary terms—the cost-effective, tradeoff argument for support and expansion. The grail of Capacity Building.

Let's say you have an idea for an afterschool program. You find an unused municipal building, granted by the city for $1 per year (this happened). A local contractor fixes and updates it to your needs, with decades to pay off the note and great terms. You outfit it for yourself and an assistant. You have a startup budget from several sources. Next, a few youngsters come before school and after, which prolongs their learning and their socialization day. They have a nutritional meal daily, which may well be the only one they have that day. You monitor school attendance, which improves. You can justify two more staff and justify outfitting two more rooms.

Over time, this expansion continues according to need and capacity. You have a board of directors and comprehensive services, all making a cost-effective "profit."

Graduation rates improve. College or trade school matriculation improves. Your program, then, translates to success in life versus failing in school and dependency on public assistance or worse. The compelling case for your idea is evident every day, *by the numbers*. And much, much more happens when an idea is also an EBP.

The importance of the chain of outcomes for Capacity Building is threefold. First, the chain keeps the program, people, and infrastructure focused on vision and mission. Secondly, impact can be measured then converted to a Return on Investment, ROI, statement. Lastly, it's aspirational as progress can be seen and noted. Now, the chain results and outcomes are proof that the idea is working.

The picture of performance is painted. It is stated in dollars saved not spent— *profit*, ROI. From the ROI, it's a quick computation to show how much more can be done incrementally with this profit. Next comes a quick tradeoff statement, which supports your program because the tradeoff, say school absenteeism, translates to suspensions or failure. It's "expensive." It makes imminent sense to continue your project, and even expand it, because not doing so would be to the detriment of your community—in compelling dollars and cents.

So, for capacity building, an evidence-based practice is a service within a program, such as a therapeutic modality with a scientific basis for a positive, measurable effect that contributes to goal accomplishment. In the case of before-and-after-school programs, EBPs include providing good nutrition, socialization, a positive environment, and child care for parents. Such provisions can be hard justification for your program or expanding it to meet the need your stakeholders want.

Caution: An EBP is well and good *if* it is guided by Capacity Building with the goal of sustainability in mind. Even an exciting EBP can be misguided, which is a tragic misdirection of resources. Program staff may be "sure" they're making progress but are not. In the worst case, funding and political will fade, and then, too, does the project.

Implementation

Implementation for Capacity Building describes the practical sequence of activities that brings a service idea from concept to permanent presence in the community. It does this by considering the functions of planning, operating, sustaining, and expanding a service over time. Learning how to implement an idea with transformative possibilities takes time, experimentation, and determination.

Successful implementation of public services is largely misunderstood in the public sector. Common failure of it prohibits many good services from being started in the first place, and misunderstanding of it causes many service projects to eventually fail.

While the Capacity Building process herein provides a promising, proven process for implementation, *every* idea for local service is unique, and practitioners must learn and adjust as they go.

Leader

The leader of today and especially tomorrow lives and works by continuously practicing virtue and developing character, and thus do the staff they lead. These leaders continuously work on the ancients' Cardinal Virtues of Justice, Wisdom, Courage, and Temperance, while pursuing well-being for self, family, organization, and community. Likewise, they constantly practice introspection and humility. They inspire the organizational body to be more than the sum of its parts, with a worthy vision of what can be. They are participatory by truly serving staff, bottom up. They see problems and obstacles as opportunities to grow and stretch. Thus they improve staff, hastening the march to individual self-worth and organizational success.

Leadership

Leadership is much contested and discussed. The Teal Trust refers to modern interpretations from noted scholars: Peter Drucker stresses that a leader simply has followers. John C. Maxwell reduces leadership to the simple ability to influence others. Warren Bennis describes the abilities of a leader such as self-awareness, building trust, and being effective.[188] This author would add humility and introspection guided by evolving morals.

Leaders who understand capacity building are essential to the successful implementation and stabilization of public service ideas. Leadership, then, consists of certain qualities in these stakeholders. They must inspire the staff of an organization to achieve defined goals and enable others to be leaders in an atmosphere of calculated risk, learning, and fun. Bottom-up leaders in this reform movement to build the business beneath the business of delivering public services are the guiding lights of social transformation.

Partner vs. Collaborator

A partner is an individual or agency bringing resources—monetary, physical, political, or human—to an endeavor. This distinguishes a partner stakeholder from a collaborator. A partner provides material support such as a donation, supplies, and perhaps a few volunteer hours. The act is important but terminal. A collaborator makes a permanent contribution to building or sustaining the idea. For example, a collaborator may regularly donate money or head up fundraising with perhaps an annual fundraiser or a series of them. Both partners and collaborators are needed—a collaborator more. While the partner brings expertise and/or resources to the project, the collaborator becomes an *integral part* of the effort and idea.

The capacity building effort may require partners who can provide labor or donate in-kind hard goods. The service idea must also have collaborators who may be able to sway political will—an elected body, for example—to support the project under development. They are believers. Put more commonly, partners are pursued for the *things* they can provide, whereas collaborators are pursued for their creativity, ideas, and connections.

The terms partnership, cooperation, and collaboration are usually used interchangeably. This can lead to confusion, especially when targeting recruiting and development strategies to each category of supporter. Partnerships are broader and longer term than those who may simply cooperate with your project in a limited way. People can cooperate on a task to get to the end of the day; a vast difference from people who see a vision and work to get there. The best partners are also collaborators who help the project achieve its vision.

You may approach a partner such as a local business representative because he upgrades his many computers every few years and donates the old ones. Or, you may approach a corporate lawyer as a partner for his expertise in writing a start-up charter for your board. If that lawyer becomes involved in the long term as a legal advisor, he or she would be considered a collaborator. The differentiation is necessary as each group of supporters needs to be courted for what they believe and can do and what they bring to the table.

Partnership

A partnership is an agreement, usually formal, between parties who agree to a common endeavor. When a partnership is successful, it's marked by cooperation, the taking of collective and individual responsibility, and being accountable for attaining stated goals. Relative to Capacity Building, partnership has several meanings depending on the phase of a project's life cycle.

- *Planning* – When planning, the essential partnership is the constellation of founding members, which includes at least the executive director.

- *Operation and stabilization* – During operations, partnerships greatly expand to include individuals and agencies that bring necessary talent and services to the effort. This goes considerably beyond necessary program staff. These partnerships may include service providers or agencies, consultants, and advisors, plus those connected to resources such as hard goods, volunteers, or funding.

- *Sustained growth* – When a service idea is in the hard-fought and won position to expand, partnerships expand, especially if the expansion is to another locale. A partnership then becomes an assembly of likeminded people of varying talents. They all have a long-term goal of delivering a service to address a social ill that continually improves the target population and thus the community.

Process

The word "process," as used in this study, has characteristics specific to the task of capacity building in the public sector. It's based on the life cycle of the project idea—from concept to reality to perpetuation. The correct process leads to *permanent solutions to permanent problems* in the local public sector.

The process of building business and administrative infrastructure to deliver a service actualizes the resources of networked entities representing a matrix of talent and skills. The multiplier effect of organized, focused networks of people allows the whole to be greater than the sum of its parts. The matrices of people and services are specifically structured by the needs of and solutions to the problem at hand.

The local project development process evolves and grows organically as Capacity Building directs resources to answer local service needs, resulting in well-being, community betterment, and social transformation.

Public service project

Many local public sector ideas are for one-time purchases of supplies, equipment, or training, for example. Other projects are part of a much larger whole. An example is an effort to enhance the academic success of elementary school children. Only one part of that project is a school readiness program that offers parenting classes and health screening for infants and preschool children. Capacity Building attacks the tangled root causes of social dysfunction.

In this study and its subsequent reform movement models, a service project is a local idea to deliver a service, over time, with the purpose of effecting positive behaviors in a target population. In turn, the project gradually, measurably, collectively, leads to improvements in a social condition and thus in community betterment.

Social capital

Social capital is the collective quality and strength of a social organization.[189] It's human capital that springs from individual qualities and strengths.[190] Social capital is understood in the context of how a community facilitates bringing people together to problem-solve when motivated by a common cause.[191] It springs from a program of human capital development that focuses on wellness, well-being, and character education and development.

Social capital in this study refers to the collective capability of networks of services and people established by Capacity Building to support and develop local social services projects.

Socially transformative

A service project is socially transformative when it fosters measurable improvements in individuals that ultimately contribute to community well-being. A post-release aftercare services program, for example, improves the employability of a former inmate, which results in long-term self- or family-supporting employment. Another example is a program for school readiness, which helps children stay in school and thus out of eventual trouble with risky behavior, drugs, or the law. This can translate to being a productive adult with skills for a self-sustaining career. As the individual becomes a productive citizen, so the community is transformed—one person at a time.

Success

A primary focus in studying the reform models highlighted herein is on the formal measurement of impact and results, or success in achieving stated goals. Analyzing the impact or result of a program is difficult. It takes years to establish a project and more years to reach a target population. Then it takes yet more years to begin to measurably change the behavior of that group. Thereafter, it can take a few additional years to conduct a sound, rigorous analysis of results, or degree of program success. Thus, few long-term studies are done that test program impact at least one year after program completion.

This presents a problem for the task of understanding the effectiveness of a process based on effective practices in Capacity Building, which is early in the timeline of documenting measurable results. While having a viable and effective service is important, it's not within the scope of this project to analyze either short- or long-term results. This study assumes that the sponsored services are worthy because project stakeholders have determined the services are both practical and successful. In other words, the program works because practitioners consistently use the ideas and effective practices they recommend and have determined to produce beneficial results.

Since project stakeholders cannot begin to assess meaningful impact until the project is self-renewing and permanent, let's use a simple funds-based criterion of success. A successful project is one that's still accomplishing originally stated goals, with permanent operational resources in place, at least one year after any start-up soft funding has evaporated.

Stability

Project stability means operational processes have become routine and are supported with staff and reliable resources. It does not necessarily mean the project has worked out the details of efficiency and effectiveness nor achieved success in making a positive difference in the local community.

Stability as used in the Capacity Building life cycle refers to Phase II: Operations, in which the project reaches its first level of daily function facilitating service delivery. It's the state of project development that focuses mainly on processes leading to permanency.

One difficulty with service project development is that it's difficult to link a program to ultimate measures of community improvement. Therefore, successful programs must focus on interim measures that link to community well-being. A school program, for example, may track graduation rates and placement in post-secondary education. This is an interim measure, as post-secondary education is only a step. There's no guarantee it will result in an individual's long-term employment in a career that will sustain a family. This distinction is relevant because many projects focus on stability as a primary end goal, whereas it's an *initial* goal and, at best, an *interim* goal of capacity building. Stability, then, is a state of routine operations with the focus on improving processes and conducting initial analysis to determine measurable impact to justify sustainability.

Sustainability

An enterprise that has reached sustainability has a reliable business infrastructure and operational capacity and especially permanent resources to persevere. The project ultimately has the *potential,* usually after years of successful operation, to become transformational in the community. Moreover, a service programming idea made permanent proves the model for other ideas to solve a social need.

Sustainability for any service project means that the project is generating adequate administrative, material, personnel, and financial resources to function productively. A sustained service project has long-term viability by continuing to provide beneficial service *after* major temporary financial resources (e.g., grants), and managerial and technical support from *external* donors terminate.[192]

Project sustainability is also determined by its contribution to general community well-being as evidenced by a thriving or at least measurably improving target population. Note, however, that this state of project development precedes a project becoming fully transformational.

Transformational

A *transformational* public service, in terms of Capacity Building, refers to a municipal public service organization that produces significant, long-term, positive behavioral changes within its community. Its goal is to build *permanent solutions to permanent problems.* When this eventually happens, the service is *fully transformational* for both the target population and the community.

Well-*being* versus Well*ness* (of a community)

A distinction between community well-*being* and well*ness* will elucidate how the terms apply to capacity building.

Wellness herein refers to public or project infrastructure devoted largely to health, the purview of the medical professions and helping arts. While health is certainly critical for thriving, wellness is only a few pixels in the whole picture of well-being.

Well-being connotes quality of life, which encompasses but expands beyond physical health. A community's well-being is determined by having positive activities and services available to support thriving and the conditions of happiness for the individual to discover. The community has little well-being if dysfunction—e.g., crime, drugs, poverty, food insecurity, mental illness, unemployment, inadequate schooling—is at toxic levels.

When discussing the ultimate result of community services, it's helpful to understand it in terms of community betterment and eventual well-being. This keeps the project focused on what it should be doing day-to-day to positively affect the community. Well-being reflects a community's strengths and attributes as a favorable place in which to live, work, recreate, and especially raise a family. A community that displays well-being is a *thriving* community.

Most programs wrongly focus on immediate results, which are usually the numbers of people going through a program, for example. This may or may not lead to a better community or effects such as higher primary school graduation rates and lower recidivism rates during court supervision. *What matters is how the behavior of service recipients changes and how that change ultimately improves the individual and consequently the community.*

Understanding well-being and how a project effects it is vital to gathering the right data, support, and decision-making, and having a successful project well beyond implementation and stabilization.

The goal is to help citizens become free of public support by being self-sufficient and thriving. Living independently is a responsibility and its own reward; it's called pride.

REFERENCES

Accel Team, "Bond-Team," 2005, viewed 30 October 2023: *http://www.accel-team.com/motivation/theory_02.html*

Agranoff, R. "Human services integration: Past and present challenges in public administration," *Public Administration Review,* 1991, vol. 51, no. 6.

American Heritage Dictionary. Boston, Mass.: Houghton Mifflin Co., 1982.

Arbreton, A. & McClanahan, W., "Targeted outreach: Boys and Girls Clubs of America's approach to gang prevention and intervention," Philadelphia, Penn.: Public/Private Ventures, 2002.

Ashburner, L., Ferlie, E., & Fitzgerald, L., "Organizational transformation and top-down change: The case of the NHS," *British Journal of Management,* vol. 7, iss. 1, 1996, pp. 1-16.

Asthana, S., Richardson, S., & Haliday, J., "Partnership working in public policy provision: A framework for evaluation," *Social Policy and Administration,* 2002, vol. 36, iss. 7, pp. 780-795.

Avison, D., Lau, F., Myers M., & Nielsen, P., "Action research: To make academic research relevant, researchers should try out their theories with practitioners in real situations and real organizations," *Communications of the ACM,* 1999, vol. 42, no. 1.

Bacal and Associates, "Management fads - Things you should know," 2005, viewed 30 October 2023: *www.work911.com/articles/mgmtfad.htm.*

Ballard, D., Reason, P., Bond, C,. & Seeley, C., "Action research and sustainable development," 2004, viewed 26 March 2008: *www.bath.ac.uk/carpp/publications/sus_dev.html*

Bardach, E., *The Implementation Game: What Happens After a Bill Becomes Law.* Cambridge, Mass.: MIT Press, 1977.

Bart, C., "Mission matters: There is a relationship between the words and concepts of a mission statement and the firm's success as a business," *Camagazine*, March 1998.

Bart, C., "Measuring the mission effect in human intellectual capital," *Journal of Intellectual Capital*, 2001, vol. 2, no. 3, pp. 320-330.

Barrett, P., "Corporate governance in the public sector context," *Canberra Bulletin of Public Administration*, 2003, vol. 107, pp. 7-27.

Bass, B. & Steidlmeier, P., "Ethics, character and authentic transformational leadership," Center for Leadership Studies, School of Management, Binghamton University, New York, 1998.

Bergen, A. & While, A., "'Implementation deficit' and 'street level bureaucracy': Policy practice and change in the development of community nursing issues," *Health and Social Care in the Community*, 2005, vol. 13, no. 1.

Bevir, M. & O'Brien, D., "New labour and the public sector in Britain." *Public Administration*, 2001, vol. 61, iss. 5, pp. 535-547.

Blore, I., "Poor people, poor services: The future of urban services as seen through 50 years of debate in *Public Administration and Development* and its predecessors," University of Birmingham, U.K., 1999, vol. 19, part 5, pp. 453-466.

Boone, H., "Saving kids from the slammer: What are the costs and benefits?" *Spectrum: Journal of State Government*, Winter, 1997, vol. 70, iss. 1, pp. 1067-8503.

Borgatti, S., *Organizational theory: Determinants of structure*, 2001, viewed 3 November 2023: *http://www.analytictech.com/mb021/orgtheory.htm*

Boyne, G., "Public services under new labour: Back to bureaucracy?" *Public Money and Management*, 1998, vol. 18, iss. 3, pp. 43-50.

Brody, J., "Earlier work with children steers them from crime," *New York Times*, 15 March 1999, p. A16.

Broom, C., "Institutionalizing performance-oriented government," *PA Times*, September 2004, p. 16.

Brown, S., Stevens, R., Troiano, P., & Schneider, M., "Exploring complex phenomena: Grounded theory in student affairs research," *Journal of College Student Development,* 2002, vol. 43, no. 2.

Bureau of Justice Assistance, "Glossary," Center for Program Evaluation, viewed 3 November 2023: *http://www.ojp.usdoj.gov/BJA/evaluation/glossary/glossary_o.htm*

Burman, A., "New marching orders," *Government Executive,* 2002, vol. 34, no. 4.

Burris, S., Drahos, P., & Shearing, C., "Nodal Governance," *Australian Journal of Legal Philosophy,* 2005, vol. 30.

Burt, R., "The contingent value of social capital," *Administrative Science Quarterly,* 1997, vol. 42.

Canadian Council on Social Development, "Measuring well-being: Proceedings from a symposium on social indicators," 1996 CCSD, Ottawa, Can.

Cartwright, J., Jenneker, M., & Shearing, C., "Local capacity governance in South Africa: A model for peaceful coexistence," Community Peace Programme, School of Government, University of the Western Cape, South Africa, 2004; originally presented at the *In Search of Security* conference in Montreal, February 2003.

Castles, I., *A Guide to Australian Social Statistics.* Canberra, Australian Bureau of Statistics, 1992.

Clarke, T. & Clegg, S., "Changing paradigms: The transformation of management knowledge for the 21st century," London: *Harper Collins Business,* 1998, pp. 9-59.

Cole, Alistair, Jones, & Glyn, "Reshaping the state: Administrative reform and new public management in France," *Governance,* 2005, vol. 18, iss. 4, pp. 567-588.

Coleman, G., Stetar, B., & Costa, J., "The measure of performance," *The Industrial Engineer,* 2004, vol. 36, no. 11.

Connell, P., Kubisch, A., Schorr, L. & Weiss, C., *New Approaches to Evaluating Communities Indicatives: Concepts, Methods and Contexts.* Washington, D.C.: The Aspen Institute, 1995.

Corbin, J. & Strauss A., "Grounded theory research: Procedures, canons and evaluative criteria," *Qualitative Sociology,* 1990, vol. 13, no. 1.

Creswell, J., *Qualitative Inquiry and Research Design: Choosing Among Five Traditions.* Thousand Oaks, Calif.: Sage Publications, Inc., 1998.

Crisp, B., Swerissen, H., & Duckett, S., "Four approaches to capacity building in health: Consequences for measurement and accountability," *Health Promotion International,* 2000, vol. 15, no. 2.

Cronbach, L., *Toward Reform of Program Evaluation.* San Francisco, Calif.: Jossey-Bass, 1980.

Cullen, F., Wright, J., & Brown, S., "Public support for early intervention programs: Implications for a progressive policy agenda," *Crime and Delinquency,* 1998, vol. 44, iss. 2, pp. 187-204.

Daft, R. *Leadership Theory and Practice.* New York: The Dryden Press, 1999.

Davis, P., "The burgeoning of benchmarking in British local government: The value of 'learning by looking' in the public services," *Benchmarking: An International Journal,* 1998, vol. 5, iss. 4, pp. 260-270.

Davis, G. & Rhodes, R., "From hierarchy to contracts and back again: Reforming the Australian public service," *Institutions on the Edge?* eds. M. Keating, J. Wanna, & P. Weller. Sydney: Allen and Unwin, 2000, pp. 74-98.

Davis, G. & Weller, P., *Are You Being Served?: State, Citizens and Governance.* Australia: Allen and Unwin, 2001.

Deich, S., "A guide to successful public-private partnerships," *The Finance Project,* 2001, viewed 13 April 2005: *www.financeprojectinfo.org/Publications/ostpartnershipguide.pdf*

Denhart, R. & Denhart, J., "The new public service: Serving rather than steering," *Public Administration Review,* 2000, vol. 60, iss. 6, pp. 549-559.

Denton, D., "Mission statements miss the point," *Leadership & Organization Development Journal,* 2001, vol. 22, iss 7, pp. 309-314.

Department of Justice, "Developing a sustainability plan for weed and seed," 2005, viewed 30 August 2006: *www.ojb.usdoj.gov/ccdo*

Dick, B., "You want to do an action research thesis?" 1993, viewed 28 March 2008: *www.scu.edu.au/schools/gcm/ar/art/artthesis.html*

Dick, B., "Action research FAQ," 1997a, viewed 2 June 2006: *www.scu.edu.au.schools/gcm/ar/arp/arp/arfaq*

Dick, B., "Approaching an action research thesis: An overview," 1997b, viewed 3 April 2007: *www.scu.edu.au/schools/gcm/ar/arp/phd.html*

Dick, B. 2000, "A beginners guide to action research," viewed 28 March 2008: *www.scu.edu.au/schools/gcm/ar/arp/guide/heml*

Dick, B., "Action research: Action and research," 2002, viewed 2 June 2006: *http://www.scu.edu.au/schools/gcm/ar/arp/aandr.html*

Dick, B., "Grounded theory: A thumbnail sketch," 2005, viewed 2 February 2006: *http://www.scu.edu.au/schools/gcm/ar/arp/grounded.html*

Dixon, J., Kouzmin, A., & Korac-Kakabadse, N., "Managerialism - Something old, something borrowed, little new: Economic prescription versus effective organizational change in public agencies," *International Journal of Public Sector Management,* 1998, vol. 11, iss. 23, pp. 164-187.

Dobbs, L., "Still failing the grade," 2003, viewed 15 June 2006: *http://www.usnews.com/usnews/opinion/articles/030915/15dobbs.htm*

Doell, D., "Application of contingency theory at opportunities for employment," *Dissertation Abstracts International,* 2003, vol. 42-05, p. 1562.

Dourado, P. & Blackburn, P., *Seven Secrets of Inspired Leaders: How to Achieve the Extraordinary ... by the Leaders Who Have Been There and Done It.* Hobokin, N.J.: John Wiley & Sons Inc., 2005.

Doyle, M., Claydon, T. & Buchanan, D., "Mixed results, lousy process: The management experience of organizational change," *British Journal of Management,* 2000, vol. 11, iss. 1, p. 59.

Dupnik, C., "Editorial," *Inside Tucson Business,* 1996, vol. 6, no. 4.

Eckersley, R. (ed), *Measuring Progress: Is Life Getting Better?* Melbourne: CSIRO Press, 1998.

Edwards, G. III, *Implementing Public Policy*. Washington, D.C.: Congressional Quarterly Press, 1980.

Ellis, H. & Kiely, J., "Action inquiry strategies: Taking stock and moving forward," Bournemouth, U.K.: Bournemouth University, 2000.

Fast, S. & Pi, C., "Getting Tough on Juvenile Crime: An analysis of Costs and Benefits," *Journal of Research in Crime and Delinquency*, 2002, no. 002-4278.

Fayol, H., *General and Industrial Management*, translated from the French edition (Dunod) by Constance Stores, Pitman, 1949.

Foley, P., "Competition as public policy: A review of challenge funding," *Public Administration*, 1999, vol. 77, iss. 4, pp. 809-836.

Friedman, T., *The World Is Flat: A Brief History of the Twenty-First Century*. New York: Farrar, Straus and Giroux, 2005.

Fulmer, W., *Shaping the Adaptive Organization: Landscapes, Learning and Leadership in Volatile Times*. New York: American Management Association, 2000.

Fulop, M., "Sustainability planning and resource development for youth mentoring programs," Portland, Ore.: Northwest Regional Educational Laboratory, 2005.

Garza, H., "Evaluating partnerships: Seven success factors," *The Evaluation Exchange*, Harvard Family Research Project, 2005, vol. 11, no. 1.

General Accounting Office, U.S., "Business process reengineering assessment guide," 1997, viewed 4 November 2023: *www.gao.gov*

General Accounting Office, U.S., "Defense pilot programs: DOD needs to improve implementation process for pilot programs," 2003, GAO-03-861, viewed 4 November 2023: *http://www.aviationtoday.com/reports/pilot080303.pdf*

George, B., "Truly Authentic Leadership," *U.S. News and World Report*, October 30, 2006.

Glaser, B., *Basics of Grounded Theory Analysis: Emergence vs Forcing*, Mill Valley, Calif.: *Sociology Press*, 1992.

Glaser, B., "Conceptualization: On theory and theorizing using grounded theory," *International Journal of Qualitative Methods,* 2002, vol. 1, iss. 2.

Glaser, B., "Conceptualization: On theory and theorizing using grounded theory," International Journal of Qualitative Methods, 2002, vol. 1, iss. 2, viewed 4 November 2023: *http://www.ualberta.ca/~ijqm/*

Glaser, B. & Strauss, A., "The discovery of grounded theory," *Strategies for Qualitative Research.* Chicago: Adeline, 1967.

Glenorchy City Council, *Community plan: A vision for the future.* Tasmania: Glenorchy, 2000.

Godoy, R., Garcia, V., Huanca, T., Leonard W., Olvera, R., Bauchet, J., Ma, Z., John, J., Miodowski, M., & Rios, O., "The role of community and individuals in the formation of social capital," 2005, viewed 5 April 2007: *http://people.brandeis.edu/~rgodoy/working%20papers/TAPS-WP-12-SC-Nov-2005.pdf*

Goggin, M., Bowman, A., Lester, J., & O'Toole, L., *Implementation Theory and Practice: Toward a Third Generation.* New York: Harper Collins, 1990.

Goldman, H., Ganju, V., Drake, R., Gorman, P., Hogan, M., Hyde, P., & Morgan, O., "Policy implications for implementing evidence-based practices," *Psychiatric Services,* 2001, vol. 52, iss. 12.

Goldsmith, S. & Eggers, W., *Governing by Network: The New Shape of the Public Sector.* Washington, D.C.: The Brookings Institution, 2004.

Gould, J., "The importance of HR practices and workplace trust in achieving superior performance: A study of public-sector organizations," *Journal of Human Resource Management,* 2003, vol. 14, iss. 1, pp. 28-54.

Goulding, C., "Grounded theory: The missing methodology on the interpretivist agenda, *Qualitative Market Research: An International Journal,* 1998, vol. 1, no. 1, pp. 50-57.

Governmental Commerce, Office of 2005, "Common causes of project failure," The UK office of Government Commerce, London, viewed 7 March 2006: *www.ogc.gov.uk*

Greenwood, D., Levin, M., *Introduction to Action Research: Social Research for Social Change.* Thousand Oaks, Calif.: Sage Publications Inc., 1998.

Grimshaw, D., Vincent, S., & Willmott, H., "Going privately: Partnership and outsourcing in UK public services, *Public Administration,* 2002, vol. 80, no. 3, p. 475.

Grol, R. & Wensing, M., "What drives change? Barriers to and incentives for achieving evidence-based practice," *MJA,* 2004, vol. 180.

Gudjonsson, G., *The Psychology of Interrogations and Confessions: A Handbook.* Chichester: John Wiley & Sons, Ltd., 2003.

Hagen, J. & Lurie, I., *Implementing JOBS: Progress and Promise.* Albany, N.Y.: Rockefeller Institute of Government, State University of New York, 1994.

Hanks, S., Watson, C., Jansen, E., & Chandler, G., "Tightening the life-cycle construct: A taxonomic study of growth state configurations in high-technology organizations," *Entrepreneurship: Theory and Practice,* 1993, vol. 18.

Harms, T., Clifford, R., & Cryer, D., "Early childhood environment rating scale: Revised edition." New York: Teachers College Press, 1998.

Hatry, H., *Performance Measurement: Getting Results.* Washington, D.C.: The Urban Institute Press, 1999.

Health and Human Services, U.S. Department of, "A guide to successful public-private partnerships for child care," 2005, viewed 9 April 2005: *www.nccic.org/ccpartnerships*

Herr, K. & Anderson, L., The Action Research Dissertation: A Guide to Students and Faculty. Thousand Oaks, Calif.: Sage Publications, Inc., 2005.

Higgins, P., James, P., & Roper, I., "An investigation into the compatibility of consultation and performance comparison in the UK's policy of best value," *International Journal of Consumer Studies,* 2005, vol. 29, iss. 2, p. 148.

Higgins, V., "Government as a failing operation: Regulating administrative conduct 'at a distance' in Australia," *Sociology,* 2004, vol. 38 no. 3, pp. 457-476.

Hill, J., *The Policy Process: A Reader.* University of Newcastle upon Tyne: Prentice Hall, 1997.

Hill, J., McNulty, I., & Stuart, S., "Early childhood education sadly overlooked in LA," *New Orleans City Business,* February, 1997.

Hill, M., Hupe, P., *Implementing Public Policy: Governance in Theory and in Practice.* Thousand Oaks, Calif.: Sage Publications, Inc., 2002.

Hjern, B. & Porter, D., "Implementation structures: A new unit of administrative analysis," *The Policy Process: A Reader.* University of Newcastle upon Tyne: Prentice Hall, 1997.

Himmelman, A., "Communities working collaboratively for a change," *Resolving Conflict: Strategies for Local Government,* Margaret Herrman ed. Washington, D.C.: International City/County Management Association, 1994, pp. 27-47.

Hoepfl, M., "Choosing qualitative research: A primer for technology education researchers," *Journal of Technology Education,* 1997, vol. 9, no. 1, pp. 47-63.

Hogwood, B. & Gunn, L., "Policy analysis for the real world," *The Policy Process: A Reader.* University of Newcastle upon Tyne: Prentice Hall, 1997.

Holmes, M. & Shand, D., "Management reform: Some practitioner perspectives on the past ten years," *Governance,* 1995, vol. 8, iss. 4, pp. 551-578.

Homel, P., Nutley, S., Webb, B., & Tilley, N., "Making it happen from the Centre: Managing for the regional delivery of local crime reduction outcomes," Home Office Research Study, 2004, 54/04, viewed 7 March 2006: *www.crimereduction.gov.uk*

Hood, C., "The 'New Public Management' in the 1980s: Variations on a theme," *Accounting Organizations and Society,* 1995, vol. 20, iss. 2/3, pp. 93-109.

HRM Guide Network 2005, Classical organizational theory modified, viewed 10 November 2023: *http://www.hrmguide.co.uk/history/classical_organization_theory_modified.htm*

Iredell County Partnership for Young Children, viewed 5 November, 2023: *http://www.iredellsmartstart.org*

Jackson, P., "Public sector added value: Can bureaucracy deliver?" *Public Administration,* 2001, vol. 79, no. 1, pp. 5-28.

Jackson, P. & Stainsby, L., "The public manager in 2010: Managing public sector networked organizations," *Public Money and Management,* 2000, vol. 20, iss. 1, p. 11.

Janis, R., "An examination of Bass's (1985) leadership theory in the project management environment," *Dissertation Abstracts International,* 1985, vol. 64-10A, p. 3753.

Jervis, P. & Richards, S., "Public management: Raising our game," *Public Money and Management,* 1997, vol. 17, iss. 2, pp. 9-16.

Johnsen, A., "What does 25 years of experience tell us about the state of performance measurement in public policy and management?" *Public Money and Management,* 2005, vol. 25, iss. 1.

Joyner, L., Miller, W., & Cage, B., "Strategic planning: A foundation for sustaining change," *National Forum of Special Education Journal,* 2000, vol. 9E.

Karr-Morse, R. & Wiley, M., *Ghosts from the Nursery: Tracing the Roots of Violence.* New York: Atlantic Monthly Press, 1997.

Keating, M. & Weller, P., "Rethinking government's roles and operations," *Are you being served? States Citizens and Governance,* M. Keating and G. Davis (eds.). Sydney: Allen and Unwin, pp. 73-96.

Kellogg, W.K., Foundation, "Using logic models to bring together planning, evaluation, & action: Logic model development guide," 2001, viewed 5 November 2023: *www.wkkf.org*

Kelman, S., "Some advice for good measure," *Government Executive,* 2001, Mar. 1, vol. 33, no. 3, p. 67.

Kemmis, S., "Action research and social movement: A challenge for policy research," *Education policy analysis archives,* 1993, vol. 1, no. 1.

Kemp, D., "Reforming the public service to meet the global challenge," Ministerial Statement to the Committee for Economic Development of Australia, Melbourne, 1997.

Kettle, D., "Models of reform," *The Global Public Management Revolution.* Washington, D. C.: Brookings Institute, 2000, ch. 2, pp. 7-29.

Kickert, W., "Steering at a distance: A new paradigm of public governance in Dutch higher education," *Governance,* 1995, vol. 8, iss. 1, pp. 135-157.

Kirkpatrick, I., "The worst of both worlds? Public services without markets or bureaucracy," *Public Money and Management,* 1999, vol. 19, iss. 4, pp. 7-14.

Kirst, A. & Richardson, J., "The utility of a longitudinal approach in assessing implementation," *Studying Implementation,* ed. Walter Williams, Chatham, N.J.: Chatham House, 1983.

Klopovic, J., Vasu, M., & Yearwood, D., *Effective Program Practices for At-Risk Youth: A Continuum of Community-Based Programs.* New York: Civic Research Institute, Inc., 2003.

Krefting, L., "Rigor in qualitative research: The assessment of trustworthiness," *The American Journal of Occupational Therapy,* 1991, vol. 45, iss. 3, pp. 214-222.

Lane, J., "Implementation, accountability and trust," *European Journal of Political Research,* 1987, 15 (5), pp. 527-46.

LaPelle, N., Zapka, J,. & Ockene, J., 'Sustainability of health programs: The example of tobacco treatment services in Massachusetts," *American Journal of Public Health,* 2006, vol. 96, no. 8.

Larson, E. & Larson, R., "How to create a clear project plan," Darwin, 2004, viewed 23 March 2005: *http://www.darwinmag.com/*

Laurie, J., "Why projects fail," JISC Infonet Case Study, JISC Centre of Expertise in the Planning and Implementation of Information Systems. Newcastle upon Tyne: Northumbria University, 2003, viewed 23 March 2005: *www.jiscinfonet.ac.uk*

Lenkowsky, L., "Reinventing government: The case of national service," *Public Administration Review,* July 2000, vol. 60, no. 4, pp. 298-307.

Leon, P., "Collaboration in the juvenile justice system and youth serving agencies: Improving prevention, providing more efficient services and reducing recidivism for youth with disabilities." Washington, D.C.: American Institute for Research, 2001.

Levy, R., "EU programme management 1977-96: A performance indicators analysis," *Public Administration,* 2001, vol. 79, iss 2, p. 423.

Lin, S. & Lee, Y., "Sustainable community indicators: Case of Mingshan Community, Taipei, Taiwan," 8th International Conference of The Asian Planning Schools Association, 11-14 September 2005.

Lincoln, Y. & Guba, E., *Naturalistic Inquiry.* Beverly Hills, Calif.: Sage Publications, Inc., 1985.

Lovelock, R., Lyons, K., & Powell, J., *Reflecting on Social Work – Discipline and Profession.* Burlington, Vt.: Ashgate Publishing Limited, 2004.

Marguerite Casey Foundation Capacity Assessment Tool, 2001, viewed 5 November 2023: *www.caseygrants.org*

Marshall, C. & Rossman, G., *Designing Qualitative Research.* Newbury Park, Calif.: Sage Publications, Inc., 1989.

Masters, J., "The history of action research," Hughes (ed) *Action Research Electronic Reader,* 1995, viewed 2 June 2006: *www.behs.cchs.usyd.edu.au/arow/Reader/rmasters.htm*

Maxwell, J., *The 21 Irrefutable Laws of Leadership: Follow Them and People Will Follow You.* Nashville, Tenn.: Thomas Nelson, Inc., 1998.

Mayne, J., "Addressing attribution through contribution analysis: Using performance measures sensibly," Material from a 1998 paper by the Office of the Auditor General and the Treasury Board Secretariat, Canada, 1999.

McKinsey, *Effective Capacity Building in Nonprofit Organizations,* for Venture Philanthropy Partners (now Youth Invest Partners), Washington, 2001. Viewed 5 November 2023: *https://youthinvestpartners.org/learning/reports/capacity/capacity.html*

McWilliam, E., *How to Survive Best Practice.* Brisbane, Australia: Always Flying Publishers, 2002.

McNiff & Whitehead, *All You Need to Know About Action Research.* Thousand Oaks, Calif.: Sage Publications, Inc., 2006.

Mead, L., "Implementing work requirements in Wisconsin," Institute for Research on Poverty, discussion paper no. 1231-01, Dept. of Politics, N.Y. University, 2001.

Mehta, D., "Urban governance: Lessons from best practices in Asia," Urban Management Programme – Asia Occasional Paper no. 40. New York: The United Nations, 1998.

Meltsner, A. & Bellavita, C., *The Policy Organization.* Beverly Hills, Calif.: Sage Publications, Inc., 1983.

Memon, A., Wark, L., Holley, A., Bull, R., & Koehnken, G., "Eye witness performance in cognitive and structured interviews," *Memory,* 1997, iss. 5, pp. 639-655.

Merriam, S., *Case Study Research in Education: A Qualitative Approach.* San Francisco: Jossey-Bass, 1988, p. 18.

Mihalic, S., Irwin, K., Elliott, D., Fagan, A., & Hansen, D., "Blueprints for violence prevention," Washington, D.C.: Office of Juvenile Justice and Delinquency, 2001, viewed 5 November 2023: *www.colorado.edu/cspv/blueprints*

Miles, M. & Hubermann, A., *Qualitative Data Analysis: A Source Book of New Methods,* 2nd ed. Thousand Oaks, Calif.: Sage Publications, Inc., 1994.

Miller, D. & Friesen, P., "A longitudinal study of the corporate life cycle," *Management Science,* 1984, vol. 30, no. 10, pp. 1161-1183.

Milne, R. & Bull, R., *Investigative Interviewing: Psychology and Practice.* West Sussex, Eng.: John Wiley & Sons, Ltd., 2000.

Mulgan, R. & Uhr, J., "Accountability and governance," Graduate program in Public Policy, RSSS, Australian National University, 2000, viewed 5 November 2023: *http://hdl.handle.net/1885/41946*

Nathan, R., *Turning Promises into Performance: The Management Challenge of Implementing Workfare.* New York: Colombia University Press, 1993.

Neale, A. & Anderson, B., "Performance reporting for accountability purposes – Lessons, issues, future." Wellington, New Zealand: Office of the Controller and Auditor-General, 2000.

NC Center for Nonprofits, "FAQ: How do I create a 501(c)(3) nonprofit organization?" 2006, viewed 19 September 2006: *http://www.ncnonprofits.org/faq/HowToStartA501(c)(3)Nonprofit.pdf*

Newcomer, K., "Performance-based management: What is it and how do we get there?" *Public Manager,* 1998, Winter, vol. 26, no. 4, p. 37.

Newman, J. "Changing governance, changing equality? New labour, modernization and public services," *Public Money and Management,* 2002, vol. 22, no. 1, pp. 7-14.

Newman, R., "Lessons from the rule breakers," *U.S. New and World Report,* September 25, 2006.

North Carolina Smart Start, viewed 23 March 2005: *http://www.smartstart.org/*

O'Brien, G., "Participation as the key to successful change – A public sector case study," *Leadership and Organization Development Journal,* 2002, vol. 23, no. 8.

O'Brien, R., "An overview of the methodological approach of action research," 1998, viewed 5 November 2023: *https://homepages.web.net/~robrien/papers/arfinal.html*

OECD 1986, The OECD list of social indicators, Paris.

Office of Management and Budget, 2007, "The budget of the US government fiscal year 2007," viewed 11 April 2007: *http://www.whitehouse.gov/omb/budget/fy2007/*

Office of Management and Budget, 2009, "Making government more effective," viewed 5 November 2023: *http://georgewbush-whitehouse.archives.gov/omb/pubpress/2009/010809_performance.html*

Olson, O., Humphrey, C., & Guthrie, J., "Caught in an evaluatory trap: A dilemma for public services under NPFM," *European Accounting Review,* 2001, vol. 10, no. 3, pp. 505-522.

Osborn, R. N., Hunt, J. G., & Jauch, L. R., "Toward a contextual theory of leadership," *The Leadership Quarterly,* 2002, 13, 797-837.

Outhwaite, S., "The importance of leadership in the development of an integrated team," *Journal of Nursing Management,* 2003, vol. 11, no. 6, pp. 371-376.

Patton, M., *How to Use Qualitative Methods in Evaluation*. Newbury Park, Calif.: Sage Publications, Inc., 1987.

Patton, M., *Utilization Focused Evaluation: The New Century Text*, 3rd ed.. Beverly Hills, Calif.: Sage Publications, Inc., 1997.

Park, T., "Toward a theory of user-based relevance: A call for a new paradigm of inquiry," *Journal of the American Society for Information Science*, 1999, vol. 45, iss. 3, pp. 135-141.

Piderit, K. & Weiss, J., "The value of mission statements in public agencies," *Journal of Public Administration Research and Theory*, 1999, vol. 9.

Pinto, J. & Prescott, J., "Variations in critical success factor stages in the project life cycle," *Journal of Management*, 1988, vol. 14, no. 1, pp. 5-18.

Podger, A., "Innovation with integrity – The public sector leadership imperative to 2020," NIPAA National Conference 2003, Brisbane, Australia, viewed 15 June 2006: *http://www.ipaa.org.au/vison2020/01_conf_Papers.htm*

Polidano, C., "The new public management in developing countries," 1999, Institute for Development Policy and Management, University of Manchester.

Pollitt, C. & Bouckaert, G., "Evaluating public management reforms: An international perspective," 2002, viewed 5 November 2023: *http://soc.kuleuven.be/io/pubpdf/IO04025_bouckaert.pdf*

Pontusson, J., "Welfare-state retrenchment revisited: Entitlement cuts, public sector restructuring and inegalitarian trends in advanced capitalist societies," *World Politics*, 1998, vol. 51, no. 1, pp. 67-98.

Prasad, A., "Avoiding failure," *Arabian Computer News*, 2005, viewed 23 March 2005: *www.ITP.net* (now *https://www.edgemiddleeast.com/*)

Pressman, J. & Wildavsky, A., *Implementation*. Calif.: University of California Press, 1984.

Program Manager, "Balancing Performance Measures: Best Practices in Performance Management," 1999, vol. 28, no. 6.

Putnam, R., *Bowling Alone: The Collapse and Revival of American Community*. New York: Simon & Schuster, 2000.

Raley, R., Grossman, J., & Walker, "Getting it right: Strategies for after-school success," Philadelphia, Pa.: Public Private Ventures, 2005.

Rao, V. & Woolcock, M., "Integrating qualitative and quantitative approaches in program evaluation," draft paper issued via The Development Research Group, The World Bank, 2002.

Reason & Bradbury, *Handbook of Action Research: Participative Inquiry and Practice.* Thousand Oaks, Calif.: Sage Publications, Inc., 2001.

Rein, M., *From Policy to Practice.* Armonk, N.Y.: M.E. Sharpe, Inc., 1983.

Rhodes, R., "Traditions and public sector reform: Comparing Britain and Denmark," *Scandinavian Political Studies,* 1999, vol. 22, iss. 4, pp. 341-370.

Rice, P. & Ezzy, D., *Qualitative Research Methods: A Health Focus.* South Melbourne Australia: Oxford University Press, 1999.

Rolfe, G., "Going to extremes: Action research, grounded practice and the theory-practice gap in nursing," *Journal of Advanced Nursing,* 1995, vol. 24, no. 6, pp. 1315-1320.

Rothgeb, J., Willis, G., & Forsyth, B., "Questionnaire pretesting methods: Do different techniques and different organizations produce similar results?" 2005, viewed 7 January 2006: *www.census.gov/srd/papers/pdf/rsm2005-02.pdf*

Ryan, C., "Australian public sector financial reporting: A case of cooperative policy formulation," 1998, Public Sector Transformation Workshop, Macquarie University.

Sabatier, P., "Top-down and bottom-up approaches to implementation research," *The Policy Process: A Reader.* University of Newcastle upon Tyne: Prentice Hall, 1997.

Sackett, D., Rosenberg, W., Muir Gray, J., Haynes, R., Richardson, W., "Evidence based medicine: What it is and what it isn't," *British Medical Journal,* 1996, 312, 71-72.

Salamon, L. (ed), "The new governance and the tools of public action: An introduction," *The Tools of Government: A Guide to the New Governance.* New York: Oxford University Press, 2002.

Sanderson, I., "Performance management, evaluation and learning in 'modern' local government," *Public Administration,* 2001, vol. 79, no. 2, pp. 279-313.

Schay, B., Beach M., Caldwell, J., & LaPolice, C., "Using standardized outcome measures in the federal government," *Human Resource Management,* Fall 2002, vol. 41, no. 3. p. 355.

Schmaltz, D., "The myths that rule our projects," *Innovative Leader,* 2003, vol. 13, no. 7.

Shearing, C., "Paradigms for policing," Center for the Study of Violence and Reconciliation, 2005, viewed 4 December 2007: *http://www.csvr.org.za/confpaps/shearing.htm*

Shearing, C., Wood, J., "Nodal governance, democracy and the new 'denizenz'," Center for the Study of Violence and Reconciliation, 2003, viewed 4 December 2007: *http://www.csvr.org.za/confpaps/shearing.htm*

Shediac-Rizkallah, M., & Bone, L., "Planning for the sustainability of community-based health programs: Conceptual frameworks and future directions for research, practice and policy," *Health Education Research – Theory & Practice,* 1998, vol. 13, no. 1.

Shors, J., "Systemic overload," *Des Moines Business Record,* January 13, 1997.

Simeon, R., "Adaptability and change in federations," *UNESCO,* iss. 167. Oxford, UK: Blackwell, 2001.

Smith, M., "What is action research and how do we do it?" *The Encyclopedia of Informal Education,* 2005, viewed 6 November 2023: *www.infed.org/research/b-actres.htm*

Smith, R., "Focusing on public value: Something new and something old," *Australian Journal of Public Administration,* 2004, vol. 63, iss. 4, pp 68-79.

Spoth, R., Greenberg, M., Bierman, K., & Redmond, C., "PROSPER community – University partnership model for public education systems: Capacity building for evidence-based, competence-building prevention," *Prevention Science,* 2004, vol. 5, no. 1, pp. 31-39.

Stake, R., *The Art of Case Study Research.* Thousand Oaks, Calif.: Sage Publications, Inc., 1995.

Steib, S., 2004, "Whatever the problem, the answer is 'evidence-based practice' – Or Is It?" *Child Welfare,* vol. 83, no. 6.

Stenbacka, C., "Qualitative research requires quality concepts of its own," *Management Decision,* 2001, vol. 39, iss. 7.

Stiglitz, J., "Public policy for a knowledge economy." London: The World Bank, 1999.

Strauss, A. & Corbin, J., *Basics of Qualitative Research: Grounded Theory Procedures and Techniques.* Newbury Park, Calif.: Sage Publications, Inc., 1990.

Szirom, T., Lasater, Z., Hyde, J., & More, C., "Working together – Integrated governance," Paper to the Institute of Public Administration Australia National Conference, Sydney, November 30, 2001(unpublished), pp. 1-18.

Tat-Kei Ho, A., "Reinventing local governments and the E-government initiative," *Public Administration Review,* 2002, vol. 62, iss. 4, p. 434.

Teal Trust, "Our definition of leadership," 2006, viewed 6 November 2023: *http://www.teal.org.uk/leadership/definition.htm*

Tellis, W., "Introduction to case study," The Qualitative Report, 1997, viewed 6 November 2023: *http://www.nova.edu/ssss/QR/QR3-2/tellis1.html*

Trochim, W., "Qualitative validity," 2006, viewed 6 November 2023: *http://www.socialresearchmethods.net/kb/qualval.php*

United Nations Development Programme 1997, "Governance for sustainable human development." New York: United Nations, viewed 13 October 2005: *http://magnet.undp.org/policy/default.htm*

Valentin, A. & Spangenberg, J., "A guide to community sustainability indicators," *Environmental Impact Assessment Review,* 2000, vol. 20, iss. 3, pp. 381-392.

Vander Kooi, G., "Camp programs provide community opportunities: Camp Henry helps community with youth diversion program," *Camping Magazine,* 2001, vol. 74, no. 5, pp. 29-31.

Van Gramberg, B. & Teicher, J., "Managerialism in local government – Victoria Australia," *The International Journal of Public Sector Administration*, 2000, vol. 13, iss. 5, pp. 476-492.

Venture Philanthropy Partners, "Effective capacity building in nonprofit organizations," 2001, viewed 6 November 2023: *http://www.vppartners.org/learning/reports/capacity/capacity.html* — Now: *http://youthinvestpartners.org/learning/reports/capacity/capacity.html*

Wallis, J. & Dollery, B., "Government failure, social capital and the appropriateness of the New Zealand model for public sector reform in developing countries," *World Development*, 2000, vol. 29, no. 2.

Webster, R., "Scary schools: Study shows suburban classrooms contain same drug, sex problems as urban counterparts," *New Orleans Citybusiness*, 29 Mar. 2004.

Weiss, J. & Piderit, K., "The value of mission statements in public agencies," *Journal of Public Administration Research and Theory*, 1999, vol. 9.

Whitehead & McNiff, *Action Research: Living Theory*. Thousand Oaks, Calif.: Sage Publications, Inc., 2006.

Wholey, J., Hatry, H., & Newcomer, K., *Handbook of Practical Program Evaluation*. San Francisco, Calif.: Jossey-Bass, Inc., 1994.

Wildavsky, A., *Speaking Truth to Power: The Art and Craft of Policy Analysis*. Boston: Little Brown, 1979.

Wiebush, R., McNulty, B., & Le, T., "Implementation of the intensive community-based aftercare program," Office of Juvenile Justice and Delinquency Prevention, 2000, viewed 9 April 2005: *www.ojjdp.ncjrs.org*

Wiebush, R., Wagner, D., McNulty, B., Wang, Y., & Le, T., "Implementation and outcome evaluation of the intensive aftercare program: Final report," 2005, Office of Juvenile Justice and Delinquency Prevention, viewed 9 April 2005: *www.ojjdp.jcjrs.org*

Williams, W., *The Implementation Perspective*. Berkeley: University of California Press, 1980.

Willis, G., "Cognitive interviewing: A 'how to' guide," 1999, viewed 7 January 2006: *www.appliedresearch.cancer.gov/areas/cognitive/interview.pdf*

Wiseman, M., "How workfare really works," *The Public Interest,* 1987, no. 89: pp. 36-47.

W.K. Kellogg Foundation, "Evaluation handbook," 1998, viewed 6 October 2006: *www.wkkf.org*

Wollmann, H., "Local government modernization in Germany: Between incrementalism and reform waves," *Public Administration,* 2000, vol. 78, iss. 4, pp. 915-936.

Woodard, C., "Merit by any other name – Reframing the civil service first principle," *The Reflective Practitioner,* Jan/Feb 2005, vol. 65, no. 1, pp. 109-116.

Wright, K. & Merrill, K., "The wilderness incident investigative interview: Mitigating memory challenges utilizing the enhanced cognitive interview (ECI) technique," 2001, viewed 7 January 2006: *www.outdoored.com/articles/Article.asp?ArticleID=141*

Yearwood, D., "Partnership advocating safety and security: An evaluation of processes and services," 2000, The N.C. Governor's Crime Commission.

Yearwood, D., "Program sustainability of Governor's Crime Commission grant funded programs," The N.C. Governor's Crime Commission Criminal Justice Analysis Center, 2004, viewed 7 March 2006: *http://www.ncgccd.org*

Yin, R., "Enhancing the quality of case studies in health services research," *Health Service Research,* 1999, vol. 34, pp. 1209-1224.

Yin, R. & Campbell, D., *Case Study Research: Design and Methods.* Thousand Oaks, Calif.: Sage Publications, Inc., 2003.

Yukl, G., *Leadership in Organizations,* third ed. Englewood Cliffs, N.J.: Prentice Hall, 1994.

Zaccaro, S. & Horn, N., "Leadership theory and practice: Fostering an effective symbiosis," *The Leadership Quarterly,* 2003, vol. 14, pp. 769-806.

ABOUT THE AUTHORS

JAMES KLOPOVIC, Major, USAF, retired, holds a Doctor of Public Policy (DPP) from Charles Sturt University, Sydney, Australia, with concentration on service program capacity building at the organizational and community levels.

James continues to work in the private and public sectors. He's helping cultivate the next generation of leaders via character-based education and development. He promotes the understanding of how to build teams that accomplish more than the sum of the parts and combines this passion with developing better ways to deliver municipal public services with collaborative capacity building.

After retiring from the United States Air Force, James continued providing leadership at federal, state, and local levels for a total of 45 years. He served as a senior staffer for 25 years on the North Carolina Governor's Crime Commission, where his responsibilities encompassed strategic planning, municipal governance, financial development, federal granting, and community and organizational development, implementation, and evaluation. Now he writes, publishes, and consults.

One of the numerous programs he created detailed the processes and procedures for School Resource Officers, which resulted in continuously improving learning environments statewide while making schools safer. Those programs continue today.

As the principal investigator/program director on a series of research programs, he analyzed and proposed model local programs leading to grant proposals for dozens of municipal and state initiatives.

James has broad experience in logistics, training, and education. His expertise in program design, implementation, and management includes ensuring program and organizational permanency. His technical support to numerous local government entities created and enhanced service ideas such as delinquency prevention, reentry, and decriminalizing people living with mental illness.

He has authored numerous publications regarding community policing, community development, and effective/efficient delivery of public services as well as books for fun. In descending order of date, they include the following:

The Good Life: My Legacy for You. A memoir. (Morrisville, N.C.: Affinitas Publishing, 2023) Available through Amazon and *http://www.affinitaspublishing.org.*

Effective Program Practices for At-Risk Youth: A Continuum of Community Based Programs. (Kingston, N.J.: Civic Research Institute, Inc., 2003). Available through Amazon and *https://civicresearchinstitute.com/index.html.*

The Honest Backpacker: A Practical Guide for the Rookie Adventurer over 50. (Morrisville, N.C.: Affinitas Publishing, 2017). Available through Amazon and *http://www.affinitaspublishing.org.*

Little Stories: A Legacy of Living, Laughing and Loving. (Morrisville, N.C.: Affinitas Publishing, 2019). Available through Amazon and *http://www.affinitaspublishing.org.*

Your Moral Compass: A Practical Guide for New Wave Leaders. (2020). Available through Amazon and *http://www.affinitaspublishing.org.*

Becoming a New Wave Leader: Principles and Practices to Live and Lead Well. (Morrisville, N.C.: Affinitas Publishing, 2021). Available through Amazon and *http://www.affinitaspublishing.org.*

Volume I, Capacity Building Series: *Building Capacity from the Bottom Up: The Key to Sustaining Local Services.* (Morrisville, N.C.: Affinitas Publishing, 2024). Available through Amazon and *http://www.affinitaspublishing.org.*

Volume II, Capacity Building Series: *Decriminalizing Mental Illness: A Practical Guide for Building Sustainable Crisis Intervention Teams.* (Morrisville, N.C.: Affinitas Publishing, 2024). Available through Amazon and *http://www.affinitaspublishing.org.*

Volume III, Capacity Building Series: *Accelerating Juvenile Reentry: A Practical Capacity Building Model for Sustaining Aftercare.* (Affinitas Publishing, 2024).

Volume IV, Capacity Building Series: *Accelerating Adult Reentry: A Practical Capacity Building Model for Sustaining Post-Release Transitional Services.* (Affinitas Publishing, 2024).

Contact: *jklopovic@gmail.com*

NICOLE KLOPOVIC is the daughter of James Klopovic. She's a certified Physician Associate (PA-C), practicing in the areas of Emergency Medicine, Urgent Care, Aesthetics, Weight Management, and Primary Care. In addition, she is a captain in the U.S. Air Force Reserves Medical Corps and is pursuing her Air Force career concurrently with her career as a PA-C.

She stays active with dance instructing, weightlifting, hiking, and cycling and enjoys cooking and traveling, striving to embrace the motto *carpe diem* while maintaining her passion to mentor, help, and teach others.

Nicole is cofounder and CEO of The Nicole and James Klopovic Family Foundation, which lends support to local social programs with funding and knowledge of Capacity Building to encourage *Permanent Solutions to Permanent Problems.*

ENDNOTES

1   J. Pressman & A. Wildavsky, *Implementation*. Calif.: University of California Press, 1984.
2   L. Salamon (ed), "The new governance and the tools of public action: An introduction," *The Tools of Government: A Guide to the New Governance*. New York: Oxford University Press, 2002.
3   R. Wiebush, B. McNulty, & T. Le, "Implementation of the intensive community-based aftercare program," Office of Juvenile Justice and Delinquency Prevention, 2000, viewed 9 April 2005: *www.ojjdp.ncjrs.org*
4   Op. Cit., Pressman & Wildavsky, 1984.
5   Op. Cit., Pressman & Wildavsky, 1984; P. Homel, S. Nutley, B. Webb, & N. Tilley, "Making it happen from the Centre: Managing for the regional delivery of local crime reduction outcomes," Home Office Research Study, 2004, 54/04, viewed 7 March 2006: *www.crimereduction.gov.uk*
6   D. Yearwood, "Program sustainability of Governor's Crime Commission grant funded programs," The N.C. Governor's Crime Commission Criminal Justice Analysis Center, 2004, viewed 7 March 2006: *http://www.ncgccd.org*
7   Op. Cit., Homel *et al*, 2004.
8   Ibid.
9   McKinsey, *Effective Capacity Building in Nonprofit Organizations,* for Venture Philanthropy Partners (now Youth Invest Partners), Washington, 2001. Viewed 5 November 2023: *https://youthinvestpartners.org/learning/reports/capacity/capacity.html*
10 Op. Cit., Pressman & Wildavsky, 1984.
11 I. Blore, "Poor people, poor services: The future of urban services as seen through 50 years of debate in *Public Administration and Development* and its predecessors," University of Birmingham, U.K., 1999, vol. 19, part 5, pp. 453-466.
12 G. Edwards III, *Implementing Public Policy*. Washington, D.C.: Congressional Quarterly Press, 1980.
13 J. Wallis & B. Dollery, "Government failure, social capital and the appropriateness of the New Zealand model for public sector reform in developing countries," *World Development,* 2000, vol. 29, no. 2.
14 D. Schmaltz, "The myths that rule our projects," *Innovative Leader,* 2003, vol. 13, no. 7.
15 Op. Cit., Homel *et al*, 2004.
16 Ibid.
17 M. Goggin, A. Bowman, J. Lester & L. O'Toole, *Implementation Theory and Practice: Toward a Third Generation*. New York: Harper Collins, 1990.
18 Ibid.
19 C. Dupnik, "Editorial," *Inside Tucson Business,* 1996, vol. 6, no. 4.
20 Op. Cit., Pressman & Wildavsky, 1984.
21 F. Cullen, J. Wright, S. Brown, "Public support for early intervention programs: Implications for a progressive policy agenda," *Crime and Delinquency,* 1998, vol. 44, iss. 2, pp. 187-204.
22 North Carolina Smart Start, viewed 23 March 2005: *http://www.smartstart-nc.org/*.
23 H. Boone, "Saving kids from the slammer: What are the costs and benefits?" *Spectrum: Journal of State Government,* Winter, 1997, vol. 70, iss. 1, pp. 1067-8503; A. Arbreton & W. McClanahan, "Targeted outreach: Boys and Girls Clubs of America's approach to gang prevention and intervention," Philadelphia, Penn.: Public/Private Ventures, 2002; G. Vander

Kooi, "Camp programs provide community opportunities: Camp Henry helps community with youth diversion program," *Camping Magazine,* 2001, vol. 74, no. 5, pp. 29-31.; S. Mihalic, *et al,* "Blueprints for violence prevention," Washington, D.C.: Office of Juvenile Justice and Delinquency, 2001, viewed 5 November 2023: *www.colorado.edu/cspv/blueprints;* J. Brody, "Earlier work with children steers them from crime," *New York Times,* 15 March 1999, p. A16.

24   J. Hill, I. McNulty, & S. Stuart, "Early childhood education sadly overlooked in LA," *New Orleans City Business,* February, 1997.

25   S. Steib, 2004, "Whatever the problem, the answer is 'evidence-based practice' – Or Is It?" *Child Welfare,* vol. 83, no. 6.

26   P. Leon, "Collaboration in the juvenile justice system and youth serving agencies: Improving prevention, providing more efficient services and reducing recidivism for youth with disabilities." Washington, D.C.: American Institute for Research, 2001.

27   S. Kelman, "Some advice for good measure," *Government Executive,* 2001, Mar. 1, vol. 33, no. 3, p. 67.

28   Op. Cit., Goggin *et al,* 1990.

29   M. C. Shediac-Rizkallah & L. R. Bone, "Planning for the sustainability of community-based health programs: Conceptual frameworks and future directions for research, practice and policy," *Health Education Research – Theory & Practice,* 1998, vol. 13, no. 1.

30   M. Holmes & D. Shand, "Management reform: Some practitioner perspectives on the past ten years," Governance, 1995, vol. 8, iss. 4, pp. 551-578; P. Jackson & L. Stainsby, "The public manager in 2010: Managing public sector networked organizations," *Public Money and Management,* 2000, vol. 20, iss. 1, p. 11; P. Jackson, "Public sector added value: Can bureaucracy deliver?" Public Administration, 2001, vol. 79, no. 1, pp. 5-28.

31   T. Clarke & S. Clegg, "Changing paradigms: The transformation of management knowledge for the 21st century," London: *Harper Collins Business,* 1998, pp. 9-59; J. Stiglitz, "Public policy for a knowledge economy." London: The World Bank, 1999.

32   Ibid., Stiglitz, 1999; R. Denhart & J. Denhart, "The new public service: Serving rather than steering," *Public Administration Review,* 2000, vol. 60, iss. 6, pp. 549-559; Op. Cit., Salamon, 2002.

33   United Nations Development Programme, 1997, "Governance for sustainable human development." New York: United Nations, viewed 13 October 2005: *http://magnet.undp.org/policy/default.htm*

34   A. Tat-Kei Ho, "Reinventing local governments and the E-government initiative," *Public Administration Review,* 2002, vol. 62, iss. 4, p. 434; Op. Cit., Jackson & Stainsby, 2000.

35   I. Sanderson, "Performance management, evaluation and learning in 'modern' local government," *Public Administration,* 2001, vol. 79, no. 2, pp. 279-313.

36   G. Davis & R. Rhodes, "From hierarchy to contracts and back again: Reforming the Australian public service," *Institutions on the Edge?* eds. M. Keating, J. Wanna & P. Weller. Sydney: Allen and Unwin, 2000, pp. 74-98.

37   Op. Cit., Sanderson, 2001.

38   P. Higgins, P. James, & I. Roper, "An investigation into the compatibility of consultation and performance comparison in the UK's policy of best value," *International Journal of Consumer Studies,* 2005, vol. 29, iss. 2, p. 148.

39   Op. Cit., Salamon, 2002.

40   M. Doyle, T. Claydon, & D. Buchanan, "Mixed results, lousy process: The management experience of organizational change," *British Journal of Management,* 2000, vol. 11, iss. 1, p. 59.

41 C. Pollitt & G. Bouckaert, "Evaluating public management reforms: An international perspective," 2002, viewed 5 November 2023: *http://soc.kuleuven.be/io/pubpdf/IO04025_bouckaert.pdf*

42 A. Neale & B. Anderson, "Performance reporting for accountability purposes – Lessons, issues, future." Wellington, New Zealand: Office of the Controller and Auditor-General, 2000; Op. Cit., Salamon, 2002.

43 Ibid., Neale and Anderson, 2000.

44 O. Olson, C. Humphrey, & J. Guthrie, "Caught in an evaluatory trap: A dilemma for public services under NPFM," *European Accounting Review,* 2001, vol. 10, no. 3, pp. 505-522.

45 Op. Cit., Dupnik, 1996.

46 Cole, Alistair, Jones, & Glyn, "Reshaping the state: Administrative reform and new public management in France," *Governance,* 2005, vol. 18, iss. 4, pp. 567-588.

47 Op. Cit., Sanderson, 2001.

48 T. Szirom, Z. Lasater, J. Hyde, & C. More, "Working together – Integrated governance," Paper to the Institute of Public Administration Australia National Conference, Sydney, November 30, 2001(unpublished), pp. 1-18.

49 Op. Cit., Pressman & Wildavsky, 1984.

50 Op. Cit., Clarke & Clegg, 1998.

51 G. Davis & P. Weller, *Are You Being Served? State, Citizens and Governance.* Australia: Allen and Unwin, 2001.

52 Op. Cit., Salamon, 2002.

53 S. Goldsmith & W. Eggers, *Governing by Network: The New Shape of the Public Sector.* Washington, D.C.: The Brookings Institution, 2004.

54 Op. Cit., Davis & Weller, 2001.

55 Op. Cit., Goldsmith & Eggers, 2004.

56 Ibid.

57 Op. Cit., Salamon, 2002.

58 I. Kirkpatrick, "The worst of both worlds? Public services without markets or bureaucracy," *Public Money and Management,* 1999, vol. 19, iss. 4, pp. 7-14.

59 L. Joyner, W. Miller, & B. Cage, "Strategic planning: A foundation for sustaining change," *National Forum of Special Education Journal,* 2000, vol. 9E.

60 Op. Cit., Kirkpatrick, 1999.

61 B. Hogwood & L. Gunn, "Policy analysis for the real world," *The Policy Process: A Reader.* University of Newcastle upon Tyne: Prentice Hall, 1997.

62 Office of Management and Budget, 2009, "Making government more effective," viewed 5 November 2023: *http://georgewbush-whitehouse.archives.gov/omb/pubpress/2009/010809_performance.html*

63 E. McWilliam, How to Survive Best Practice. Brisbane, Australia: Always Flying Publishers, 2002.

64 Op. Cit., Hogwood & Gunn, 1997.

65 Op. Cit., Pressman & Wildavsky, 1984.

66 J. Hill, *The Policy Process: A Reader.* University of Newcastle upon Tyne: Prentice Hall, 1997.

67 B. Hjern & D. Porter, "Implementation structures: A new unit of administrative analysis," *The Policy Process: A Reader.* University of Newcastle upon Tyne: Prentice Hall, 1997.

68 Op. Cit., Pressman & Wildavsky, 1984.

69 J. Klopovic, M. Vasu, & D. Yearwood, D., *Effective Program Practices for At-Risk Youth: A Continuum of Community-Based Programs.* New York, Civic Research Institute, Inc., 2003.

70   Op. Cit., Hogwood & Gunn, 1997.

71   Op. Cit., Salamon, 2002.

72   Op. Cit., Hogwood & Gunn, 1997.

73   Op. Cit., Klopovic, Vasu, & Yearwood 2003; R. Webster, "Scary schools: Study shows suburban classrooms contain same drug, sex problems as urban counterparts," *New Orleans Citybusiness,* 29 Mar. 2004.

74   Op. Cit., F. Cullen *et al,* 1998.

75   Op. Cit., Boone, 1997; Op. Cit., Arbreton & McClanahan, 2002; Op. Cit., Reynolds, Temple, & Robertson, 2002; Op. Cit., Vander Kooi, 2001; Op. Cit., Mihalic *et al,* 2001; Op. Cit., Brody, 1999.

76   Op. Cit., Hill, McNulty, & Stuart, 1997.

77   Habermas, cited in Whitehead & McNiff, *Action Research: Living Theory.* Thousand Oaks, Calif.: Sage Publications, Inc., 2006, p. 52.

78   L. Dobbs, "Still failing the grade," 2003, viewed 15 June 2006: *http://www.usnews.com/usnews/opinion/articles/030915/15dobbs.htm*

79   Op. Cit., Homel *et al,* 2004.

80   Op. Cit., Reynolds, Temple, & Robertson, 2002.

81   Ibid.

82   J. Shors, "Systemic overload," *Des Moines Business Record,* January 13, 1997.

83   Op. Cit., Klopovic, Vasu, & Yearwood, 2003.

84   Op. Cit., Homel et al, 2004; P. Foley, "Competition as public policy: A review of challenge funding," *Public Administration,* 1999, vol. 77, iss. 4, pp. 809-836.

85   Ibid., Foley, 1999.

86   P. Sabatier, "Top-down and bottom-up approaches to implementation research," *The Policy Process: A Reader.* University of Newcastle upon Tyne: Prentice Hall, 1997; J. Mayne, "Addressing attribution through contribution analysis: Using performance measures sensibly," Material from a 1998 paper by the Office of the Auditor General and the Treasury Board Secretariat, Canada, 1999.

87   Op. Cit., Goggin *et al,* 1990.

88   Op. Cit., Pressman & Wildavsky, 1984.

89   U.S. Department of Health and Human Services "A guide to successful public-private partnerships for child care," 2005, viewed 9 April 2005: *www.nccic.org/ccpartnerships*

90   Op. Cit., Pressman & Wildavsky, 1984.

91   B. Van Gramberg & J. Teicher, "Managerialism in local government – Victoria Australia," *The International Journal of Public Sector Administration,* 2000, vol. 13, iss. 5, pp. 476-492; H. Wollmann, "Local government modernization in Germany: Between incrementalism and reform waves," *Public Administration,* 2000, vol. 78, iss. 4, pp. 915-936.

92   D. Miller & P. Friesen, "A longitudinal study of the corporate life cycle," *Management Science,* 1984, vol. 30, no. 10, pp. 1161-1183.

93   J. Pinto & J. Prescott, "Variations in critical success factor stages in the project life cycle," *Journal of Management,* 1988, vol. 14, no. 1, pp. 5-18.

94   Op. Cit., Miller & Friesen, 1984.

95   S. Hanks, C. Watson, E. Jansen, & G. Chandler, "Tightening the life-cycle construct: A taxonomic study of growth state configurations in high-technology organizations," *Entrepreneurship: Theory and Practice,* 1993, vol. 18.

96   Op. Cit., Hanks *et al,* 1993.

97   Op. Cit., Holmes & Shand, 1995.

98   Op. Cit., Homel *et al,* 2004.

99   C. Polidano, "The new public management in developing countries," 1999, Institute for Development Policy and Management, University of Manchester.

100   Ibid.

101   Op. Cit., Stiglitz, 1999.

102   A. Podger, "Innovation with integrity – The public sector leadership imperative to 2020," NIPAA National Conference 2003, Brisbane, Australia, viewed 15 June 2006: *http://www.ipaa.org.au/vison2020/01_conf_Papers.htm*

103   Outhwaite, S., "The importance of leadership in the development of an integrated team," *Journal of Nursing Management,* 2003, vol. 11, no. 6, pp. 371-376.

104   Op. Cit., Salamon, 2002; Op. Cit., Klopovic, Vasu, & Yearwood 2003.

105   Op. Cit., Clarke & Clegg, 1998; R. Smith, "Focusing on public value: Something new and something old," *Australian Journal of Public Administration,* 2004, vol. 63, iss. 4, pp 68-79.

106   D. Schmaltz, "The myths that rule our projects," *Innovative Leader,* 2003, vol. 13, no. 7.

107   Op. Cit., Salamon, 2002; Op. Cit., Homel *et al,* 2004; Op. Cit., Sabatier, 1997.

108   Reason & Bradbury, *Handbook of Action Research: Participative Inquiry and Practice.* Thousand Oaks, Calif.: Sage Publications, Inc., 2001.

109   M. Miles & A. Hubermann, *Qualitative Data Analysis: A Source Book of New Methods,* 2nd ed. Thousand Oaks, Calif.: Sage Publications, Inc., 1994.

110   S. Kemmis, "Action research and social movement: A challenge for policy research," *Education policy analysis archives,* 1993, vol. 1, no. 1.

111   D. Ballard, P. Reason, C. Bond, & C. Seeley, "Action research and sustainable development," 2004, viewed 26 March 2008: *www.bath.ac.uk/carpp/publications/sus_dev.html*; B. Dick, "You want to do an action research thesis?" 1993, viewed 28 March 2008: *www.scu.edu.au/schools/gcm/ar/art/artthesis.html*

112   Friedman cited in Op. Cit., Reason & Bradbury, 2001, p. 159; Heron & Reason, 2001, cited in Op. Cit., Reason & Bradbury, p. 179.

113   Habermas cited in Op. Cit., McNiff & Whitehead, 2006.

114   D. Greenwood, M. Levin, *Introduction to Action Research: Social Research for Social Change.* Thousand Oaks, Calif.: Sage Publications Inc., 1998; Op. Cit., McNiff & Whitehead, 2006.

115   Iredell County Partnership for Young Children, viewed 5 November, 2023: *www.iredellsmartstart.org*

116   Section 501(c)(3) is a federal tax law provision granting nonprofit organizations exemption from federal income tax.

117   Boys and Girls Club of Henderson County, viewed 10 November, 2023: *bgchendersonco.org/*

118   Op. Cit., Klopovic, Vasu, & Yearwood, 2003.

119   *http://www.juvjus.state.nc.us/cpsv/index.html*

120   North Carolina Partnership for Children, viewed 10 November, 2023: *www.smartstart.org*

121   The Mediation Center of Eastern Carolina (now MCEC Peacemakers), viewed 10 November, 2023: *mceconline.org/*

122   Op. Cit., Boys and Girls Club of Henderson County.

123   P. Barrett, "Corporate governance in the public sector context," *Canberra Bulletin of Public Administration,* 2003, vol. 107, pp. 7-27; Op. Cit., Salamon, 2002.

124   Op. Cit., Homel et al, 2004; R. Mulgan & J. Uhr, "Accountability and governance," Graduate program in Public Policy, RSSS, Australian National University, 2000, viewed 5 November 2023: *hdl.handle.net/1885/41946*; Op. Cit., Klopovic, Vasu, & Yearwood, 2003.

125   Op. Cit., Pollitt & Bouckaert, 2002; Op. Cit., Davis & Rhodes, 2002.

126 J. Dixon, A. Kouzmin, & N. Korac-Kakabadse, "Managerialism – Something old, something borrowed, little new: Economic prescription versus effective organizational change in public agencies," *International Journal of Public Sector Management*, 1998, vol. 11, iss. 23, pp. 164-187; R. Levy, "EU programme management 1977-96: A performance indicators analysis," *Public Administration*, 2001, vol. 79, iss. 2, p. 423.

127 R. Wiebush, D. Wagner, B. McNulty, Y. Wang, & T. Le, "Implementation and outcome evaluation of the intensive aftercare program: Final report," 2005, Office of Juvenile Justice and Delinquency Prevention, viewed 9 April 2005: *www.ojjdp.jcjrs.org*; R. Rhodes, "Traditions and public sector reform: Comparing Britain and Denmark," *Scandinavian Political Studies*, 1999, vol. 22, iss. 4, pp. 341-370; Op. Cit., Salamon, 2002; Op. Cit., Klopovic, Vasu, & Yearwood, 2003.

128 Op. Cit., Pressman & Wildavsky, 1984; S. Deich, "A guide to successful public-private partnerships," *The Finance Project*, 2001, viewed 13 April 2005: *www.financeprojectinfo.org/Publications/ostpartnershipguide.pdf*; Op. Cit., Salamon, 2002.

129 Op. Cit., Pressman & Wildavsky, 1984; Op. Cit., Salamon, 2002; J. Lane, "Implementation, accountability and trust," *European Journal of Political Research*, 1987, 15 (5), pp. 527-46. M. Hill, P. Hupe, *Implementing Public Policy: Governance in Theory and in Practice*. Thousand Oaks, Calif.: Sage Publications, Inc., 2002; Op. Cit., Hogwood & Gunn, 1997.

130 Op. Cit., Clarke & Clegg, 1998; Op. Cit., Kirkpatrick, 1999.

131 Op. Cit., McWilliam, 2002; Op. Cit., Kirkpatrick, 1999.

132 J. Pontusson, "Welfare-state retrenchment revisited: Entitlement cuts, public sector restructuring and inegalitarian trends in advanced capitalist societies," *World Politics*, 1998, vol. 51, no. 1, pp. 67-98.

133 Op. Cit., Homel *et al*, 2004; Op. Cit., Foley, 1999; M. Bevir & D. O'Brien, "New labour and the public sector in Britain." *Public Administration*, 2001, vol. 61, iss. 5, pp. 535-547; E. Larson & R. Larson, "How to create a clear project plan," *Darwin*, 2004, viewed 23 March 2005: *http://www.darwinmag.com/*

134 Op. Cit., Holmes & Shand, 1995; Ibid., Bevir & O'Brien, 2001; Op. Cit., Jackson, 2001; Gould 2003)

135 Op. Cit., Holmes & Shand, 1995; Op. Cit., Jackson & Stainsby, 2000; Op. Cit., Jackson, 2001.

136 A more comprehensive human and social capital development of staff produces a better result. For example, pre-hire can occur with a multi-phasic personality profile to determine job suitability with strengths and weaknesses to improve. Better people are hired, developed, retained, and promoted. It effects everything from improved turnover to reductions in risk and liability claims and payouts.

137 Op. Cit., Shediac-Rizkallah & Bone, 1998.

138 R. Agranoff, "Human services integration: Past and present challenges in public administration," *Public Administration Review*, 1991, vol. 51, no. 6.

139 Op. Cit., Shediac-Rizkallah & Bone, 1998.

140 Department of Justice, "Developing a sustainability plan for weed and seed," 2005, viewed 30 August 2006: *www.ojb.usdoj.gov/ccdo*

141 R. N. Osborn, J. G. Hunt, & L. R. Jauch, "Toward a contextual theory of leadership," *The Leadership Quarterly*, 2002, 13, 797-837.

142 C. Bart, "Mission matters: There is a relationship between the words and concepts of a mission statement and the firm's success as a business," *Camagazine*, March 1998; J. Weiss & K. Piderit, "The value of mission statements in public agencies," *Journal of Public Administration Research and Theory*, 1999, vol. 9; C. Bart, "Measuring the mission effect in human intellectual capital," *Journal of Intellectual Capital*, 2001, vol. 2, no. 3, pp. 320-330;

D. Denton, "Mission statements miss the point," *Leadership & Organization Development Journal,* 2001, vol. 22, iss. 7, pp. 309-314.

143 Ibid., Bart, 2001.

144 Op. Cit, Bart, 1998.

145 Op. Cit, Denton, 2001.

146 W.K. Kellogg Foundation, "Evaluation handbook," 1998, viewed 6 October 2006: *www.wkkf.org*

147 H. Garza, "Evaluating partnerships: Seven success factors," *The Evaluation Exchange,* Harvard Family Research Project, 2005, vol. 11, no. 1.

148 Tradeoff in this instance is the numeric benefit or lack of benefit from delivering one service over another. In other words, suppose a municipality chooses to fund a new recreation center that comes at the expense of not being able to fund a school readiness program. Data is used to determine at what tradeoff cost that decision comes. While the recreation center is justifiable in its contribution to quality of life, not having good school readiness has ultimate repercussions. Those may be not having a better workforce and perhaps increases of youth and adults on public assistance or involved in the criminal justice system. No decisions are simple; making them based on the tradeoff argument hopefully helps elected officials make the optimal decision.

149 Planned giving is big money! Billions are given away every year. Anyone can start a foundation for a thousand dollars or even less and be a philanthropist. As their foundation funds grow, these philanthropists can make regular tax-deductible donations to your program. People who want to do something for their communities also are concerned with legacy—theirs and their heirs. It is proven that regular giving can translate into estate planning where substantial amounts are bequeathed to a favorite charity. Court these people as part of your resources development plan.

150 The Triangle Residential Options for Substance Abusers (TROSA) in Durham, North Carolina, and Leading Into New Communities (LINC) in Wilmington, North Carolina, are supported by sustainable enterprises such as a moving company, carpentry, picture framing, and even sustainable agri-aquaculture, which is done at LINC. While they take years to develop, as with TROSA, they are not only part of the therapeutic model, but they provide most of the operational resources, which at the time of this writing are just over $3M annually. As of 2022, they have their first satellite campus. It took over 30 years and was worth the work to prove TROSA successful.

151 R. Raley, J. Grossman, & Walker, "Getting it right: Strategies for after-school success," Philadelphia, Pa.: Public Private Ventures, 2005.

152 R. Daft, *Leadership Theory and Practice.* New York: The Dryden Press, 1999.

153 B. George, "Truly Authentic Leadership," *U.S. News and World Report,* October 30, 2006.

154 Ibid., p. 52.

155 Marguerite Casey Foundation Capacity Assessment Tool, 2001, viewed 5 November 2023: *www.caseygrants.org*

156 V. Rao & M. Woolcock, "Integrating qualitative and quantitative approaches in program evaluation," draft paper issued via The Development Research Group, The World Bank, 2002, p. 9.

157 Op. Cit., Garza, 2005.

158 A. Himmelman, "Communities working collaboratively for a change," *Resolving Conflict: Strategies for Local Government,* Margaret Herrman ed. Washington, D.C.: International City/County Management Association, 1994, pp. 27-47.

159 T. Harms, R. Clifford, & D. Cryer, "Early childhood environment rating scale: Revised edition." New York: Teachers College Press, 1998.

160 Op. Cit., George, 2006.
161 Op. Cit., Shediac-Rizkallah & Bone, 1998.
162 B. Crisp, H. Swerissen, S. Duckett, "Four approaches to capacity building in health: Consequences for measurement and accountability," *Health Promotion International,* 2000, vol. 15, no. 2.
163 Op. Cit., Shediac-Rizkallah & Bone, 1998.
164 Op. Cit., McKinsey, 2001.
165 Venture Philanthropy Partners (now Youth Invest Partners), Washington, 2001. Viewed 5 November 2023: *https://youthinvestpartners.org/learning/reports/capacity/capacity.html*
166 Op. Cit., Pressman & Wildavsky, 1984.
167 Op. Cit., Pressman & Wildavsky, 1984; Op. Cit., Holmes & Shand, 1995; Op. Cit., Jackson & Stainsby, 2000; Op. Cit., Jackson, 2001.
168 Op. Cit., Stiglitz, 1999; Op. Cit., Denhart & Denhart, 2000; Op. Cit., Salamon, 2002.
169 Op. Cit., Boone, 1997; Op. Cit., Arbreton & McClanahan, 2002; Op. Cit., Reynolds, Temple, & Robertson, 2002; Op. Cit., Vander Kooi, 2001; Op. Cit., Mihalic *et al,* 2001; Op. Cit., Brody, 1999.
170 G. Yukl, *Leadership in Organizations,* third ed. Englewood Cliffs, N.J.: Prentice Hall, 1994; J. Maxwell, *The 21 Irrefutable Laws of Leadership: Follow Them and People Will Follow You.* Nashville, Tenn.: Thomas Nelson, Inc., 1998; W. Fulmer, *Shaping the Adaptive Organization: Landscapes, Learning and Leadership in Volatile Times.* New York: American Management Association, 2000.
171 Ibid., Fulmer, 2000.
172 Op. Cit., Yukl, 1994.
173 Op. Cit., Daft, 1999.
174 Ibid.
175 Op. Cit., Weiss and Piderit, 1999.
176 Op. Cit., W.K. Kellogg, 1995.
177 M. Fulop, "Sustainability planning and resource development for youth mentoring programs," Portland, Ore.: Northwest Regional Educational Laboratory, 2005.
178 Op. Cit., Raley, Grossman & Walker, 2005.
179 R. Newman, "Lessons from the rule breakers," *U.S. New and World Report,* September 25, 2006.
180 Ibid.
181 Op. Cit., Pressman and Wildavsky, 1984.
182 Op. Cit., McKinsey, 2001.
183 Op. Cit., Marguerite Casey Foundation Capacity Tool, 2001.
184 D. Sackett et al, "Evidence based medicine: What it is and what it isn't," *British Medical Journal,* 1996, 312, 71-72.
185 Pennsylvania's Juvenile Justice System Enhancement Strategy, p. 5.
186 Teal Trust, "Our definition of leadership," 2006, viewed 6 November 2023: *http://www.teal.org.uk/leadership/definition.htm*
187 R. Putnam, *Bowling Alone: The Collapse and Revival of American Community.* New York: Simon & Schuster, 2000; Op. Cit., Salamon, 2002.
188 R. Burt, "The contingent value of social capital," *Administrative Science Quarterly,* 1997, vol. 42.
189 R. Godoy *et al,* "The role of community and individuals in the formation of social capital," 2005, viewed 5 April 2007: *http://people.brandeis.edu/~rgodoy/working%20papers/TAPS-WP-12-SC-Nov-2005.pdf*
190 Op. Cit., Shediac-Rizkallah & Bone, 1998.

www.ingramcontent.com/pod-product-compliance
Lightning Source LLC
Chambersburg PA
CBHW051317020426
42333CB00031B/3391